LATINX LITERATURE UNBOUND

Latinx Literature Unbound

Undoing Ethnic Expectation

Ralph E. Rodriguez

FORDHAM UNIVERSITY PRESS

New York 2018

Fordham University Press has no responsibility for the persistence or accuracy of URLs for external or third-party Internet websites referred to in this publication and does not guarantee that any content on such websites is, or will remain, accurate or appropriate.

Fordham University Press also publishes its books in a variety of electronic formats. Some content that appears in print may not be available in electronic books.

Visit us online at www.fordhampress.com.

Library of Congress Cataloging-in-Publication Data available online at https://catalog.loc.gov.

Printed in the United States of America

20 19 18   5 4 3 2 1

First edition

For my parents, Sophie and Gumaro,
always for Sophie and Gumaro

CONTENTS

LATINX LITERATURE UNBOUND

What We Talk about When We Talk about Latinx Literature

Classification is a condition of knowledge, not knowledge itself,
and knowledge in turn dissolves classification.

—MAX HORKHEIMER and THEODOR W. ADORNO,
Dialectic of Enlightenment

Two pedagogical moments in the spring of 2012 brought this project to life. The first came while teaching poetry in my annual survey of Latinx literature.[1] The class, while giving students a historical grounding in the literary production of Latina/os, principally focused on the post-national period of the 1980s to the present. As I was reviewing the poetry I was teaching on that particular April morning, which included works by Julia Alvarez, Benjamin Alire Sáenz, and Ana Castillo, I was suddenly taken aback by the poem "I Ask the Impossible," which I had selected from the well-known and prolific Chicana writer Ana Castillo. It is a poem in which the persona asks for the unqualified love of the addressee. The theme is universal. There is not one instance of linguistic code-switching, and none of the figurative language marks it as uniquely Latinx. In short, it bears none of the hallmarks of Latinx literature.[2] Had I concealed the author's name from the students, there would have been no reason for them to suspect it was a Latinx poem, which led me to ask myself, "When is a work of literature written by a Latinx author not a work of Latinx literature?" It is both odd and counterintuitive to suggest that a writer is sometimes but not always a Latinx writer. Complicating matters further, Castillo's poem is not an exception. There are numerous pieces of Latinx literature that do not thematically register as Latinx.

Relatedly, there is the burden of representation that Latinx writers seemingly labor under because of community expectations, marketing pressures, and perhaps writerly desires. Much pressure is imposed either from external or internal forces requiring that writers with Latinx surnames produce work that is recognizably Latinx. While there are numerous examples like "I Ask the Impossible," where recognizable Latinx themes are absent, the majority of Latinx works call up familiar stories of migrant workers, embattled barrios, tightly knit *familias*, and so on. I will take up the burden of representation at greater length below, but let me return for a moment to the site of my Latinx literature class.

A little later that same semester, definitional matters grew more complex when I asked the students to listen to an installment of Michael Silverblatt's *Bookworm* podcast entitled "Hispanic Identity in Writing" (July 21, 2005). His guests were the celebrated Chicana writer Sandra Cisneros and the then up-and-coming writer Nina Marie Martínez, whose novel *¡Caramba!* Anchor Books had recently published. In a lead-in to a discussion about Martínez's identity, Silverblatt says, "I'm fascinated. I was told before the interview that you are an Arymex." Martínez calmly explains that it is a label meant to capture both her German and Mexican roots. It signifies, that is, the complexity of her identity, a complexity that marks many Latinx identities, but that is often obscured by the seemingly homogeneous signifier *Latinx*. Indeed, later in the same interview, Martínez describes herself and ostensibly all Latina/os when she says, "We are somebody in between." It was not as if I was naïve about these matters. I grew up the child of parents with ties to Mexico, Italy, and Ireland, and I have been reading in the field long enough to know how varied are the themes Latinx writers take up and how varied are the racial and ethnic subjects hailed as Latinx. Having to work through these complexities made me realize, nevertheless, just how often we, in the field of Latinx studies, take that label for granted. Moreover, despite an increased literary output from a growing, ever more diverse Latinx population, little sustained scholarly attention has been paid to the very category (i.e., *Latinx* or *Hispanic*) under which we group this literature.

We have missed an important opportunity to ask and answer a question fundamental to the field: What is it that labeling a work of literature *Latinx* allows us to know? Let me be clear. I am not interested in a zero-sum game of deciding what Latinx literature "authentically" means. Indeed, I find authenticity politics unproductive. I am interested, instead, in the effects produced by laboring under our current definitions of Latinx literature. I am interested in the ways the criticism circumscribes what we talk about when we talk about Latinx literature and how we talk about it. It is this critical act that, perhaps, more than any other, keeps us working in limited ways with Latinx literature. Critical studies determine what counts. They influence what works we put in conversation with each other, and which ones we *might* put in conversation with each other. By dint of the approved channels through which they circulate and are validated, they create an authoritative bias, influencing what gets taught, talked about, and read. We critics may not mean to create a canon, but our critical acts generate one. I want to suggest that the limits of employing the political fiction of *Latinx* to organize and analyze a corpus of literary texts outweigh the benefits.

In the coming pages, I argue that there are more satisfying taxonomies and heuristics for grouping and analyzing literature than what scholars now recognize as the biological fiction but social reality of race. Even if one accepts the fiction of *Latinx* as a strategically instrumental tool in the struggle for social justice, it nevertheless confounds all reason to think that the heterogeneous communities and peoples from more than twenty different nations (who now reside in the United States) gathered under its mantle would produce a body of literary works that could be said to be recognizable because of the supposedly shared racial or ethnic identity of the authors.[3] Furthermore, if you accept that *Latinx* is a strategic category—a fiction employed to effect political outcomes—then you must forgo using it as an aesthetic marker. Categories strategically imagined and employed for social and political ends do not serve intellectual analyses well. Thus, we arrive at the question of scale: What is an appropriate and justifiable scale for organizing a corpus or network of literary texts?

I want to argue that genre has much to recommend it as a scale that might allow us to understand better the complexities and nuances of what we have heretofore considered Latinx literature. It also would allow us to make more regular and compelling connections to literatures that fall outside of the Latinx parameters. The latter, I believe, has been neglected because critical studies have heretofore largely tended to place Latinx authors in conversation only with each other.[4] This study will organize its chapters around genres, but before we arrive at that discussion, much more has to be said about why I find *Latinx* wanting as a taxonomical and aesthetic category.

Over the last two decades, there has been unparalleled growth in the field of Latinx literary analysis. None of it, however, has taken up the taxonomic, formalist, and aesthetic concerns at the heart of my project. Numerous scholars have made significant and compelling inroads into re-periodizing Latinx literary production, showing us its deep, pre–twentieth-century roots.[5] Scholars have charted a hemispheric and trans-national approach to Latinx literature that disrupts exclusively national understandings of this body of literary production.[6] They have also attended to dominant and key themes in the literature and to analyses of specific genres such as detective novels and graphic novels.[7] In the areas of queer, feminist, and gender approaches to literature, we have witnessed significant critical appraisals.[8]

I want, at the outset, to underscore an important point about my approach to the extant scholarship. I am not, by any stretch of the imagination, suggesting that some harm has been done by the insightful, existing work on Latinx literature. When I was attending graduate school in the 1990s, there had been a tendency (it continues in limited quarters today) in much scholarship to review the literature only to show how one's predecessors had failed and how you had the singularly correct interpretation. I have no interest in undertaking such triumphalist, scorched-earth criticism. Instead of pointing to harm or some type of failure, I am attending to what I see as a notable absence in the scholarship. In short, the field has been conspicuously quiet in evaluating the very rubric under which we do our work.

Only three books—Karen Christian's *Show and Tell* (1997), Marta Caminero-Santangelo's *On Latinidad* (2007), and Claudia Milian's more recent *Latining America* (2013)—engage this matter of taxonomy, aesthetics, and Latinx identity. Christian focuses her argument on the debates of the 1990s regarding social construction, essentialism, and the process of identity formation. Caminero-Santangelo is interested in how, when, and why the panethnic label *Latino* gets employed both sociologically and culturally. In the first twenty-plus pages of her book, Caminero-Santangelo reviews the relevant critical literature that discusses the complications with the label, but then she makes the following rhetorical move to show that there may be some merit in using the label as a literary marker: "This evolving sense of panethnic Latino communities—or at least panethnic contact—in U.S. cities is born out in some examples of literary production in the last two decades" (25). In other words, she now hopes to show that there is something identifiable as *Latino literature*. She does, however, caution, "Perhaps it is fair to say that, as the conditions emerge in the United States for a collective Latino identity, we can begin to observe more 'narration' of that identity in Latino literature. *But* it is nevertheless still striking how very tentative that particular form of narration seems to be" (26; emphasis added). Despite, however, recognizing just how tentative that form is, she accepts the category *Latino* and works with it to see how the literary texts she examines imagine a collective Latino identity (31–33). Milian believes Latinx studies, as currently practiced, misses the rich diversities—epistemological, ontological, and existential—that inhere in the various peoples who fall under the heading *Latina/o* and whose subjectivities and culture constitute that which we have come to call *Latinidad*. To "offer a conceptual framework that plots other subjectivities and localities that have yet to be charted within and beyond the configurations of Latinidad" (6), Milian proposes the neologism *Latinities*. In doing so, she hopes "to initiate a dialogue with writers, narratives, and experiences that have been previously ignored or written out of Latina/o studies: the southern, the black, the dark brown, the indigenous, and the Central American" (8–9). While my argument certainly builds on Christian's, Caminero-Santangelo's, and Milian's important work, I diverge considerably from their projects insofar as I concentrate on the formal features of the literature, reading as event, and the shaping role organizational rubrics like "Latinx literature" play in the interpretive process.

Finally, I want to draw attention to Paul Allatson's recent essay "From 'Latinidad' to 'Latinid@des.'" His essay offers "an overview of key critical positions that assist in recognizing new Latin@ literary aesthetics and in tracking how their authors challenge essentialist understandings of Latinid@d as the framework for interpreting their texts" (129). In addition, he correctly observes that the complex language matters that have regularly been a part of Latinx literature are now "increasingly accompanied and bolstered by cosmopolitan, international typologies, references, and settings that either exceed homeliness in the United States, or imply a rejection of what an orthodox creative Latin@ text is, should be, and ought to contain in terms of its cultural references, settings, and context. In short, numerous Latin@ writers are contributing to the emergence of new post-identitarian latinid@des that reflect the constant flux of transculturations and their potential to modulate the United States' twenty-first-century future" (129). Allatson's is a welcome addition to this important conversation, but given the brevity of the essay form, he is unable to undertake the detailed close readings that a book-length argument allows. Assessments such as Allatson's, nevertheless, help push critics to question the taxonomies under which we labor.

Furthermore, in placing pressure on the taken-for-granted paradigms we use to evaluate cultural production, *Latinx Literature Unbound* finds

itself in conversation—at times implicitly and at other times explicitly—
with works such as Kenneth W. Warren's *What Was African American
Literature?*, Caroline Rody's *The Interethnic Imagination: Roots and Passages
in Contemporary Asian American Fiction*, and Vijay Prashad's *Everybody Was
Kung-Fu Fighting: Afro-Asian Connections and the Myth of Cultural Purity*.
These works, along with mine, ask questions about first principles such
as, "What constitutes a meaningful and illuminating group of literary
production?" Getting this grouping right matters because, as Jonathan
Culler explains, "[T]he literary work is dependent for its meaning and
effects on a system of possibilities, which needs to be described" (*Literary in Theory* 8). Working from a flawed grouping—a faulty system of
possibilities—means our interpretations will, by definition, be flawed.
Latinx Literature Unbound aims to understand what those systems of possibility are for the body of literature we have heretofore labeled *Latinx*.

As we left the cultural nationalist period of the 1960s and 1970s, when
people regularly spoke of Chicana/o literature, Puerto Rican or Nuyorican literature,[9] and to a lesser extent Cuban American literature, we found
ourselves more regularly employing the umbrella terms *Latinx* and *Hispanic*. These terms first appeared on the 1970 census and gained even more
momentum in the 1980s, when the news media regularly referred to it as
the "decade of the Hispanic." Already in 1982, Juan Bruce-Novoa was
pointing out the problem with this umbrella: "Although it is convenient
for government agencies—as well as some leftist organizations—to lump
Chicanos and Puerto Ricans (and any other Hispanics) together under any
of several rubrics, this is as much an illusion as that of a monolithic U.S.
national character" (*Retrospace* 28).[10] Moreover, the very moment at which
the umbrella label was gaining more traction in the media was also the very
moment in which the Latinx population was growing ever more diverse
and geographically dispersed.

In *From Bomba to Hip-Hop: Puerto Rican Culture and Latino Identity*, Juan
Flores suggests that one way to deal with the complication that umbrella
terms entail "without becoming paralyzed by the sheer complexity and
contradictoriness of it all" would be to distinguish between "a *demographic*,
an *analytic*, and an *imaginary* approach to Latino unity and diversity" (194;
emphasis in original). The demographic approach is about the way agencies
conceive of and aggregate Latina/os—"count them therefore they are"
(194). He ties the analytic approach to a positivist social science, one "bent
on deaggregation; it presumes to move closer to Latino 'reality' by recognizing and tabulating the evident diversity of Latino groups and experiences" (195). Finally, the imaginary approach has to do with how the Latino

population imagines itself. He writes, "[A]nalysis is guided above all by a lived experience and historical memory, factors that tend to be relegated by prevailing sociological approaches as either inaccessible or inconsequential" (197). I can fully appreciate that these three approaches yield different results and that, as Flores rightly points out, they are not mutually exclusive and are very often complementary. This tripartite approach, however, still leaves the fiction of the collectivity in place. Let me begin by tackling two of the crucial reasons why I remain unconvinced about the efficacy of this grouping, particularly as it applies to literary analysis.

First, the necessary and sufficient criteria we have created to label a piece of literature *Latina/o literature* are not illuminating. We often take the category for granted without thinking hard about what we mean when we invoke it. Some thirty years ago, Juan Bruce-Novoa wrote a brief essay entitled, "Hispanic Literatures [note the plural] in the United States," in which he delineated in specific terms the differences between Chicano and Puerto Rican literature. He did not include Cuban literary production in the United States as one of the Hispanic literatures at the time because he argued that it did not engage the U.S. experience and that the writers considered themselves exiles, though he did maintain that it would likely become a Hispanic literature in the coming decades. Even more important for my argument are the essay's closing sentences. Bruce-Novoa writes, "But at present [1982] the cultural differences between Chicanos and Puerto Ricans are still stronger than the will to unify. Their writing reflects those differences as much as it constitutes a literature different from the mainstream writing of the United States" (*Retrospace* 32). Those differences have become even more pronounced for the community labeled and frequently self-identified as *Latinx* because the populations that make up its ranks have grown more diverse and more geographically dispersed than ever before.

Consider, for instance, the *Norton Anthology of Latino Literature*, published in 2011. It offers a contemporary take on what defines Latino literature, and because it comes with the institutional imprimatur of Norton, it holds a certain amount of critical weight in this debate.[11] In the anthology's preface, Ilan Stavans, the general editor, uses identity as a central principle for inclusion in the volume: "*The Norton Anthology of Latino Literature* celebrates five centuries of diverse writing *by Latinos* in what is now the United States" (liii; emphasis added). As he develops the three central ideas that "define the 'library'" that the anthology seeks to be, his definition gets more complex. He adds, "Latino literature is about the tension between double attachments to place, to language, and to identity" (liii). In elaborating this point, he would like us to believe two things, which, though partially true, are not unequivocally true. First, he needs us to recognize that many Latinos did not come as immigrants to the United States, but that the United States came to them in the form of colonial enterprises. One can certainly point to Mexico as an example. With the redrawing of national boundaries at the end of the U.S.-Mexico War in 1848, the border crossed Mexicans rather than the other way around. Many Mexicans, however, have come to the United States as immigrants, to say nothing of the numerous other heterogeneous groups colligated under the signifier *Latino* (e.g., Puerto Ricans, Salvadorans, Costa Ricans, Guatemalans, Dominicans, and so on). Moreover, I am not wholly persuaded by his claim that those Latinos who came as immigrants "are unlike any other immigrant group in the United States, because for centuries they have maintained strong ties to the places once called home and with the languages of those homelands" (liii). There is certainly an argument to be made about geographic proximity for some immigrants' home countries as opposed to immigrants from more distant geographic regions, but proximity does not guarantee attachment, nor does distance preclude it. If attachment implies travel back and forth between homeland and newly adopted country, one would need a historical analysis of available modes of travel (steamer ship vs. airplane say) and economic means, among other factors. Furthermore, in the absence of empirical data, I am not convinced that one need accept the argument that Latina/os feel a stronger tie to a place once called home than, say, Asian Americans or immigrants from Italy, Poland, Russia, and so on. Generational factors would also need to be considered. In other words, to say, "Latino literature is about the tension between double attachments to place, to language, and to identity," is not what one might call a distinguishing feature.

Second, Stavans's definition highlights the multinational quality of Latinos as a group. Noting that feature, however, does more to underscore the group's cultural heterogeneity and differences than to serve as support for a unifying aesthetic. Sensing this tension, Stavans attempts to shore up his definition by adding his third definitional criterion. He writes, "For a long time, because of their different national backgrounds the individual groups of people within this minority perceived themselves as independent from one another. From the 1980s onward . . . a feeling of unity has begun to emerge" (liii). His support for this unity is thin. He first turns to the Census Bureau, which has observed that in the twenty-first century Latinos are the largest and fastest growing ethnic group in the United States. Size and rate of growth, however, do not imply or guarantee unity. He then focuses on the shift from the emphasis during the civil rights era on Chicano studies and Puerto Rican studies to the 1990s turn to Latino studies in the academy. He correctly notes that departments as diverse as sociology, history, anthropology, literature, linguistics, and political science are "devoted to understanding the Hispanic experience" (liv). Other disciplines taking up the mantle of *Latino* does not, however, mean it is a useful or meaningful label for assessing cultural, historical, or political formations. In its grand lumping together of these diverse populations, *Latino* likely conceals more than it reveals about these heterogeneous communities and their cultural productions. Implicitly acknowledging that there may be differences among the various national subgroups organized under the rubric *Latino*, Stavans and his editorial board offer an alternate table of contents that is grouped around the various nations (Chile, Colombia, Cuba, and so on) that constitute Latino America.[12]

Following Stavans's rationale for a nationally organized table of contents is a telling paragraph regarding the limits of *Latino* as an aesthetic label. In that paragraph, Stavans offers a revealing qualification. He declares, "Not every 'Latino' author in the anthology has an equally rounded Latino identity" (lvi). In the subsequent sentences, he attempts to clarify the peculiar phrasing of "equally rounded."[13] In so doing, he must acknowledge the porosity, the historical contingency, and the linguistic variability of the seemingly monolithic label *Latino*. He asks if Fray Bartolomé de Las Casas is perhaps a "proto-Latino" given his fight against the Spanish abuse of the indigenous populations of the Americas and given that he never set foot in the United States. He asks if Isabel Allende, who writes in Spanish, is a Latina. "Or is she a Chilean émigré living permanently in the United States?" (lvii).

A well-versed, prolific scholar, Stavans is cognizant of the complicated matters that go into defining both Latino identity and Latino literature, but despite the various complications, he and his editorial board are not ready to abandon the rubric *Latino literature*. Rather, as Stavans notes, "[T]he editors have defined Latino literature in elastic terms, as the artistic, written manifestation, in Spanish, English, Spanglish, or any combination of these three, by an author of Hispanic ancestry who has either lived most of his or her existence in the United States or, while having only some tangential connection to the Latino community, has helped define that community through his or her work" (lvii). Thus, the definition resides in language, ancestry, geography, and a vague idea of defining community.[14]

Following the editors' concise definition of Latina/o literature, Stavans offers a full paragraph of representative, but by no means exhaustive "gray areas": Rudolfo A. Anaya occasionally writes about countries other than the United States (e.g., *A Chicano in China*). The editors claim William Carlos Williams as a part of the tradition.[15] Herberto Padilla, who "never perceived himself as a Latino," is included in the anthology. María Luisa Bombal, despite her sometime residence in the United States, and who writes and/or translates in the requisite languages—Spanish and English—is not, however, included in the anthology because "her oeuvre has no connection to Latino identity" (lvii).

My project does not intend to attack the *Norton Anthology of Latino Literature*, nor does it suggest that other anthologies have done a better job of defining Latino literature. For instance, in his anthology *Hispanic American Literature*, Nicolás Kanellos—who as director of Arte Público has been instrumental and perhaps singular in his efforts to bring and keep the majority of Latinx writers in print—fails to offer a definition of what constitutes Hispanic literature beyond the idea that it is the literary output of Hispanics (e.g., "Hispanic literature, a literature created by the people proudly emerging from the fusion of Spanish, Native American, and African cultures, has always been part of the mosaic of the United States" [1]). Stavans, Kanellos, and all of the other editors and publishers of Latinx literature have performed a tremendous service in bringing greater attention to Latinx writers. I do not wish to be misunderstood on that score. Their attempts, however, to define Latinx literature illustrate its decided porosity rather than its integral unity.

Furthermore, even as a marker of ethnic or racial identity, *Latinx* is a troublingly unstable signifier. In her recent book, *The Trouble with Unity: Latino Politics and the Creation of Identity*, the political scientist Cristina Beltrán notes, "[W]hile the mass media and other political elites often portray Latinos as a collective body with common interests, the actual existence of Latino unity—of a collective political consciousness and will distinct among Latinos—is far less certain. . . . Characterizing a subject as either 'Hispanic' or 'Latino' is an exercise in opacity—the terms are so comprehensive that *their explanatory power is limited*" (6; emphasis added). The referent *Latinx* attempts to index a community of people not in the least as homogeneous as that group label suggests, as Beltrán and other social scientists have been quick to point out.[16]

We, literary scholars, too, often note the social construction of the term, but then we regularly go about our business as if noting that constructedness were enough. Consider, for instance, Angie Chabram-Dernersesian's impressive argument, made some fifteen years ago, about Chicana/o studies' failure to attend to the multiplicity of identities gathered under the label *Chicana/o*, including her own Chicana–Puerto Rican identity. Of the Chicana/o movement's flattening out of complex identities, she writes,

> For years I had witnessed Central Americans, Latina/os, even Spaniards/ *españoles* joining the ranks of the Chicana/o movement, consciously assuming a Chicano political identity and strategically glossing over their ethnic and cultural distinctions, and being expected to do so for a chance to join in to forge an alliance—*una relación con la causa chicana/* a relationship with the Chicana/o cause. But they were not alone in this endeavor; there was already a blueprint for containing ethnic differences engraved in important documents such as the epic poem *I am Joaquín/ yo soy Joaquín*, where the speaking subject infers that la raza—mexicanos, españoles, latinos, hispanos, and Chicanos; Yaquis, Tarahumaras, Chamulas, Zapotecs, mestizos . . . and *indios* are all the same because of *his* [Corky Gonzales's] authenticating discourse of the universal Chicano. ("Refashioning the Transnational Connection" 267)

Despite her careful critique, we continue talking about our identities as if they were monoliths—be they narrower group designations like Chicanx, Puerto Rican, Cuban American, or larger umbrella terms like Latinx and Hispanic. Chabram-Dernersesian is equally critical of these larger group fictions. She is not seeking to rectify the problems of identity and Chicana/o nationalism "by unproblematically adding Caribbean or Central American or Latin American linkages to it or *by making the fatal move into an unmarked collectivity*" (270; emphasis added).[17]

Similarly, the performance studies theorist José E. Muñoz expressed his own dissatisfaction with the "incoherence" of the term *Latino*. It is unable "to index, with any regularity, the central identity tropes that lead to our understandings of group identities in the United States. 'Latino' does not subscribe to a common racial, class, gender, religious, or national category, and if a Latino can be from any country in Latin America, a member of any race, religion, class, or gender/sex orientation, who then is she? What, if any, nodes of commonality do Latinas/os share?" ("Feeling Brown" 67). Muñoz suggested turning to affect and feeling rather than "identity politics" as a way to better understand the "affiliations and identifications between racialized and ethnic groups" (68). In an essay that served as a prolegomenon to the continued research and writing he was doing on the "brown commons" and "brown feeling" prior to his death, Muñoz wrote of the way "Latina/o (and other minoritarian) theatre and performance set out to specify and describe ethnic difference and resistance not in terms of simple being, but through the more nuanced route of feeling. . . . I am interested in plotting the way in which Latina/o performance theatricalizes a certain mode of 'feeling brown' in a world painted white, organized by cultural mandates to 'feel white'" (68).[18] Despite critiques such as Muñoz's, Beltran's, and Chabram-Dernersesian's, we have yet to take the next step that asks us to consider how working with a social fiction—*Latinx*—perhaps limits our literary analysis by forcing us into what Vijay Prashad argues are narrow, static boxes of cultural authenticity that end up causing us to misunderstand the dynamic nature of culture and its historical specificity.[19]

Given our historical remove from the height of the Chicana/o movement (1965–1975), we can certainly ask, following Kenneth Warren's example, "What was *Chicana/o* literature?" We are not yet, however, at the point where we can ask, "What was *Latinx* literature?" In his *Concise History of Latino/a Literature*, Frederick Luis Aldama notes, "The Latina/o novels, short stories, drama, and poetry of the early- and mid-twentieth century are more limited in focus and generic range than those of today. At the same time, the literature of today is made by authors who are clearly more integrated socioeconomically than those of yesteryear. The paradox holds. The results, if they go the way of other minority literatures, might lead in the future to the erasure of the category Latino/a Literature itself. Only time will tell" (xv). Aldama does not deal with the very fiction of the cultural category *Latino/a*. He seems willing to accept it and only to note that this population is becoming more "integrated socioeconomically."[20] Similarly, Marta Caminero-Santangelo, after an elaborate scrutiny of *Latino*, concludes,

> I have chosen (after all my laborious dissection of it) to accept the category "Latino" and to use it, without assuming any more fundamental connections between the various groups but in acknowledgement of the fact that a sense of a larger group identity has tentatively been constructed—often by popular culture—in the United States. Since the category "Latino" or "Hispanic" has acquired very real meaning and power in U.S. public discourse, inevitably, those named by the category must therefore engage with it somehow. (*On Latinidad* 31)

While the umbrella labels are, no doubt, operational in social and political arenas, that does not mean they have an aesthetic force. Shared political and social features do not necessarily mean a shared aesthetic practice or practices.

My study means to unbind us from the preconceived, unquestioned notion that there is something called "Latinx literature" and from the identity and thematic expectations attendant to that formulation. The Latinx literature category is often an unthinking one into which much gets un-critically stuffed because of the racial and ethnic identity of the writer. As a marketing tool, the Latinx label can also limit the aspirations of the writers themselves. Agents, editors, and publishers come to expect, even demand, that writing from an author with a Latinx surname deal with "recognizable Latinx themes." A number of fiction writers have commented on this limiting aspect. Julia Alvarez, for instance, writes,

> I get nervous when people ask me to define myself as a writer. I hear the cage of a definition close around me with its "Latino subject matter," "Latino style," "Latino concerns." I find that the best way to define myself is through the stories and poems that do not limit me to a simple label, a choice. Maybe after years of feeling caught between being a "real Dominican" and being American, I shy away from simplistic choices that will leave out an important part of who I am or what my work is about. (*Something to Declare* 169)

Or consider the Chicano author Alfredo Vea who, when asked in a 2000 interview for the *Bloomsbury Review* about the future of Latino literature, makes a similar argument about how the category has restricted, and still restricts, the aesthetic quality of the literature:

> There was a time when it was necessary for the Latino community to embrace its artists, whether that embrace was motivated by artistic or political reasons. These artists spoke and speak for us. Unfortunately, much of what was embraced was and is not high art. We are capable of high art. We have and will demonstrate this truth.
>   While Latinos in South and Central America and Mexico have long ago developed an intelligentsia that has operated on the world stage (witness Paz, Borges, Fuentes, Márquez), we have allowed ourselves to applaud the provincial in literature. That time is over. The artistic bar of "literary fiction" has been set for our time by Nabokov, Bellow, Faulkner, et al. We should study that bar—aim at it with every intention of leaping over. (Biggers, "More Than Measuring Up")

Although Vea is being more forceful than I might be about the aesthetic accomplishments of Latinx writers, he nonetheless marks yet another way in which the category has restricted the field's horizons. These matters of limiting taxonomies concern not only well-established writers but also a younger generation of writers. Consider Veronica Gonzalez's comments to Michael Silverblatt in an interview for *Bookworm* on November 1, 2007. They were discussing the theme of identity in her novel, *twin time: or, how*

death befell me [*sic*], and her reception of a Latina fiction prize selected by
Rudolfo Anaya, and Silverblatt inquired into "her desire to be and not be
Mexican":

> I went to school in the early '90s. . . . I went to NYU for writing
> school, and it was really . . . kind of the height of the identity novel and
> the ethnic identity novel, and I think that there's some wonderful
> books that have come out of that vein of writing. But I didn't want my
> book to be easily categorized. I found that when I started trying to
> publish, I had a really hard time because people expected a certain
> kind of story from me, and only that kind of story was acceptable
> because I was Mexican. And . . . because my writing is experimental, it
> plays a lot with philosophical ideas that there was this sense that I
> couldn't be an intellectual, experimental writer and a Mexican writer
> at the same time in the publishing, the larger publishing world, and so
> I found ways to continue doing what I was doing in quieter ways. I ran
> a zine; I started a little publishing company; my friend Laura—who is
> a Filipina-American writer—and I published this anthology with Soft
> Skull, and I found these ways to continue to do the work I feel I want
> to do without having my Mexicanness be categorized or my self be
> categorizable because of my Mexicanness. (Silverblatt, *Bookworm*)

As critics, we can do better than yoke writers beneath a label that they
themselves resist because of its limiting qualities. If labels and taxonomies
fail to advance our critical understanding, then they should be abandoned.
In the following pages, I mean to unbind this literature from this, at times,
limiting aesthetic rubric.

I fully understand and appreciate that given the racism of the publishing industry and the academy, there has been and continues to be a great
need to get Latinx writers published, reviewed, and taught. To fail to appreciate the ongoing struggles in this field is to misunderstand the long
genealogy of Latinx writing in the United States. Yet, while these struggles are important for understanding the history of how Latinx literature
came to be, they are not relevant to a discussion of the taxonomy and interpretation of this literature. A recounting of these battles can give us a list
of the proponents who made it possible for this literature to exist, and it
can give us insight into how it found its way into the classroom. It is
important that we record that history and even pay tribute to those figures.
I certainly do not wish to diminish that valiant work. But such homage,
such memorializing, can create provincial boundaries and borders around

the literature, giving some rights to enter, and forbidding passage to others on the thinnest of identity politics.

Moreover, this policing can lead to a cult of ethnicity that has deleterious effects on the literature, for, wittingly or not, it places a burden of representation on the writer. Publishing houses come to expect Latinx writers (all ethnic writers for that matter) to write on a certain set of themes, and if they do not, an agent or editor will often tell them that it is not ethnic enough, stifling their imaginations by forcing them into knowable boxes.[21] Similarly, readers become trained to expect books on recognizable Latinx themes from Latinx writers, and in the worst cases, perhaps will not buy or read them if they are not Latinx enough. So while we must appreciate the struggles that Latinx writers have undergone to get published and taught, we must also avoid saddling these writers with the need to represent "their people." In my critique of the burden of representation, I concur with Carmen Giménez Smith and John Chávez, who, in the introduction to their anthology of "new Latin@ writing," assert,

> [T]he roles of Latino writers are too often conflated with those of cultural attachés, the narrative representatives of our so-called minority states. Rather than sit at our drafting tables as aesthetic innovators, we Latino poets are expected to normalize our histories and tell the ancestral tales of our colorful otherness. We are supposed to write about our *abuelitas*, our cultural heritages. (xii)

The spirit of their anthology is, then, akin to the spirit of *Latinx Literature Unbound*. They want to break open the canon of Latinx literature and the expectations that are imposed on Latinx writers. As critics, I maintain, we must unbind such expectations from how we understand and evaluate what we have heretofore called "Latinx literature" in order to create rich, nuanced, and complex analyses, which returns me to my argument about scale and why I think genre is a more felicitous way than *Latinx* to group and analyze literature.

Scale matters because it sets in place the "system of possibilities" for analyzing a text or group of texts. That system of possibilities sets, in other words, the interpretive horizon. It determines what we can know about a given text, and not all systems or scales are created equal. I have been arguing that the grouping of a body of literary texts beneath the label *Latinx* is a flawed scale and that we see that flaw in the inability of scholars to generate the necessary and sufficient criteria to define it. There are many other taxonomic scales to which critics turn to create literary groupings. Those most regularly employed are nation, region, hemisphere, and transnationalism or globalism. Each has merits to recommend it, but each, as numerous scholars have shown, has its limitations as well.[22] We can perhaps presume that, because a given nation's inhabitants are subject to its political and governmental doctrines and labor under its economic machine, those inhabitants might produce a literature that is recognizable and unique. Indeed, much ink has been spilled to demonstrate national traditions in literature. In a reverse trajectory of influence, Benedict Anderson, in his classic study *Imagined Communities*, has shown how print culture—the novel and the newspaper in particular—helped imagine the nation. Nevertheless, numerous critics, coming at the national problematic from different angles, have demonstrated that it is a scale with its own flaws and limitations. Wai Chee Dimock, in her argument in favor of a "deep time"[23] analysis of literature, for instance, points out the following flaws in the national approach:

> [W]hat does it mean to set aside a body of writing as "American"? What assumptions enable us to take an adjective derived from a territorial jurisdiction and turn it into a mode of literary causality, making the latter reflexive of and indeed coincidental with the former?
>
> Nationhood, on this view, is endlessly reproduced in all spheres of life. This reproductive logic assumes that there is a seamless correspondence between the temporal and spatial boundaries of the nation and the boundaries of all other expressive domains. And, because this correspondence takes the form of a strict entailment . . . it is also assumed that there is a literary domain lining up in just the same way. This is why the adjective "American" can serve as a literary epithet. Using it, we limit ourselves, with or without explicit acknowledgement, to an analytic domain foreclosed by definition, a kind of scholarly unilateralism. Literature here is the product of one nation and one nation alone, analyzable within its confines. (3)[24]

Numerous other critics have also shown that culture does not respect national boundaries and that it would be more felicitous to think hemispherically and/or transnationally. Close to home for this study of "Latinx literature" are, among others, Kirsten Silva Gruesz's *Ambassadors of Culture: The Transamerican Origins of Latino Writing*, and José David Saldívar's *The Dialectics of Our America: Genealogy, Cultural Critique, and Literary History*; his *Border Matters: Remapping American Cultural Studies*; and his more recent *Trans-Americanity: Subaltern Modernities, Global Coloniality, and the Cultures of Greater Mexico*. Gruesz and Saldívar both argue that—given imperial concerns in the Americas, historical immigration, and migration patterns of Latin American communities into and throughout the United States—the category of the singular nation, namely, the United States, is insufficiently supple to capture the robustness of the cultural production in the Americas. Moreover, Saldívar contends that there is a rich genealogy and shared cultural production that we must attend to in the Americas. He writes forcefully and at length about this in *The Dialectics of Our America* (1991):

> During the past generation the new cultural history of America has been fractured into various professional shards: social history, ethnic history, women's history, African American history, and Chicano history. No longer is American history conceived exclusively as the story of Anglo-Saxon men from the first settlements in the Chesapeake Bay area in 1607 to the present. Looking at American history "from the bottom up," this revisionist scholarship has shattered the traditional consensus. But there has not been enough major revisionist scholarship. Moreover, a stark fragmentation of American intellectual history has plagued some of our revisionist historians, and the literary history of the Americas must be made whole again. Efforts to achieve this wholeness have been begun in the genealogical texts of Martí and Fernández Retamar who in their oppositional discourses attempted to unify the history of the Americas. By looking at the Americas as a hemisphere and by analyzing the real and rhetorical, often hostile, battles between the United States and what Martí called "Nuestra América"—"Our America"—it is possible to perceive what the literatures of the Americas have in common. (4–5)

Saldívar makes an impassioned call here, and one can see that there is much to gain from drawing lines of affiliation among, say, Gabriel García Márquez, William Faulkner, and Rolando Hinojosa or among Clarice Lispector, Renata Adler, and Cecile Pineda.

In his critique of José David Saldívar's transnational imaginary, José E. Limón suggests that we take up a critical regionalism, which, at least in the case of U.S.-Mexican border cultures, he argues, offers a more salutary mode of analysis. Drawing on the work of Fredric Jameson and Kenneth Frampton, among others, Limón contends that the critical regionalist model has the benefit of being attentive to local specificity (something he finds lacking in Saldivar's work) without precluding the influence of the global. Limón writes, "We thus have in this concept [critical regionalism] an abiding and fulsome respect for and rendering of the complexity of local cultures in comparison to others in the world, while recognizing that all are in constant but critical interaction with the global. Such, I think, is an alternative way to render literary histories, at least those involving the US-Mexico border, a desirable goal, in my view . . ." (*American Encounters* 168).[25]

These models—the national, the transnational, and the regional—have attributes to recommend them, and much interesting work has been done beneath their banners, but these scales have not been used to free Latinx literature from its thematic and identity strictures. Indeed, each of these models views the political fiction of *Latinx* as an acceptable aesthetic category and merely articulates it to another scale (i.e., the nation, the hemisphere, or the region). I aim to unbind *Latinx literature* from those identity and thematic strictures and to use the category of genre to understand the literary corpus by authors known as *Latinx*.

Genre is a durable taxonomic category that has persisted across time and space. It can, of course, move across all of the scales mentioned thus far, and it is a more logically justifiable category for grouping literature than "the impossible diversity of the term 'Latino'" (Silva Gruesz, *Ambassadors of Culture* x–xi). In addition, it by no means precludes us from taking up matters of race and identity that have filled the pages of Latinx literary criticism. Genre gives us a systematic way to put categorically similar texts in conversation with one another and to analyze how their formal features generate a host of meanings within and across texts. Moreover, since genres are dynamic forms that change over time, they can even, if the sample is large enough, tell us much about the historical moment in which they were produced. Though I am by no means a Marxist critic, Fredric Jameson's appraisal of the power of genre criticism holds equally true for this project. He writes that the value of generic concepts is that their mediatory function "allows the coordination of immanent formal analysis of the individual text with the twin diachronic perspective of the history of forms and the evolution of social life" (*Political Unconscious* 105). Genres, that is, help us understand literary history, aesthetics, and the broader category of the social. In this book, I focus on the novel, the poem, and the short story. Furthermore, I examine texts that have yet to receive much attention in Latinx literary criticism. In addition, when possible, I move us away from "preapproved, recognizable" themes to further unbind us from our limiting preconceptions about just what it is we talk about when we talk about *Latinx literature*.

While my project is historically minded throughout, particularly in its focus on the 1980s to the present (the period during which the term *Latina/o* and, subsequently, *Latinx* gained ascendancy), it is methodologically driven by a reinvestment in formalist approaches to literature. Although one might tie this reinvestment to any number of recent scholarly publications, I date it to the special issue of *Modern Language Quarterly* dedicated to reading for form published in 2000. In her introduction to that special issue, Susan Wolfson, writes,

> The readings for form that follow [in the included essays] show, if no consensus about what form means, covers, and implies, then a conviction of why it still has to matter. All share a sense that the reductive critique of formalism, in publication and pedagogy, has had unfortunate results, not the least a dulling of critical instruments and a loss of sensitivity to the complexity of literary form: its various and surprising work, its complex relation to traditions, and its interaction with extraliterary culture. "Reading for form" implies the activity as well as the object. (9)

Hence I hope to sharpen the sense of what is at stake in reading Latinx literature and understanding its complex aesthetic. Wolfson's emphasis on the activity of reading, moreover, highlights a tendency in my approach, namely, an emphasis on the significance of reading as a meaning-making event. Meaning does not inhere in the reading object itself, but is produced in the act of reading. Whether reading the paratext of a dust-jacket blurb and cover design or the text of a novel or secondary material such as interviews, I ask throughout my project what sentences do—what their effect is—rather than presume what they mean in and of themselves.

Some forty years ago, in "Literature in the Reader: Affective Stylistics," Stanley Fish argued that the sentence "is no longer an object, a thing-in-itself, but an *event*, something that *happens* to, and with the participation of, the reader. And it is this event, this happening . . . that is, I would argue, the *meaning* of the sentence" (125; emphasis in original).[26] Fish's strategies, though they focus on the participation of an informed reader and reading as an event, are not at all inconsistent with my neo-formalist tendencies, for the event of reading depends on paying close attention to the syntax, tropes, diction, structure, juxtaposition, and all of the other particular linguistic and literary characteristics that animate formalist readings. Indeed, Fish's method "is simply the rigorous and disinterested asking of the question, what does this word, phrase, sentence, paragraph, chapter, novel, play, poem, *do*; and the execution involves *an analysis of the developing responses of the reader in relation to the works as they succeed one another in time*" (127; emphasis in original). He continues, "Essentially what the method does is *slow down* the reading experience so that 'events' one does not notice in normal time, but which do occur, are brought to our analytical attentions. It is as if a slow motion camera with an automatic stop action effect were recording our linguistic experiences and presenting them to us for viewing" (128; emphasis in original).

Such an attention to form and to reading as event abets my goal of thinking through the complexities of the cultural representation of what Nina Marie Martínez referred to as the "somebody in between." My study's attention to the formal features of Latinx literature helps us see the dynamics of difference rather than static sameness. It will demonstrate, to borrow phrasing from Judith Butler, how the label *Latinx* does not represent the category it presumes to index, but rather produces it. In paying attention to the discursive production of the category, we can begin to shine a light on the diverse experiences the nomenclature hides beneath its seeming sameness. The result could well be a richer understanding of what we too often carelessly lump together as Latinx life and culture. Through a series of socially attuned close readings, I aim to demonstrate how an analytic attentive to the texts' cultural dynamism can open up a rich array of readings responsive to the complexities, contradictions, and nuances of culture.

Before embarking on a full-scale generic analysis of the work we have heretofore identified as Latinx, I develop more fully in Chapter 1 the limitations of both authorial identity and recognizable themes as the key criteria defining Latinx literature. It is an argument whose complexity and nuances warrant further elaboration. I pursue that argument through a case study of three writers—Danny Santiago, Brando Skyhorse, and Eduardo Halfon—not readily recognizable through the conventions we use to define Latinx literature. These are exemplary cases, not exceptional ones, and as such, they sharpen my argument that *Latinx* is a politically efficacious label, but not a clarifying, aesthetic one. The three subsequent chapters analyze contributions of Latinx writers to the postmodern novel, the short story, and the poem. The Conclusion not only draws together the arguments from the previous ones and reminds readers where the argument has taken them over the preceding pages, but also suggests ways in which my investigation may affect future studies of Latinx literature.

Let us move on to the work of unbinding Latinx literature from the usual critical, racial, and sociological perspectives that restrict what it is we know about this corpus of texts and see where that might lead us. There are many conversations to have about this literature, and I believe our insights—rich as they have been—can be broadened even further.

CHAPTER I

Brown Like Me? The Author-Function, Proper Names, and the Rise of Fictional Nobodies

It is said that when Linnaeus "found an insect that resisted classification he crushed it immediately" (Behar, "Juban América" 163). This chapter takes up the case of three writers whom Linnaeus, given his purported propensity to eradicate all matter of complexity, might indeed wish to crush. The first is the author of a novel that was heralded, upon its publication in 1983, as an authentic tale of life in a Chicano barrio, *The Catcher in the Rye* for the Chicano canon. It received the Richard and Hinda Rosenthal Foundation Award, given to one painter and one American work of fiction, which, "though not a commercial success, is a considerable literary achievement." The publishers also wished to nominate the book for the Pulitzer Prize. This new Chicano voice turned out to be that of a seventy-three-year-old, blacklisted, Anglo playwright. The second is a writer with an American Indian surname who, raised by five stepfathers, did not know for years that he was Mexican.[1] He has written a powerful first novel about Mexicans and Mexican Americans in Los Angeles's Echo Park. The novel received the 2011 PEN/Hemingway Award and the Sue Kaufman Prize for First Fiction from the American Academy of Arts and Letters. The third is a writer who was born in Guatemala City and raised in the

United States. He writes in Spanish (his books are published in Spain) on topics not recognizably Latinx, including the novel I will focus on, which is, among other things, the tale of the author's Polish grandfather and his imprisonment in Auschwitz. The author also happens to be an award-winning Latin American novelist. All three of these writers indisputably illustrate the complexities of literary classification. The novels and their authors raise important questions about the definitional limits of Latinx literature, limits that might be understood as "Who speaks?" and "What is spoken?" Such questions wrap us in a web of authenticity, appropriateness, and cultural expectations. If you can't crush the insects, how do you classify them? What does their disruption of the system tell you about the system's shortcomings and blind spots?

The Rise of the Novel and Fictional Nobodies

Let me begin with an inquiry into authority, fictionality, and mimesis in the modern and contemporary novel, for it will abet us in tackling the pressing definitional matters raised by the three authors I examine in this chapter. In an insightful essay that claims historians and theorists of the novel have left the term *fictionality* "unexamined," Catherine Gallagher rectifies that neglect by moving us through a compelling history of the rise of the novel and the concept of fictionality. Gallagher maintains that the "novel is not just one kind of fictional narrative among others," but rather the two terms are "mutually constitutive" ("Rise of Fictionality" 337). It is the modern novel, as opposed to earlier forms such as fables, fairy tales, romances, and allegories, in which the special relationship between a plausible story and purely imaginary individuals takes hold (338–341). Working within this nexus of the plausible and the imaginary, the mid–eighteenth-century novel takes proper names as its "key mode of nonreferentiality." The mid–eighteenth-century novel established this special relationship of the plausible story full of "fictional nobodies" (341, 353). If we are thinking in terms of contemporary literature as, for instance, with the novel *The Brief Wondrous Life of Oscar Wao*, there is no referent outside of the pages of the novel for Oscar Wao. He is a fictional nobody with a proper name inside a plausible story about Dominicans and Dominican Americans. Gallagher's argument, however, is more complex than the truism not to confuse characters with people, and as such it undertakes an analysis of the relationship between belief, disbelief, volition, and readers' expectations.

Although the proper names in novels "do not take specific individuals as their referents, and hence none of the specific assertions made about them can be verified or falsified" (341), we still must think through the various paradoxes this generates about referentiality, nonreferentiality, and belief. Indeed, "the founding claim of the form . . . was a nonreferentiality that could be seen as a greater referentiality" (342). These eighteenth-century novelists were distinguishing their work from the *chroniques scandeleuses* and the charges of fraud, libel, and scandal they generated by creating a world of fictional nobodies, but unlike fables and fairy tales, they were creating fictions we might recognize, if not verify or falsify, in the everyday world.

Aristotle's *Poetics* legitimized and lent them the formula they needed to square the probable and the fictive. "The difference between the historian and the poet," writes Aristotle, "is this: the one tells what has happened, the other the kind of things that can happen" (qtd. in Gallagher 343). But Aristotle's work had long been available, so why this recent squaring of the probable and the fictive? The rise of modernity, argues Gallagher, made early eighteenth-century England an auspicious location for the birth of the novel: "Modernity is fiction-friendly because it encourages disbelief, speculation, and credit" (345). These attitudes of disbelief and speculation put the reader in a position to sympathize with certain characters while also feeling superior to the characters' innocence and using the "reality of the story" as a means to speculate on how the reader might behave, act, react, and so on. "Novels," writes Gallagher, "promoted a disposition of ironic credulity enabled by optimistic incredulity; one is dissuaded from believing the literal truth of a representation so that one can instead admire its likelihood and extend enough credit to buy into the game" (346).

Gallagher, then, persuasively illustrates how the connection between belief and disbelief in the rise of fictionality is tied to the modern epoch. Unlike other forms of speculation that attended the rise of modernity—the economy and marriage—the novel allowed readers "to indulge in imaginative play," in which they were protected from any dire consequences (346–348). The individual's willing suspension of disbelief, which Coleridge made famous, "set novel reading apart from those mandatory suppositional acts that required the constant maintenance of active skepticism" (347). The reader could immerse herself and enjoy fiction's illusion because voluntary disbelief protects you from delusion (349). Gallagher brings us back again to the paradox of the novel form: It both discovers and obscures fiction. "The novel," she reiterates, "gives us explicit fiction and simultaneously seems to occlude it; the novel reader opens what she knows is a fiction because it is a fiction and soon finds that enabling knowledge to be the subtlest of the experience's elements. Just as it declares itself, it becomes that which goes without saying" (349). It is this paradox of dis-covering and obscuring fiction, I contend, that underwrites the agonistic relationship many readers and critics have had with novels that push Latinx literature outside of its comfort zone and that trouble our mainte-nance of the category Latinx literature, particularly the poles of authen-ticity and ethnicity around which it oscillates.

As with any other fiction, readers of Latinx fiction (perhaps especially Latinx readers), need to believe that the fictional world presented is plau-sible, but we readers of Latinx fiction (or at least a group of vocal critics) often forget the catalyst that drives the history of the novel, namely, a uni-verse of fictional nobodies. We take the novels' proper names and read them, not as nobodies, but as somebodies. We read them, that is, not as the novel form demands we do, but as the romance does. Characters in the ro-mance were considered exemplary individuals. As Gallagher observes, "Cer-vantes . . . introduces the difference between the novel, with its fictional nobodies, and the romance, with its exemplary individuals, as, first of all, a matter of names" (353). We overlook these fictional nobodies' non-referentiality and insist on their referent. When a novel fails to conform to a knowable universe or, better put, fails to conform to what readers believe are acceptable political, racial, social, gender, sexual, and other practices, we often deem it fraudulent and inauthentic; we consider it a sell-out.

Famous All Over Town

What makes Danny Santiago's *Famous All Over Town* (1983) especially in-teresting is not that its representations failed the callow test of authentic-ity. In every way, the novel conformed to a knowable Latinx universe.[2] In brief, the novel tells the story of Rodolfo "Chato" Medina, Jr., growing up in a barrio in East Los Angeles. Medina, now an adult, recalls his youth and the various obstacles he and his family faced. By novel's end his par-ents have split up, and his barrio has been razed. It is a coming-of-age story that follows Medina through tough times, with all the expected tests of his masculinity and male prowess. Things go too far when Medina is caught throwing up graffiti on a bank building and is subsequently arrested. This arrest will, however, see Medina's life turned around as he is put on his path to becoming a successful writer. Critics at the time praised it as a mas-terpiece. Lauro Flores, for instance, called it a "remarkable achievement," and added that it "joins the ranks of the foremost contemporary Chicano prose fiction works. Many more valuable contributions can be expected from this very talented artist" ("Response to Chaos" 147).[3]

What set the novel apart, and what makes it particularly interesting for my study of Latinx literature, was the discovery that Danny Santiago was not Danny Santiago. He was not, as had been supposed, a twenty-something Chicano author publishing his first novel. He was, rather, Daniel James, "a septuagenarian ex-Stalinist aristocrat from Kansas City" (Dunne, "Secret"). Danny Santiago—as if a character in a modern novel—was indeed a fictional nobody, rather than a unique individual. Or perhaps to make this complex case more interesting, we should give the screw another turn and say that we had a romance character (i.e., not a specific individual, but an exemplary one) writing a modern novel. That is, many readers and critics turned the person they believed to be writing the novel—Danny Santiago—into a representative for the group, a Chicano exemplar. It is a move often made in regards to Latinx fiction. Authors are often read as ambassadors for their culture. To add a layer of complexity, we had in the case of Danny Santiago, not just the readers' typical move of making the author a romance character—an exemplar—but we had a double fiction. Daniel James had not only invented the story known as *Famous All Over Town*, he had also invented a "character," a persona, to be the author. That invention seems, for many readers and critics, to have gone beyond the pale, to have pushed the willing suspension of disbelief necessary to read a novel onto the figure of the author as well, where readers have displayed a recalcitrance to suspend disbelief. To create an authorial fiction—even if that author is writing novels, not nonfiction[4]—is somehow going too far. We expect novels to be fictions, but not author's names.

Yet the pages of literary history are filled with such fictions. Mark Twain is Samuel Clemens. George Eliot is Mary Ann Evans. Jane Somers is Doris Lessing. Mary Westmacott is Agatha Christie. Robert Galbraith was revealed to be J. K. Rowling. Benjamin Black is John Banville. María Amparo Ruíz de Burton published her 1885 novel *The Squatter and the Don* as C. Loyal, a play on *Ciudadano Leal* (Loyal Citizen), a conventional way to close official letters in nineteenth-century Mexico. Fernandes, Rae Jolene Smith, Rosamond Smith, and Lauren Kelly are all Joyce Carol Oates. The names of some very famous authors even appear on the covers of the books they publish pseudonymously—Stephen King writing as Richard Bachman. There are hundreds, if not thousands, more that could be listed.

After an author's identity is disclosed, many want to know the motivations for the pseudonym. Some, like Mary Ann Evans, use a pen name to avoid gender discrimination. Some, like María Amparo Ruíz de Burton, use one to avoid gender and racial discrimination. Some, like Lessing, are testing the integrity of the publishing industry. In a July 2013 article for the *Guardian*, Rowling said that writing under a male pseudonym was intended to "take my writing persona as far away as possible from me" and that she was "yearning to go back to the beginning of a writing career in this new genre, to work without hype or expectation and to receive totally unvarnished feedback. It was a fantastic experience" (Bury, "J. K. Rowling Tells Story," par. 6, 12). The possible motivations are many and sundry, and I'm not certain we can (or need to) arrive at a generalizable rule for their use.

Let us consider, however, two pressing factors in assessing Daniel James's writing as Danny Santiago: (1) the distinction between a pseudonym and a heteronym, and (2) what Foucault has called the "author-function." While there may not be bright line distinctions between a pseudonym and a heteronym, there is a difference, and in the case of Danny Santiago, it merits our attention. A pseudonym, as we well know, is a pen name—a name other than the writer's own under which she publishes and may have adopted, as noted earlier, for a variety of reasons. A heteronym, on the other hand, though also a name other than the writer's own, carries with it the distinction of being not just a "false name," but a persona, an alter ego. The Portuguese writer Fernando Pessoa (1888–1935) "referred to the many names under which he wrote prose and poetry as 'heteronyms' rather than pseudonyms, since they were not merely false names but belonged to invented others, to fictional writers with points of view and literary styles that were different from Pessoa's" (Zenith 505). He endowed these heteronyms "with their own biographies, physiques, personalities, political views, religious attitudes and literary pursuits" (Zenith viii).

Given what we know of Daniel James's relation to Danny Santiago, of which I will have more to say in a moment, we are speaking of a heteronym—the persona—not a pseudonym. James, for instance, would write his agent, his editor, and his close friends John Gregory Dunne and Joan Didion in the voice of Danny Santiago, with all of its bravado, machismo, and interlingual (Spanish/English) language usage (Dunne, "Secret"). Daniel James inhabited Danny Santiago, and it freed his writerly voice. As he told William McPherson in a *Washington Post* interview on July 24, 1984, "The book. The book. That's the important thing. Not the skin color or the ancestry of the author. I had to become Danny Santiago to write. I couldn't explain it to my friends or wife. Perhaps a psychiatrist in two or three years might find the root causes of my need to be someone else. But the fact is I have that need" (A15).[5] To reduce this complex case of Danny Santiago and Daniel James to a mere case of ethnic fraud is to miss what makes this tale interesting for the history and definition of Latinx literature.

Before we undertake an investigation of the Danny Santiago persona and the controversy it stirred, we need to keep in mind one more crucial factor, namely, the author-function. In 1969, Michel Foucault published "What Is an Author?," an essay that interests itself, not in *who* an author is (not, say, at what point a writer becomes an author), but *what* an author is and how her name functions. The name of the author "is more than a gesture, a finger pointed at someone; it is, to a certain extent, the equivalent of a description," writes Foucault. "When we say 'Aristotle,'" he continues, "we are using a word that means one or a series of definite descriptions of the type: 'the author of the *Analytics*,' or 'the founder of ontology' and so forth" (121). In contemporary parlance, the author-function is much like what we call the brand. This author-function, this branding, creates expectations. Even before you open the cover of a Stephen King novel, you have expectations about its content, based solely on King's name. It does not just index a man who is a writer; it signals to you that you are going to read a novel by one of the masters of the horror genre. Indeed, you expect a book with King's name on it to be a horror novel and to be consistent affectively with the thrills and terrors generated by his earlier works, such as *The Shining, Cujo, It,* and so on.[6]

Let us imagine now that we are encountering *Famous All Over Town* upon its publication in 1983. The author-function, while still at work, is not as strong as it would have been with an established author. If you were an avid reader of fiction, you may have seen a Danny Santiago story in *Redbook* or *Playboy* in 1970 or 1971. You may have read his story, "The Somebody," in Martha Foley's annual *Best American Short Stories.* But Santiago was, relatively speaking, a little-known quantity when *Famous All Over Town* came out. To the extent that the author-function was in play, it was around the name Santiago. Being a Latinx surname, it served, for many readers, to authenticate the Chicano experience captured in the two hundred–plus pages of *Famous All Over Town.* Add to this author-function all of the other paratextual cues that tell us how to read a book—cover design, dust jacket blurbs, encomia gathered from reviews—and *Famous All Over Town* has you primed for an urban tale before you have even launched into the first paragraph.

As you open the cover of the paperback edition, you encounter excerpts from the reviews that appeared in the *Pittsburgh Press* and the *New York Times Book Review.* The one from *NYTBR* notes,

> Danny Santiago is a natural. . . . His *Famous All Over Town* is full of poverty, violence, emotional injury and other forms of major disaster,

all vividly and realistically portrayed, yet, like a spring feast-day in a barrio, it is nevertheless relentlessly joyous. Best of all is its language . . . a rich street Chicano English that pleases the ear like sly and cheerful Mejicana music . . . *Famous All Over Town* is a classic of the Chicano urban experience. And Danny Santiago is good news" (n.p.; ellipses in original).

Using no less a literary authority than the *NYTBR*, the publisher's design team lets the prospective buyer know that she can expect the "real thing" in this novel. That real thing trades on the reading public's stereotypical ideas of barrio life—"poverty, violence, and emotional injury" among others—and primes them for a voyeuristic reading experience. What, then, when a year later the author-function cannot perform as expected because that which the author's name designates and describes is not what was once believed? The heteronym—the persona and its connection, not to a Latino writing under a Latino surname, but to an aging Anglo writer—significantly changed the author-function and certain readers' experiences of the novel.[7] So it is not the persona *qua* persona that causes the disturbance to this particular author-function and the reading experience (though knowledge of an author's alter ego does modify the author-function) but the persona that makes a claim on an identity other than James's own. John Gregory Dunne knew this well.

In 1968, Daniel James approached Dunne with some stories he had written about East Los Angeles, a community that had been his home for twenty years. Dunne, who admired the stories, "was not enthusiastic" about James's desire to publish them under the pseudonym Danny Santiago ("Secret"). Dunne writes, "I had nothing against pseudonyms . . . but the idea of an Anglo presenting himself as a Chicano I found troubling" ("Secret"). Knowing, however, that James felt he had been unable to write for nearly twenty years under his own name, both because of being blacklisted and "because he had lost confidence in his own ability," Dunne went ahead and, with "an obfuscating cover letter," introduced Danny Santiago to his agent, Carl Brandt ("Secret"). The stories that would become the basis for *Famous All Over Town* enjoyed quick success, but it would be another fifteen years before the novel appeared. And for those fifteen years, from 1968 until 1983, John Gregory Dunne and his wife, Joan Didion, guarded Daniel James's secret.

But on August 16, 1984, in the *New York Review of Books*, Dunne—with Daniel and Lilith James's consent—published "The Secret of Danny Santiago," the article that brought Daniel James out. The article explains at great length the history of Daniel James, who was born an Anglo-American in 1911 and was seventy-two years old at the time *Famous All Over Town* was published. We learn of his Yale education, his struggles to become a writer, his work with Charlie Chaplin on *The Great Dictator*, his days as a member of the Communist Party, his blacklisting, his brief period of success as a writer and as a cowriter with his wife, Lilith, and his twenty-five-year period of unproductivity as a writer that would lead to the creation of Danny Santiago, during which time he would be an active member of the Mexican American community in East Los Angeles. Nevertheless, it is Dunne's unease with James's adoption of a Latinx surname that highlights the concerns over the novel and makes it an especially interesting object with which to embark on this investigation of the category of Latinx literature.

As a final note on Dunne's article and the controversy over James's use of the surname Santiago, I argue that Dunne makes a peremptory and savvy rhetorical move in opening his essay with direct testimony from Daniel James's hearing before the House Un-American Activities Committee (HUAC). Contra Alexander Cockburn, who says the use of the testimony and the essay itself "had the whiff of the witch hunter while purporting to be something else" (71), I contend that the testimony places the reader, who might be tempted to accuse Daniel James of various misdeeds, in an uncomfortable position from the very start. A far cry from witch-hunting, the essay—written with the consent of both Daniel and Lilith James by their own friend John Gregory Dunne—puts any potential detractors in the awkward position of aligning themselves with the HUAC and its nefarious hunting of "Reds" (i.e., anyone who dared to think in ways the committee deemed unpatriotic). In addition, opening the essay with an excerpt from James's HUAC hearing leaves no space for the questioning of his left, radical politics, the very politics the Chicana/o movement held dear.[8] Dunne's shrewd rhetorical opening forces anyone who would resort to the politics of ethnic authenticity into the position of having to run her own moralizing witch hunt. One can even imagine how the hypothetical trial might begin:

Q: Will you state your full name, Mr. *James*?

A: Daniel Lewis James.

Q: Are you now or have you ever been a Latino?

A: No.

Q: Have you ever consorted with Latinos?

As Dunne's article and numerous other essays and newspaper articles make clear, James had, of course, "consorted" with Latinos, Mexicans, and Mexican Americans in particular. He and his wife lived for decades in East Los Angeles. Beginning in the late 1940s, they served as volunteer social workers with the Los Angeles Church Federation, working to improve social, educational, and economic opportunities for youth in the area, to say nothing of the numerous families who asked them to serve as godparents to their children. Be that as it may, not all opening gambits win the game, so it matters little that Dunne's rhetorical gesture failed to keep the detractors at bay. It suggests he knew they would be coming, and he tried to stave them off. Writing under a fictitious name often creates no controversy, but in the case of Danny Santiago, it most certainly did.

The claiming of another's identity can register as profiteering, turning the plight of others into one's own success. In 1968, Daniel James attempted to convince Dunne of his legitimate reasons for adopting the name Danny Santiago, with the hope that Dunne would introduce James to his agent. He writes to Dunne:

> He's [Santiago] so much freer than I am myself. He seems to know how he feels about everything and none of the ifs, ands and buts that I'm plagued with. I don't plan to make a great cops and robbers bit out of him, but now at any rate I can't let him go. Maybe he'll prove a strait-jacket later on. We'll see. ("Secret")

If we are to trust this letter (and perhaps we don't), James's motivations appear more complex than a simple taking advantage of, but motivations are dicey and complex matters. We may never be able to ascertain them or arrive at some unimpeachable verdict. It is with good reason that we, literary critics, have a long-standing doctrine that encourages us to stay away from an author's intention when analyzing a piece of literature. Should we presume that knowing an author's intention about the adoption of a name would be any easier to apprehend than the intended meaning of a piece of literature?

In June 1984, when Dunne was discussing the possibility and contents of the article he wished to publish about Daniel James, he went to visit James. He says he was struck by "how deeply ingrained the character of Danny Santiago was on Dan James. Danny was the only persona in which Dan could write."[9] The moment when Dunne asks James if "he had considered the possibility of being accused of manufacturing a hoax" is especially revealing for thinking about the limits and boundaries of Latinx literature. Dunne writes, "[James] shrugged and said the book itself was the only answer. If the book were good, it was good under whatever identity the author chose to use, the way the books of B. Traven were good" ("Secret"). The book, however, was not "the only answer." The debate over the book has largely built itself around ethical inquiries about aggrieved groups and their cultural production—though at times this has bogged down in simplistic name calling[10]—but what has been missed or avoided is a discussion of the ways the novel troubles what it is we know or think we know about the category of Latinx literature.

I am not attempting to claim Daniel James as a Latinx subject; he certainly did not. What I am suggesting is that the case of Daniel James brings into sharp relief the definitional complexities of identifying a proper Latinx subject, and that, then, must bring along with it the complexities of defining the body of literature known as Latinx because, as matters currently stand, the identity of the author is one of the necessary and most heavily leaned-upon criteria for defining Latinx literature. Moreover, if we deal with the rich array of subject positions that might be called "Latinx," does that then not raise interesting, vexing, and wonderfully complex questions about what constitutes recognizably Latinx themes, as well as yet another referential conundrum about mimesis and the world outside of the fictional text?

If something with a genuinely "authentic" feel such as *Famous All Over Town* could be written by someone with a fictitious Latinx name (i.e., Danny Santiago), it presents not only an ethical dilemma of who can speak or who can speak for whom, but it creates a taxonomic problem that is hinged to a problem of poetics, "mak[ing] explicit the conventions of the literary system that make possible the production and interpretation of literary works" (Culler, *Literary in Theory* 9).[11] By every measurable standard, Daniel James is working with the formal conventions that render a work of Latinx literature recognizable as such, but there has been a critical desire to remove *Famous All Over Town* from the system because of the author's identity. Danny Santiago can be revealed as Daniel James. It is a one-time mystery that is easily solved. The conundrum he poses, however, for the classification of Latinx literature is not easily remedied.

Take, for example, the following two passages (purposefully selected at random). If both can and do look, sound, and feel like what we have come to call Latinx literature, are we to accept the one and dismiss the other because one writer is a "genuine" Latina/o and the other is a "fraud"? Could you distinguish these passages without the accompanying title or author name? Could they pass a blind test?[12]

That word [trucha] might mean trout in the dictionary, but to us it has
a different meaning. I looked down the street. A black-and-white had
just turned into Shamrock and now it came prowling up the street. A
black-and-white on Shamrock is like a cloud passing across the sun, it
chills you. Loud guys get quiet, quiet guys get loud. Some walk casually
into backyards, others start flaky conversations and everybody feels
Wanted For Murder. The cops raked the sidewalk with those glassy
eyes of theirs, and I stared right back at them. They don't like that. (90)

She raged with fear and revenge, waiting for the police to arrive. She
tipped the slats of the Venetian blinds to watch the boys standing in a
circle passing a joint, each savoring the sweet taste of the marihuana
cigarette as they inhaled. She remembered Toastie as a child. She had
even witnessed his baptism, but now he stood tall and she wondered
where he had learned to laugh so cruelly. She lowered her head. The
world was getting too confusing now, so that you even had to call the
police in order to get some kindness from your neighbors. (108)

These two passages capture the scene of much Latinx writing—that of the
local barrio, the urban landscape, the tough life in the city, the ubiquitous
presence of the police, and the navigation of gang violence. If one were
being honest, it would be difficult to claim that, on any formal basis of style
or content, one could tell these two passages apart. It just so happens that
the first passage is from Danny Santiago's *Famous All Over Town*, and the
second is from the Chicana writer Helena María Viramontes's story
"Neighbors." So, since Danny Santiago turned out to be Daniel James, is
what was once thought of as a great piece of Chicano writing about the
barrio now no longer part of the Chicanx and Latinx canons? If it is ruled
out, is this not then the very moment at which the whole definitional project of Latinx literature begins to founder on its need for referentiality? On
its utter dependence on the author-function and authenticity?

   In their annotated bibliography, *Chicano Perspectives in Literature* (1976),
the scholars Francisco Lomelí and Donaldo Urioste attempted to handle
the issue of non-Chicanos writing about Chicana/o matters with their invented category, *Chicanesque* writing.[13] However, as Juan Bruce-Novoa
points out, this category "has not really solved the problem, rather only
served to focus our attention more acutely on the unresolved nature of Chicano ethnicity" (*Retrospace* 140). Indeed, in this scenario, the project of
Latinx literature becomes the project of the author's identity. Not only is
this a questionable standard for defining a literary aesthetic, but it could
also harken back to dangerous nineteenth-century, pseudoscientific racial

understandings based in blood, for it would seem to lead one into debates over the author's heritage and bloodline. What percentage Latinx does one have to be to be a Latinx author? Are we willing to define Latina/os as "quadroons," "octoroons," and "quintoons"? While any self-respecting scholar would wince at those terms and deny using them, such language makes manifest what is really at play in defining who is an actual Latinx author. Daniel James is not of Latinx descent, but that is precisely the interest of this case; it forces us to bring into the open, and carry out to their logical conclusions, the identity criteria we are using to define the literature we call Latinx.

The history of *Famous All Over Town* is essentially an extended blindfold test—one that lasted over a year rather than a mere few seconds or minutes. And in that protracted time span, it gave critics and readers a chance to evaluate and appraise the novel, unaware that they were participating in a blindfold test. They offered their honest and laudatory assessments of the novel, but when, in August 1984, John Gregory Dunne untied the knot and let the veil drop from their eyes, suddenly the standards of evaluation had shifted because one of the definitional criteria had changed. The author was no longer the author. The author was a work of fiction, and because he was a work of fiction that did not accord with the standards and criteria of what counts as Latinx, his novel was no longer a classic work of Chicano fiction. I concur with Henry Louis Gates, Jr., when he writes that what we learn from the literary blindfold test "is not that our social identities don't matter. They do matter. And our histories, individual and collective, do affect what we wish to write and what we are able to write. But that relation is never one of fixed determinism. No human culture is inaccessible to someone who makes the effort to understand, to learn, to inhabit another world" ("Authenticity" 522).[14]

Daniel and Lilith James inhabited the world of East Los Angeles, and Daniel James's regular circulation in that world fired his imagination and ability to tell the story he told of the rise and fall of *Famous All Over Town*'s fictional Shamrock Street and its inhabitants. Indeed, he did so with the help of many of his friends who were the former residents of Clover Street— the barrio James fictionalizes as Shamrock Street. As he was polishing his manuscript, these friends helped him, for example, with matters of accuracy and language. Bobby Verdugo, a bus driver dispatcher, recalls, "He brought over the rough draft because he wanted us to help with slang expressions, the time references, things that were happening, what were some of the fashions. We were going, 'Wow! This is neat. This is a trip. Why couldn't I have done something like this?' Here was this man, at the time

71, I guess, and he's writing as a teen-ager and he's doing it believable" (Abrams, par. 13–14). There was clearly a sustained and affirming relationship between James and his neighbors, one that included all manner of education and cultural sharing. To return to Gates's comment, this is not to say that social identities do not matter. They do. They certainly affect how we see, approach, and inhabit the world, and while those are important social and personal matters, they are not the foundation upon which one can build an intellectual argument about aesthetics, poetics, and cultural taxonomies. If we continue to put pressure on this identity category, as I intend to do, we see its flaws and weaknesses. How does it deal, for instance, with multiracial people or with non-Latinx children adopted by Latinx parents or vice versa? The monolithic signifier *Latinx* is anything but monolithic. It is porous and fractured. It might be a useful tool for taking a census, but its indeterminacy—a constant state except when *Latinx* is strategically marshaled as a necessary fiction—dramatically limits its usefulness for theorizing the tenets and contours of a literary corpus.

In my probing of the Daniel James case, I have been trying to capture the deep story.[15] I have wanted to see what happens if we avoid an outright rejection of Daniel James and his heteronym Danny Santiago. To continue deepening our understanding of what we talk about when we talk about Latinx literature, I turn to Brando Skyhorse—the writer with the "Indian" surname, five stepfathers, and, for many years, a lack of knowledge that he is Mexican. It may serve as a helpful analog and reminder to recall the complicated backstory to a quintessential work of American literature, namely, *The Autobiography of Benjamin Franklin*. A tale little recited outside of specialist conversations among historians of early American literature is that, "Franklin's autobiography was first published in Paris and in French in 1791 as *Mémoires de la Vie Privée*, that the first English translation, *The Private Life of the Late Benjamin Franklin, LL.D. Originally Written by Himself, and Now Translated from the French*, was published in London in 1793 rather than in the United States, and that Franklin self-identified as English rather than American until at least 1772" (Levander, *Where Is American Literature?* 18).

The Madonnas of Echo Park

As you first read the paratext of *The Madonnas of Echo Park* (2010), you may find yourself in a similarly topsy-turvy world. It is perhaps a bad idea to judge a book by its cover, but the cover is the starting point for understanding the book's contents. Attempting to make sense of the novel before deciding to purchase or read it, you scan the book for clues about its content. You note the catchy cover design. The title and author's name are spray-painted on a white brick wall, surrounded by floral flourishes and a green stencil of a woman caught mid-dance pose, wearing a large hoopearring and a wrist full of jangly bracelets. If you happened to have grown up in the 1980s, you may even immediately recognize her as an iconic new wave figure. The cover gives the novel an urban feel.

If you happen to know much about Los Angeles, you immediately imagine the Echo Park neighborhood and its predominantly Mexican and Mexican American inhabitants, so you perhaps begin to think you are in the world of Latinx literature. In that frame of mind, you associate the "Madonnas" of the title with the Blessed Virgin Mary and then link that up to a history of representations and (stereo)types in Latinx literature, but you also perhaps look again at the stenciled new wave icon on the cover and think of the pop sensation Madonna, not a figure well-circulated in the pages of Latinx literature. Your eyes move left again to the author's surname, and it fails to register as Latinx. Thus the front cover leaves you in a world of not easily squared signifiers.

You flip the book over and begin reading the back cover. If you are an avid reader of contemporary fiction, you will note that the blurbs come from a powerful group of literary fiction writers—Glen David Gold, Aimmee Bender, and Peter Matthiessen among others. If you happen to be looking for a book of Latinx fiction, or if you happen to be a critic of Latinx literature, you note that of the six blurbs not one of them is from a Latinx author. Moreover, not one of them associates the novel with a Latin American writer or a Latinx writer, and not one makes any reference to magical realism or the Latin American boom. It lacks, in other words, all of the typical packaging of Latinx fiction. The blurbs address the urban quality of the fiction, Skyhorse's talent as a writer, and the care with which he handles his characters. You may discern that you are in the world of a master fiction writer, but the blurbs do not give you cause to think you may be entering a world of Latinx fiction—no comparisons, for instance, to the works of recognizable Latinx writers, which would have been easy to make. Yxta Maya Murray, Abraham Rodríguez, and Helena María Viramontes come immediately to mind. But perhaps these are the names that a specialist in the field associates with the urban tradition in which Skyhorse writes, and not the names that strike a familiar chord with general readers— names that might bring them from the shelves to the cash register. In short, the paratext simultaneously works on multiple levels for multiple readers.

But as soon as you begin reading the inside flaps of the dust jacket of *The Madonnas of Echo Park*, you are on more familiar thematic turf. The synopsis of the novel begins as follows:

> *We slipped into this country like thieves, onto the land that once was ours.*

> With these words, spoken by an illegal Mexican day laborer, *The Madonnas of Echo Park* takes us into the unseen world of Los Angeles, following the men and women who cook the meals, clean the homes, and struggle to lose their ethnic identity in the pursuit of the American dream. (emphasis in original)

This dust jacket copy places us in a world of readily recognizable Latinx fiction—the border crossing, the day labor, the way in which immigrants are treated as expedient labor, and the cost of the American dream. If before the *Famous All Over Town* scandal broke, Danny Santiago—a Latino-named author—brought us into a recognizable Latinx-themed novel, we have something different with *The Madonnas of Echo Park*. We have an author with a Native American surname bringing us into a recognizable Latinx world, and that pairing unsettles the semiotics of books we recognize as Latinx.

You flip to the back inside flap in search of information about the author, and you find a cropped headshot of Mr. Skyhorse. The photo engages the phenotypic talents with which you have been indoctrinated to read race, and, admit it or not, you think, "Dark hair, dark eyes, brown skin. A book about Echo Park. He's Latino."[16] You then read the author's note below the picture and learn that Skyhorse was born and raised in Echo Park, fulfilling your desire for a credible and authoritative voice, someone who can place you in a world of plausible, fictional nobodies. Moreover, you learn he completed an MFA at one of the top writing programs in the country and has worked for a decade in the world of New York publishing, confirming the claims of the encomia that you are in the hands of a "unique talent" and "gifted writer." Then you come to the final sentence of the note and discover that Skyhorse is writing a memoir about growing up with five stepfathers. While this may not undercut the feelings of authenticity the author's photo generated, nor his credentials as a denizen of the very neighborhood about which he writes, it sets your curious mind wandering— Who are these stepfathers? Was one of them Native American? Who is his biological father? Is he really the Latino I think he is?

Things grow more complex as you move from paratext to text. As you embark on reading the novel, you are greeted with three epigraphs:

They thought I was a Mexican, of course; and in a way I am.

JACK KEROUAC, *On the Road*

I wish I was born Mexican, but it's too late for that now.

MORRISSEY

It's no fun to pick on Mexicans. You guys got a country.

RICHARD PRYOR

Given the semiotic function of the epigraph, you know these sentences telegraph a central theme or idea about the pages of the novel to follow. Richard Pryor's lines are the easiest to situate because they register familiar themes in Mexican and Mexican American history and literature—ideas of national belonging; the relationship between borders, citizenship, migration, and xenophobia; and the feelings of dislocation many Mexican Americans, among others, feel. The Morrissey and the Kerouac passages are trickier because they deal with identity and the claiming of or the desire to be Mexican from an American author of French-Canadian descent and from a British pop singer.[17] Positioned as telegraphs, these two epigraphs—which cannot but be read in conjunction with the information about Skyhorse's "five stepfathers"—give knowing readers pause to speculate on how they relate to the content of the novel and/or the author.

When you then turn the page and find not the beginning of the novel but rather a ten-page "Author's Note," you fully realize you are in the hands of a self-conscious fiction writer—one who is aware of the terrain and debates over ethnic literatures and authenticity, and one who, like Kerouac and Morrissey, is thinking about his Mexican identity. The note begins, "This book was written because of a twelve-year-old girl named Aurora Esperanza. In the 1980s, before I knew I was Mexican . . ." (Skyhorse, *Madonnas of Echo Park* xi). And there you have it—the Latina-named personage who is the catalyst for the novel and the author's claim to a Mexican identity. That latter claim is, however, couched in a narrative clause of intrigue: "before I knew." It signals to the reader that there is a complex, complicated, and nuanced story to the author's identity, that his ethnic identity was one of discovery. This knowledge unleashes a string of questions for the reader, the principal one being, "How could this be so?" The syntax of Skyhorse's phrasing, combined with the expectations the reader brings to something called an "author's note," makes the reader hunger for an explanation, but it is one Skyhorse only hints at. He tells us that his sixth-grade class mostly comprised "American-born Mexicans and first-generation Vietnamese immigrants" and that he felt he belonged to neither group, but that on occasion his "Mexican-ness would peek out every so often from under the shadow of my stepfather's last name" (xi).

Most of the note is dedicated to explaining why he has written the book for Aurora Esperanza, which is no small detail, given my analysis of Brando Skyhorse and the limits and possibilities of labeling a work of literature as Latinx literature. In short, he wrote the book as an apology, because when Aurora asked him to dance at their classroom party, he told her he couldn't dance with her because she was Mexican, a response he had practiced with his mother (xvii). His comment, of course, caused Aurora great pain, and she reciprocated by rendering him invisible, staring through him in horror. When, following the dance, he wanted to apologize, Aurora was gone and never showed up to class again. I cite the closing of this note at length, not only for what it tells us about the anti-Mexican episode with Aurora, but also for what we come to learn of this note in subsequent interviews with Skyhorse:

> Twenty-five years later, I think I have found my way [to apologize], in the book you're reading now. This is the story of Aurora Esperanza and why she disappeared, told through the people of Echo Park who ultimately led me back to her. And while I've changed some details to protect those who drifted in and through this project over the duration of its writing, these voices are their real voices. I want to add that everyone in this book insisted he or she was a proud American *first*, an American who happened to be Mexican, not the other way around. No one emphasized this more than Aurora. I *am* a Mexican, she said when I caught up with her, but *a Mexican* is not *all that I am*. . . . she was gracious enough to ask about my mother's attempts to raise me as someone other than a Mexican in a curious rather than an accusatory way.
>
> "I don't blame her," she said. "I must confess—and I guess this *is* a confession—why would anyone want to be a Mexican in *this* country at a time like this?" I understood what she meant. When writing this book, originally called *Amexicans*, there was such a vitriolic fever against illegal immigration (translation: Mexicans) that it made me grateful I had an Indian last name, and ashamed that I felt grateful. (xix–xx; emphasis in original)

This closing does much significant work. It shows us an author who has found a means to apologize, an author full of remorse for his behavior. It lets us know that the tale of Echo Park will be told through "real voices." It captures feelings of national pride and national rejection, xenophobia, and racism. And it underscores, again, the complexity of Skyhorse's own identity—coming to an awareness (though we know not how) of his Mexicanness and the resonance of his American Indian surname. The candor of the note and the painful tale of racism and remorse that it tells draws the reader in, and what follows in the subsequent two hundred pages is a compelling tale of recognizable fictional nobodies, principally Mexicans and Mexican Americans, and their intertwined lives in Echo Park. We hardly have to suspend our disbelief to recognize the urban tale he tells of racial strife, class antagonisms, chased-after dreams, and "urban revitalization," among other themes. The author's note has let us into Brando Skyhorse's world, or we have every reason to believe so, given its genre, the language of "real voices," and his explanation for why he came to write the book.

I was, thus, caught off guard when I read Skyhorse's response in a 2010 interview for *Publisher's Weekly*, when he was asked about the author's note and how his upbringing affected his "view of ethnicity." Skyhorse responded,

> In case there's been any confusion: the author's note is fictional. It was always sold as fiction. When I was writing the book, I assumed there would be questions about why a guy named Brando Skyhorse is writing about Mexican-Americans in East L.A., and it's a totally fair question. The part about me not knowing I was a Mexican until I was 12 or 13 years old, that part is true. I wanted to acknowledge that part of my life in this book in some fashion and I felt that the best way to do that was in a fictional author's note. The idea of ethnicity is a little weird for me because, for a number of years, I believed that my biological father was Native American. I'm a Mexican, but a Mexican is not all that I am. That probably sums it up best, at least for me. (Manning, "Becoming Mexican," par. 5)

Leaving aside that many readers probably never read this interview from April 2010 and have gone on trusting the veracity of that author's note, Skyhorse's response remains intriguing. On the one hand, it reveals his knowledge of the authenticity politics and mimetic expectations that many readers bring to a work of fiction. On the other hand, his registered surprise that the interviewer might have read the author's note as nonfiction is in itself surprising. As mentioned earlier, readers have every reason to believe that a prefatory document that calls itself an "author's note" is a work of nonfiction. And while it is helpful for Skyhorse to clarify that the part of not knowing he was Mexican until he was twelve or thirteen is true, he has created a hermeneutic conundrum around questions of veracity.

Moreover, the narrative play that Skyhorse engages in by claiming that a seemingly nonfictional text about his autobiography is principally fiction brings to the fore the problematic position of using an author's identity as a definitional criterion in literary taxonomies. The interview and the author's note reveal, that is, the limits to ascertaining a person's identity. Who would want to make herself the arbiter of someone else's identity, and on what basis would she be suited to make that assessment? In cases such as Danny Santiago/Daniel James, one can easily ascertain the crossing of ethnic and racial boundaries, or at least as we have come to inherit and understand those boundaries. We hardly live, however, in a world of pure, authentic, discrete racial and ethnic boundaries, even if the racial taxonomy in the United States would have us believe otherwise. In Skyhorse's case, as we will see, the search for his own identity was particularly acute, but that is not to say rare.

Whereas it was John Gregory Dunne—Daniel James's friend—who told us the complicated story of how and why Daniel James came to write as Danny Santiago, it is Brando Skyhorse himself who tells us his own amazingly complex life story in his memoir, *Take This Man* (2014). This memoir sees the racial bet of the fictional "Author's Note," with which *Madonnas* begins, and raises it tenfold. To the extent that the memoir gives us a greater autobiographical sketch of Skyhorse, what role does it play in shaping how and if we classify *Madonnas* as a work of Latinx literature and Skyhorse as a Latinx novelist? As Skyhorse asks, "How is it that someone with the most American Indian of names came to write a story set among Mexicans? It's impossible to talk about that book [*Madonnas*] without telling my and my mother's stories" (*Take This Man* 239–240). And to reiterate one of the guiding principles of *Latinx Literature Unbound* in particular and poetics in general—how we classify a work or corpus of literature matters because it sets in place the semiotic system that shapes what we can know about that work or corpus. Similarly, but from a temporal perspective, Kenneth Warren, in treating African American literature as a historical phenomenon, notes, "Of course, any insistence on historical periodization is justified only if it leads to interpretive clarity" (9).[18] "Interpretive clarity" must be the guiding principle in any classification of literature.

The memoir charts Brando Skyhorse's search "for a father and who I was" (5). While I cannot retell that entire tale, I want to focus on the ways Skyhorse's complex identity formation not only shows us the limits of relying on identity as a criterion for defining a corpus of literature, but also how the nomenclature we have and use for defining ethnic and racial groups, itself, masks the complexity of the groups it presumes to index and thereby their presumably shared cultural expression as well. So who is Brando Skyhorse? The encapsulated version with which he opens the memoir runs as follows:

> My mother, Maria Teresa, a Mexican who wanted to be an American Indian, transformed me into Brando Skyhorse, a full-blooded American Indian brave. I became the son of Paul Skyhorse Johnson, an American Indian activist incarcerated for armed robbery who my mother met through the mail. She became Running Deer Skyhorse, a full-blooded "squaw" who traded in her most common of Mexican names for the most stereotypical of Indian ones.
>
> . . .
>
> I lived most of my childhood without knowing who I really was. All I knew was the power in my own name: *"Brando Skyhorse? That's beautiful."* (*Take This Man* 1; emphasis in original)

Skyhorse spends the next 250 pages unpacking that capsule version of his life, as he brings us to understand his mother's "fabrications," his participation in the various narratives his mother weaves of her and him, his struggle to latch onto any of the five men his mother "marries" as a father, and his search for the man he finds out to be his biological father—Candido Ulloa. I have no desire to make myself the arbiter of Skyhorse's identity or to determine if he is "authentically" or "officially" Latino. My goal is antithetical to those authenticity politics.

Whereas Skyhorse's case may seem like an exceptional one, it stands in well as a representative example of how complex identity is and can be. I am tempted to use the language of exogenous and endogenous marriages, but to do so presumes that there are, in fact, discrete groups into and out of which one could marry. I want to dismantle those reified group categories because when we employ them, they conceal more than they reveal; they limit rather than unbind; they present a dynamic of difference as a static sameness. Thus, an attention to a figure such as Brando Skyhorse forces us to analyze the pat categories we use to label people and, by extension, their cultural production. He makes us wrestle with race and ethnicity, not as preternatural categories waiting to be "discovered," but as narratives that are invented and imposed. While in Skyhorse's case they are largely his mother's self-fashioning ones, she does not invent them *de novo*, but rather constructs them through available discourses of Native American politics and stereotypes, biology and phenotype, immigration and assimilation, and linguistics and acculturation. As for his role in this self-fashioning, Skyhorse tells us, "I found out I was Mexican when I was around twelve or thirteen. My mother forbade me from telling anyone our story. I kept our secret long after I needed to because my mother's lie had become my whole truth" (3). Let us continue working through that "whole truth," for it gives us a sense not of an alter ego or heteronym, but rather insights into the complexity of an identity in formation, the identity that will undergird the author who gives us that most compelling of urban tales and gentrification—*The Madonnas of Echo Park*.

Brando Skyhorse is the biological son of a mother whose identity itself is hard to track in Skyhorse's memoir. In interviews and even in most of the memoir, he tells us that his mother—Maria Teresa (her surname is never given)—is Mexican American, but he also tells us that Maria Teresa's mother—June—"was, in fact, a Plains Indian from Oklahoma, making Maria half Indian" (*Take This Man* 22), but also that his grandmother is "a lightish mix of Mexican, Spanish, and Swiss" (9). Thus, if we are following lines of ancestral descent to ascertain Maria's identity, we fail to come up with an easy answer. We also know that Maria was raised by her Mexican mother, June, and her Filipino stepfather, Emilio, and if culture is something learned—not exclusively about ancestry and or biology—Emilio certainly complicates the story further, but he appears too infrequently in the memoir to allow any clear assessment of how Filipino culture may have figured into Maria's upbringing. Skyhorse will refer to her identity throughout as Mexican, an identity she bears with shame and rescripts as Native American around the time that Candido (Brando's biological father) leaves Maria and Brando.

Brando was only three years old when Candido left, and his "life as Brando Kelly Ulloa, the son of a 'good-for-nothing wetback' [his mom's phrasing] ended" and his "life as Brando Skyhorse, the American Indian son of a political activist" began (26). Thus, for nine or ten years he genuinely believed he was American Indian and did not realize he was Mexican American. In 1977, Brando's mother began a correspondence with Paul Skyhorse Durant, a member of the American Indian Movement (AIM), who, with Pat "Mohawk" Billings, had been arrested in 1974 for the robbery and murder of a taxi cab driver. They were both acquitted in 1978. During the trial, Maria attempted to pass herself off as Paul Skyhorse Durant's wife, but when she realized that was unfeasible, "she found—or created—in another prison . . . a second Paul Skyhorse" (28).[19] This Paul Skyhorse became Brando's father. By the fall of 1978, Maria became "Running Deer," a name she claimed "Paul bestowed on her" (31). As Brando notes, the name fulfilled her dream of "being an Indian somebody instead of a Mexican nobody" (31). The mother went as far as rescripting Candido as

"Uncle Candy" on the backs of family photos and rewriting any instances of Brando Ulloa as Brando Skyhorse as well (31). For his part, Brando had no reason to believe he was anything other than who his mother said he was. Consider as illustrative the following act of civil disobedience. In first grade, when his "Mexican and Vietnamese" classmates rise to say the Pledge of Allegiance, he refuses and recites the words his mother had him memorize, "'Because of this country's treatment of my race and my people, I cannot pledge allegiance to this flag or country'" (52).

Skyhorse is living the identity he thinks is his own, but as he grows older, matters become more complicated. When he discovers around age twelve or thirteen that Candido Ulloa is his biological father,[20] not Paul Skyhorse or any of the other men who enter his life, he grows frustrated with his mother's evasions of his questions and with her refusal to give him his "first story" (101). Moreover, simply knowing the biological origins of his existence provides little ontological clarity, and when Paul Skyhorse deserts him and his mother, the confusion simply mounts:

> Was I no longer a Skyhorse? I was still "Indian," closing yearbook signatures the way I had in seventh and eighth grades, "May the Great Spirit guide you," the same signature Paul used in his letters. If I wasn't a Skyhorse—the only part of my identity I felt was "me"—then who *was* I? A Mexican who had no idea what being Mexican meant, pretending to be an American Indian in name only? (131; emphasis in original)

What I find so rich in this retelling of his confusion as a young boy is how it captures the tension between a blood identity and a lived identity. On the one hand, he is the biological product of a Mexican mother and father, but the mother kept that biological identity from him, including disallowing his grandmother, June, from teaching him Spanish and doing so much to conceal that they were Mexicans that he has "no idea of what being Mexican meant" (and he evidently believes there is some uniform or clear way to be Mexican).[21] On the other hand, though he seems to have no blood ties to a particular Native American nation (his grandmother's Plains Indian identity being difficult to ascertain), he has been raised in perhaps the most stereotypical ways as if he were Native American, so much so that that it is the part of him he "feels" to be real. Yet he also remains cognizant that that identity is a manufactured one: "For me, being 'Indian' wasn't different from what any other kind of ghetto raconteur in Echo Park did: talk fast and hide the truth. Or tell my mother's version of the truth that I had memorized" (105).

This "feeling" and narrating of his identity seems to me to be the more interesting point, more so than the setting up of what Juan Bruce-Novoa once flippantly referred to as a *prueba de sangre* (a blood test) for determining who is an authentic Chicano author (*Retrospace* 141).[22] I say more interesting because it treats identity not as something simplistic that one could use, say, a litmus test to prove, but as something one regularly negotiates, practices, and performs. Or as Skyhorse would have it, this performance, this narrating of a life, is important because it is through our stories that we "sustain" ourselves: "They carry us through the lives we convince ourselves we can't escape to get to the lives we ought or *need* to live instead. They create out of endless chaos a beginning, a middle, and an *end*" (*Take This Man* 239; emphasis in original). But this sustaining, this ordering of chaos, does not mean landing in a space of surety, of an easily codified, neatly boxed identity. For although Skyhorse is now forty years old and has been reunited with his biological father and Candido's three daughters with whom Skyhorse has developed budding relationships, he still feels himself in an in-between place:

> I'm not an Indian . . . but feel I'm still somewhere between two names and two cultures. It's difficult because I can't even occupy the gray space mixed children try to claim for themselves. I get emails from Stanford's American Indian alum network that say, "Dear Native Alum," while I struggle to learn Spanish beyond a second-grade level. In New York, where I live, I'm less Mexican or American Indian and more some kind of ethnic superhero—*Passing Man!* Capable of passing for whatever any member of another ethnicity wants me to be! . . . The feeling of another man claiming me as a member of his own people and his own homeland is irresistible to someone who feels he truly has neither. (240–241)

Skyhorse, then, does not strike me as someone who, in Browder's parlance, we might want to categorize as a slippery ethnic subject. Rather, he illustrates the very slipperiness of subjecthood in general. His story makes manifest the multiple ways—complex family histories, adopting the stories one hears about oneself, concealing one's identity because of xenophobia and racism, being seen and claimed by others for the ethnic group they feel you belong to—subjects come into being. That becoming is never one of racial purity. Such a thing does not exist. Let us remind ourselves, as Stuart Hall says, that "The future belongs to the impure. The future belongs to those who are ready to take in a bit of the other, as well as being what they themselves are" (299). It is perhaps in this space of impurity and in-betweenness, not one of racial authenticity, that we should look for the story of Latinx literature, a story that takes yet another turn as we consider Eduardo Halfon.

THE POLISH BOXER

If Danny Santiago turned out not to be a new Chicano voice telling his "authentic" tale of the barrio, but rather an aging, blacklisted, Anglo writer, and if Brando Skyhorse is the writer who was "raised as a piecemeal Native American" (Morrison, "Brando Skyhorse," par. 13), who didn't realize he was Mexican until he was twelve, and who even then intermittently embraced and rejected that identity over the years, then Halfon gives us yet further pause as we consider the definitional parameters and limits of what we currently understand to be Latinx literature. In many ways he is a recognizable figure—especially for scholars of Latinx literature such as José David Saldívar and Kirsten Silva Gruesz who profitably push us within and beyond national boundaries to transnational or hemispheric understandings of literary production—and in other thematic ways, he is an outlier. I should note, as well, that my analyzing Halfon as someone who helps us question the limits and possibilities of the category *Latinx literature* is an anticipatory gesture. He has been the recipient of the José María de Pereda Literary Prize in Cantabria, Spain, and in 2007 the Hay Festival of Bogotá named him one of the best young Latin American writers. He has yet, however, to the best of my knowledge, to be claimed as a Latinx writer. If we rely, however, on the typical identity grounds, he certainly could be. Thus, it is in that prospective frame of mind that I consider him.

Born and raised in Guatemala until he was ten years old, Halfon came to the United States (Florida more specifically) in 1981, eventually studied engineering at North Carolina State University, and moved back to Guatemala in his early twenties, where he was a professor of literature at Universidad Francisco Marroquín. He currently resides in Nebraska. It is not an especially unique biography in the annals of Latinx migration and immigration. Like many, but by no means all, Latina/os, he accentuates how he feels out of place—*desubicado* in Spanish. In a *3:AM Magazine* interview with Des Barry, Halfon says,

> I went to the United States when I was ten and went back to Guatemala in my early twenties. When I returned to Guatemala, I could barely speak Spanish. I felt totally out of place. Living in the United States, I was seen as a Guatemalan. When I returned to Guatemala I

was an outsider there, too. I suppose I've always been an outsider. Still
am. I never understood Guatemala. I felt completely *desubicado*. Maybe
you could translate that as a sense of profound displacement, of not
belonging anywhere. ("Eduardo Halfon," par. 43)

This is not an uncommon story. One hears many stateside Puerto Ricans
and Chicana/os, for example, claiming to live in a space in between.
Mexican nationals often describe Mexican Americans as *pobre pochos del otro
lado*, and many Chicana/os who made roots journeys to Mexico during the
heydays of the movement found themselves not in the warm embrace of
"their people" but cast as outsiders in the drama of that particular nation.
Thus, many Chicana/os find themselves at home neither in the United
States nor Mexico. A similar story can be told of Puerto Ricans who live
in the United States. One is likely to hear a Nuyorican declare herself "Ni
de acá, ni de allá." I am painting with broad brushstrokes. There are, of
course, a host of complicating factors to consider—where one lives in the
United States, which generation one hails from, what one's language fa-
cility is in Spanish and English, how frequently one travels back and forth
between the United States and the country of origin or one's family's country of origin, and so on. Moreover, many Latina/os, of course, feel very
much at home in the United States, and in fact, the United States is their
home by birth and/or choice. So while I think it is important to note the
long history of Latina/os feeling both in and out of place, I avoid all too
easy generalizations about national belonging.

In the case of Halfon, displacement becomes interesting in how it works
with and against the literary traditions that have laid claim or may lay claim
to him. Through that heavy leaning on the ethnic identity of the writer,
one could imagine that Latinx critics would be quick to claim him as a
Latinx writer, though he himself never does.[23] Indeed, in a 2013 interview
for *Guernica* magazine, he refers to himself as an international writer: "It's
very hard for any international writer—Spanish, Japanese, Russian, Chi-
nese—to get their work into English. There is very little room for all of
us. We just don't fit. In my case, although I was so close to the English
language, it still took a long time to break through" (Murphy, "Origin Stories," par. 31; emphasis in original). When, in a 2012 interview for literary
magazine *Sampsonia Way*, he is asked if he considers himself a "citizen of a
particular country," Halfon remarks, "Not at all. . . . I've just never felt that
I belonged anywhere—not in Guatemala, not in the United States, not in
Spain. I don't know why that is, but it's my reality. It's a very fluid existence.
I can pretend to be where I'm at: I'm very American if I'm in the U.S., and

I'm very Guatemalan if I'm in Guatemala, and I'm very Spanish in Spain. I can modify my voice and my physical appearance and pretend to be from where I'm living at the moment.[24] Yet I'm not really there" (Barnes, "No Borders," par. 16). There is not one mention in either of these interviews—nor in any of the extant available material on Halfon—of a Latino identity. He says that he's "very American in the U.S.," not very Latino. And whereas Santiago/James and Skyhorse write on recognizable Latinx themes in recognizable Latinx places—a criterion scholars also put much weight on in assessing Latinx literature[25]—Halfon does not. He writes of famous authors' literary origins (*El ángel literario*), of the search for a Serbian pianist (*La pirueta*), and of his childhood in the tumultuous 1970s in Guatemala (*Mañana nunca lo hablamos*), among other topics. I want to push this point of authorial identity and theme to its logical limits to see how it might help us unbind, or perhaps even break open, Latinx literature.

Let me add that while its pronunciation can easily be Hispanicized, Halfon is not a Latinx surname, but rather a Lebanese one, and if we are to believe there is some connection between Eduardo Halfon the author and Eduardo Halfon the narrator of *The Polish Boxer*—I address that overlap below—Halfon is also of Polish ancestry. His mother's last name is a Polish one—Tenenbaum (*Polish Boxer* 73). In Eduardo Halfon, then, we have a *desubicado* Guatemalan national with Polish, Lebanese, and Jewish roots. On this latter point, his "novel" *The Polish Boxer*, which I will focus on here, is among other things his attempt to tell the story of his grandfather's survival in Auschwitz, a story his grandfather had kept hidden from Halfon for years. More generally, the book is a search for lost stories, lost people, and lost things. In that search, the collection moves through some geographic sites largely unfamiliar to Latinx literature—Serbia, Portugal, and Guatemala. In addition, he says of his then forthcoming novel *Monastery*, which is set in Israel, "It's about something that happened during my sister's Orthodox wedding in Jerusalem" (Murphy, "Origin Stories," par. 24). Again, neither a typical locale nor common theme in Latinx literature. What can we stand to learn from Halfon's example?

I begin by tracing the curiously protean history of *The Polish Boxer* because it highlights Halfon's penchant for pushing on boundaries that circumscribe rather than open a text up. *The Polish Boxer* is an ever growing text that exists in many forms, not a singular, definitive one. The novel was originally published in 2008 as *El Boxeador Polaco*. In 2012, it was translated into English—Halfon's English-language debut—by Halfon and a team of five translators. The two books are, however, distinct from one another—the English version contains four additional stories or chapters. It is a generically elusive text, and it is hard to tell whether we are dealing with linked stories or a novel.[26] Moreover, the ordering of the stories differs, as does some of the content. The book will also be coming out in "different formats" in German, Portuguese, and Italian. As Halfon notes, "Each country has decided which stories they want, in what order, and which book-length they prefer" (Barry, "Eduardo Halfon," par. 47). In addition, the story of his grandfather, and the Polish boxer who helped save him, has been present in all nine of Halfon's books. It is part of a "bigger project that is constantly growing" (Barry, "Eduardo Halfon," par. 47). When, in his interview, Des Barry suggests that *The Polish Boxer* is perhaps like Walt Whitman's ever growing *Leaves of Grass*, Halfon replies, "I keep writing more chapters, more stories, more episodes, and they all fit in at different places in the narrative. New stories grow out of the existing ones. Old stories become new ones. Shorter stories become longer ones. Maybe in thirty years *The Polish Boxer* will be one huge book. Maybe I'm just writing one huge book. Maybe all of my writing is part of one huge project. Maybe it'll never end" ("Eduardo Halfon," last par.). This protean, dynamic, ongoing narrative is also tied to the qualities of selfhood, of the very construction of Eduardo Halfon through an act of narrative doubling. Halfon is both author and narrator. This is not the act of an author's identity being revealed by a close friend, or of an author defining himself through an author's note and subsequent memoir. This is an author writing himself into an ever changing, ever growing text and into a discourse of literary classification that has come to rely on authorial identity and fictional themes. All of these factors ramify into how we measure Halfon vis-à-vis the Latinx canon and vice versa. Additionally, *The Polish Boxer* is not only an ever growing story, it is also a story whose author and narrator like to push at the limits of truth and reality, verisimilitude and artifice—traits employed to differing effects in Daniel James's performance of Danny Santiago and in Brando Skyhorse's production of himself.

The first place we perhaps notice this pushing of boundaries in *The Polish Boxer* is with the introduction of the narrator as none other than Eduardo Halfon, which is both similar to and different from Daniel James's use of the heteronym Danny Santiago. The proper name Eduardo Halfon is both a fictional nobody—*pace* Gallagher's formulation of novels, referentiality, and naming—and a specific somebody. Halfon does and does not have a specific referent. As *The Polish Boxer* opens, we find a narrator pacing amongst his students and reviewing with them an essay by the Argentinian writer Ricardo Piglia. Fittingly, and by no accident, the argument of that essay is that "a story always tells two stories . . . that the visible narrative always hides a secret tale" (Halfon 9). This narrative scene of instruction registers not only the tenor of the story we are reading, but our very experience of the event of reading *The Polish Boxer*, for just a few pages later we learn that this narrator, who will be the narrator throughout the book, is none other than Eduardo Halfon. The pages of what we have come to call "postmodern fiction" or "metafiction" (i.e., fiction that draws attention to itself as an act of fiction) are filled with such acts as giving the narrator the author's name. These acts both break the illusion of the narrative and ask us to consider that our own lives are narratives and that fiction does not occupy some space outside of the real, but is also constitutive of it.[27] For his part, Eduardo Halfon the author wants to tie the play of this narrative ambiguity to "an emotional response" in the reader. In one interview he notes,

> There's a game that I like playing—blurring all types of preconceptions or genres or borders between what's real and what isn't. I'm lulling the reader—lulling myself, even—into not knowing what's real anymore. Similar to achieving a hypnotic state, I suppose, while writing, while reading. You're just in. You don't doubt anymore. It's all true, though you know it's not all real. I'm usually asked why I do that. Why isn't it just a differently named version of me, a thinly disguised narrator? I do it because I want to create an emotional response in the reader, and part of the way in which I do that is by drawing him into a comfort zone, into a more real experience. Then there can be a reaction to the book as though it were not fiction. Readers can completely erase the line between the narrator and myself. They absolutely believe—or should believe—that the narrator is me. And he's not. Yet he is. (Murphy, "Origin Stories," par. 50)[28]

In Halfon's response, we hear echoes of Gallagher's claim about the nature of belief and disbelief in the rise of fictionality and the novel, particularly the paradox that the novel "gives us explicit fiction and simultaneously seems to occlude it" ("Rise of Fictionality" 349). However, I cannot help but wonder if—unlike those modern readers of the novel who could enjoy fiction's illusion because voluntary disbelief protected them from delusion (349)—something else is going on in Halfon's desire to blur borders of all types and in his insistent coyness in saying that the narrator is him, isn't him, is him.

Indeed, it would seem impossible to read a collection like *The Polish Boxer* whose opening chapter is about a professor of literature talking to his students about the illusion of literature without wondering about the borders Eduardo Halfon is blurring. To explain the illusive character of literature, Halfon—quoting Plato—tells one student, "[L]iterature is a deceit in which he who deceives is more honest than he who does not deceive, and he who allows himself to be deceived is wiser than he who does not" (*Polish Boxer* 18). If Eduardo Halfon the author winks at us through Halfon the narrator, what is the deception of *The Polish Boxer*? While that magic act applies to all literature, it seems especially freighted in a chapter ("Brown Like Me?") about myriad conceals and reveals—pseudonyms, heteronyms, and author's notes that are presented as fact but are fictitious, and narrators and authors who bear the same names but are not necessarily coterminous—in a corpus of literature that all too often prizes "authenticity" and mimetic fidelity. In a mental state of such authorial illusion, one begins to see a Daniel James behind every Danny Santiago, Brando Skyhorse, Eduardo Halfon, and so on, and that vigilance is not in itself a bad thing, not because it keeps us on the hunt for "real" or "authentic" Latinx authors, but precisely the opposite—it forces us to question why we lean so heavily on an author's identity in valuing a work of literature. It forces us to wonder what that authorial identity contributes, if anything, to a world of fictional nobodies. The indeterminacy that underwrites the distinction between Eduardo Halfon the author and Eduardo Halfon the narrator is not one to be resolved, but rather one that pushes the limits of the coherency of the term *Latinx* and thereby the coherency of the category *Latinx literature*. If the identity category lacks a coherency, then nothing it names or categorizes can have an illuminating coherency. It cannot result, in other words, in interpretive clarity.

The necessary and sufficient definitional criteria of any taxonomic order are there to help us understand what we see before us, and as the definitional parameters of Latinx literature currently exist, we can perhaps register Halfon as a Latinx writer based on his personal biography, but his tales of teaching literature in Guatemala, of hunting for a Serbian pianist in Belgrade, and of understanding how a Polish boxer came to save his grandfather's life in Auschwitz do not square with the thematic definitions and expectations critics have of Latinx literature. What we stand to learn from the example of Eduardo Halfon in regards to Latinx literature is not unlike what the legend Halfon the narrator recounts in regards to what we see in our everyday worlds and how we incorporate that into our sense of reality.

In his search for Milan Rakic (the Serbian pianist), Halfon recalls the legend his girlfriend Lía had told him about Columbus and the conquest of the Americas:

The legend says that as Columbus's fleet was approaching the shores of America, the native Indians didn't see it, since the concept of galleons in full sails was so alien to them, so unimaginable, that it didn't enter into their version of reality, and as such, their minds simply decided not to register it. There's nothing there, I remember Lía saying to me, with her hand on her forehead, as though she was watching the horizon. I construct my reality solely on the basis of that which I know, she said. (*Polish Boxer* 155–156)

The veracity of this particular legend does not concern me, but its lesson does. Out on the horizon are a host of authors and works to which we may be unnecessarily blind. We are perhaps not ready to see an Eduardo Halfon as a Latinx writer because he writes on themes that fall outside of the purview of recognizable Latinx literature, or perhaps we want to assign him strictly to the category of Latin American author. Instead of being a Linnaeus who squashes bugs that he cannot readily classify, I think we want to follow in Halfon's path, "blurring all types of preconceptions or genres or borders." We must blur them, because to hold them too tightly is to blind ourselves to the realities that surround us. It is this rigid adherence to boundaries that makes characters such as Ralph Ellison's eponymous narrator invisible. He cannot be seen in his full humanity because racial preconceptions and racial hatred preclude others from seeing him as the man he is. It is a similar fate that Halfon's Rakic faces: "To Serbs I've always been a piece of shit Gypsy, a filthy good-for-nothing Gypsy. And to Gypsies I've always been a piece of shit gadje, a piece of shit non-Gypsy. My mother's family rejected us. My father's family rejected us. I'm a Gypsy who can't be a Gypsy and a Serb who can't be a Serb" (106). Episodes such as this, and even the opening tale of Halfon lecturing his students about literature's two stories—the visible and invisible—indicate that the takeaway from *The Polish Boxer* is to keep pressure on the boundaries, as Halfon's many characters do. We must push the boundaries to their limits to see what lies beyond them, to get past limits to our understanding, not for the mere sake of pushing limits, but so that we might see the galleons on the horizon.

Lia Brozgal, a professor of French and Francophone literatures, has written a fascinating essay about the French author Jack-Alain Léger's impersonation of a *Beur* author (whom Léger calls Paul Smaïl),[29] an impersonation whose contours resemble those of Daniel James/Danny Santiago. Writing under this pseudonym, Léger published four novels between 1997 and 2001. The one Brozgal focuses on is the 1997 sensation *Vivre me tue*—which at one point was selling six hundred copies per day ("Hostages of Authenticity" 114)—and the strenuous critique of the novel by the sociologist and prize-winning novelist Azouz Begag. Begag takes exception with the work on linguistic and ethical grounds, finding it "'fatally flawed, both aesthetically and ethically' (54)" (118). In her critique of Begag's criticism, Brozgal closes her essay with some questions that I think we might bear in mind when assessing the works of those writers who do not easily fit into our current conceptions of Latinx literature, as well as those considered in this chapter and in the following ones. She writes, "Begag puts forth a totalizing view of the *Beur* author, of what kind of language he uses, and how he situates his narratives culturally. While this may have allowed Begag to 'frame' Smaïl as an impostor, has he not subsequently pigeon holed [*sic*] writers of his own ethnic background into a literary impasse? Is he not imitating the champions and purveyors of doxa and 'high-culture'—those who police the canon—and in the process creating an *exception beure?*" (126). While crushing insects and pigeonholing writers may make our work as critics easier, a generative, enduring, and robust analysis demands that we prove ourselves equal to the complexities of the literature with which we grapple. If the category *Latinx literature* is to have any meaning at all, we cannot afford to generate a taxonomy or poetics that swerves around the nuances of the literature or the complexities and even contradictions of its authors. James/Santiago, Skyhorse, and Halfon are only exceptions if we operate with a narrow definition of the Latinx subject. Beneath that homogenizing umbrella label—*Latinx*—resides a group of people more complex and heterogeneous in their cultural practices and cultural productions than that label would have us believe. Indeed, we must take these supposedly "exceptional" cases and use them to enrich our understanding of Latinx literature. Or, as Brozgal maintains, "Rather than as a hijacker of *Beur* subjectivity, Léger may be read as helping to problematize questions of authorial subjectivity, identity, narrative, literary discourse, and cultural purity" (125). Turn the limit case into limitless.

And in such turning, we might find ourselves returning to Foucault's essay "*What* Is an Author?" (emphasis added). The essay not only gives a fine account of the author-function, but also at its conclusion, we see Foucault—the staunch anti-humanist—return. At essay's end, he imagines what a critical world without the subject would look like. The author-function is "far from immutable," he writes, and then he launches into a speculative pondering, which we might keep in mind as we think about the identity matters that have come to define Latinx literature:

We can easily imagine a culture where discourse would circulate without any need for an author. Discourses, whatever their status, form, or value, and regardless of our manner of handling them, would unfold in a pervasive anonymity. No longer the tiresome repetitions:
"Who is the real author?"
"Have we proof of his authenticity and originality?"
"What has he revealed of his most profound self in his language?"
New questions will be heard:
"What are the modes of existence of this discourse?"
"Where does it come from; how is it circulated; who controls it?"
"What placements are determined for possible subjects?"
"Who can fulfill these diverse functions of the subject?"
Behind all these questions we would hear little more than a murmur of indifference:
"What matter who's speaking?"[30] (138)

Can we hear those new questions? Can we wonder not about the author-function but about the unfolding of the various discursive moves that lend themselves to the creation of the thing we think we know as Latinx literature? Perhaps not just yet. We have more thinking to do and more analyses to perform in the coming chapters before we might reach that conclusion. I would like such questions to echo in our minds as I examine, in the following chapters, a series of texts that are dissonant in one fashion or another with how we have come to think and write about Latinx literature. Moreover, I have organized the following chapters around genres—the metafictional novel, the short story, and the lyric poem. I find the taxonomy of genre to be a historically durable one that has much to recommend it as setting in place a rich system of interpretive possibilities. I turn, first, to Salvador Plascencia's *The People of Paper*, which confounds many critics' desires to value literature according to its mimetic fidelity and its representation of a world that is faithful to what they believe is *Latinx*.

CHAPTER 2

Confounding the Mimetic:
The Metafictional Challenge
to Representation

The vision I have of Latinx literature includes an openness to thinking about the complexities of racial categories and their representations so that a label like *Latinx* can no longer operate as a taken-for-granted marker. Rather than abandon or denounce the label, I want to think about how it gets produced and circulated. In this chapter, I examine how characters in Salvador Plascencia's *The People of Paper* come into being—characters whom readers would be inclined to label, or who label themselves, as Latinx. The novel represents a world we seemingly know—Mexico and El Monte, California—but it also places us in a metafictional world that travels beyond mimetic boundaries. While metafiction employs strategies and conventions that exceed the boundaries of the real, it perhaps thereby makes the real more perceptible and more knowable by defamiliarizing it. It is from those conventions that depend upon the so-called real as referent (i.e., the world we think we know and that we inhabit) and those that clearly surpass it that we stand to learn something about the discourses we employ to construct our everyday lives. My aim here is not to tread new ground in theorizing metafiction or the postmodern; rather I aim to analyze how Plascencia and the form in which he writes further unbind us from our heretofore conventional understandings of Latinx literature. Characters such as Plascencia's Federico de la Fe, who enlists members of the El Monte Flores street gang in his war against Saturn (the omniscient narrator), drive this chapter. With the cast of Plascencia's *The People of Paper*, that is, we enter into a new and different world of *lo Latino*.

Salvador Plascencia's *The People of Paper* breaks away from realist imperatives for mimetic fidelity. The story is a story about story. "As we read along," Max Benavidez observes, "we know we are witnessing the conscious creation of a novel, yet we allow ourselves to be pulled into the ruse because the ruse is so beautiful, so true, and so fleeting" ("Salvador Plascencia," par. 2). There are place names (e.g., El Monte, California) and references to real people (e.g., Rita Hayworth) that connect the narrative to referents outside of the novel, but the novel's radical indecidability, its self-referentiality, and its several non-realist characters trouble any claims to verisimilitude. While the majority of the action takes place in El Monte, California, it happens at an unspecified and indeterminate time. Additionally, there are characters made of paper and mechanical tortoises that speak in an indecipherable binary code.

When I say that it is a story about story, I mean that the driving force of the narrative is the struggle between a group of characters led by Federico de la Fe against Saturn, one of the narrators of the novel and the only "omniscient one." The narrative is about "a war for volition and against the commodification of sadness" (*People of Paper* 53). Through the use of various stratagems—for instance, the building of lead homes and the thinking of only banal and repetitive thoughts—the characters endeavor to keep Saturn out of their heads and thereby their lives. Paradoxically, the characters—who can only exist if there is a narrator to tell their story—are fighting to crush the very source that brings them into being. I return to these matters of form and metafiction in greater detail later in this chapter. But to understand this story about story—particularly its implications for thinking about *lo Latino* and its relation to and representation in literature—we must first begin with a cursory account of the novel's publishing history and Plascencia's authorial identity, particularly how he sees himself vis-à-vis Latinx writing.

Publishing History and the Authorial Self

Those familiar with the novel will know that McSweeney's originally published it in 2005 and that Harcourt brought out a slightly modified paperback version in 2006.[1] Readers may not, however, know that on its march toward publication it was rejected by every major press, and those rejections had to do with its not easily pitched storyline and form. In recounting the publishing history to Angela Stubbs for *Bookslut*, Plascencia recalls, "Trying to summarize the book was a big problem. . . . You've got to sell this book and so you say, 'It's a war-novel, it's a memoir, it's about immigration, it's a meta-fiction, and it's a love story.' If you read the McSweeney's description, it's absurd.[2] No major publisher would use that description, you're going to find a tag like, 'It's a father-daughter story.'"

Although "memoir" would be a tough sell, one could imagine pitching the novel as any of the other subgenres Plascencia mentions. Nevertheless, branding it for the marketing and sales teams of a major press would present difficulties. Compounding these branding issues, the structure of the novel also exceeds "standard" conventions. At times, the chapters follow the typical page layout of a novel, but just as often, if not more so, they are laid out in columns. There are even pages toward the end where the column structure—in the service of a thematic point—is irregular and challenging to follow. Furthermore, for one character—Baby Nostradamus—all we get are blacked out columns because Saturn cannot tell what Baby Nostradamus thinks. Thus, the combination of the novel's "experimental" layout and its not conforming to a recognizable genre led to publishing obstacles for this first-time author.

This publishing history, moreover, is not divorced from the author's identity and from presses' expectations for "ethnic" authors. In an April 2010 interview, Matthew Baker asks Plascencia if he "identif[ies] as a Latino writer." Plascencia replies, "To be honest, I'm not really sure what that means. Professionally . . . I'm a writer. But I'm not a professional Mexican; that's Ruben Navarrette's gig. I'm a Latino. I'm a writer. I identify as both, but not when 'Latino' is serving as a modifier" (Baker par. 10).[3] This is a familiar reply. A number of writers who are Latinx say that they prefer not to have the "cage" of an ethnic identity close the door on who they are and what they write about. While many are happy to take on the mantle of "Latinx writer," none want to be pigeonholed. What makes Plascencia's reply intriguing and noteworthy is its relationship to the subsequent answer he gives Baker regarding the question of publishing an "experimental novel":[4]

This might seem like I'm contradicting what I said earlier—I'm not—but what was a major [publishing house] going to do with an experimental Mexican-American writer? The reality is that—aside from the [*sic*] Cisneros and Dagoberto Gilb, writers who reinforce a parochial view of Latinidad—there are very few of us on the majors. Name them. Off the top of my head, I can only think of Alex Espinoza, Joe Loya, and my fellow El Montian Michael Jaime-Becerra.[5] But Joe and Michael were under Rayo, some HarperCollins specialty imprint aimed exclusively at Latinos. The Houghton Mifflin's and HarperCollins don't see us as marketable to the general public. There is Luis Rodriguez—a writer that heavily informed me—but even he is pushed as some sort of exotic criminal. (par. 16)

Although Plascencia refers to himself as a "Mexican American writer," perhaps he is correct in asserting that he is not contradicting himself. For he is not talking about how he labels himself; rather he is stating how *presses* position him. Once again we are back to expectations created by an author's ethnic identity. While he is unnecessarily sharp in his mention of Cisneros and Gilb—two talented and well-received authors—the point Plascencia is making is that their fictions are legible to agents, editors, and presses because they write on familiar "Latinx themes" that fulfill those publishing figures' expectations. I take this also to be his point regarding Rayo, HarperCollins's imprint. It is clear from his dismissive tone ("some HarperCollins specialty imprint") that he sees Rayo as a niche marketing strategy that precludes "Latinx writers" from the "universalism" of the general HarperCollins label. The analog here in terms of national literary traditions would be to say that Cisneros is a Latina writer, not an American one. She fits a particular category, not a general or universal one. In the remainder of Plascencia's response, he continues with and then complicates his line of reasoning about ethno-racial identity and expectations:

True, eventually *The People of Paper* ended up at Harcourt as a paperback. But even then, it didn't receive the same amount of muscle and push that similar paperbacks received. The problem is, even if you don't think of yourself as a "Latino writer," there are a lot of people who get stuck on your last name.

But there are obvious advantages, too. Sometimes, for no good reason aside from the fact that I were [*sic*] born south of the Rio Grande [he was born in Guadalajara, Jalisco, Mexico], my name gets tangled up with the greats: Bolaño, Borges, García Márquez. I'm never going to complain when that happens. (Baker, "Interview," par. 17–18)

Plascencia sees himself caught in the double-bind of being an "ethnic writer." On the one hand, as an "ethnic writer" you are expected to write on recognizable "ethnic themes." On the other hand, if you write on those themes, you supposedly have a more limited consumer market, and thus get less weight thrown behind your PR campaign. Capitalism has no complaints with identity. In fact it loves your identity. It makes establishing niche markets that much easier. All niche markets do not, however, have the same buying power.[6]

Plascencia is not naïve about the process. Indeed, what his final comments make clear is that he is quite happy to straddle the line that typically divides histories of Latin American and Latinx literature. Latin American writers like Borges, Márquez, and Bolaño have more cachet and better sales figures than (almost) any Latinx writer. There are a host of prejudices and reasons for this disparity. I need not elaborate them here. Rather, I mean to underscore Plascencia's ambivalent and shifting responses to how he thinks of himself as a writer, and how publishing industry expectations factor into how he is marketed and affect the content and the form of his writing.

On this latter score, Plascencia is well versed in the "experimental" tradition in which he situates *The People of Paper*. He is a graduate of the MFA program in creative writing at Syracuse University, where he studied with George Saunders, and then he subsequently enrolled in the English PhD program at USC to study with Aimee Bender.[7] He understands his novel's play on the page as consistent with that of Jonathan Safran Foer's *Extremely Loud and Incredibly Close*, Steven Hall's *Raw Shark Texts*, and the works of Mark Z. Danielewski, such as *House of Leaves*. In his interview with Matthew Baker, Plascencia explains,

> For whatever reason, the standard formatted novel kept breaking on me. Out of my frustration with the single-column I went looking for other ways. I found Cris Mazza, John Edgar Wideman, even a chapter of Denise Chavez—writers who had reengineered the page for their own purposes. Somehow this led me to Lawrence Sterne, to early books, and to the realization that the way we understand the book is only a domesticated version of the wild, feral, origins of the book. We have housecats, when we once had sabertooths." (par. 3)

The People of Paper is a sabertooth. It is a demanding, but, by no means, impenetrable novel. It is not simply formalist pyrotechnics. Beneath its formal play and self-reflexivity beats the heart of a moving story.

That beating heart, however, is in a tradition of "experimental" fiction not common to Latinx letters. It certainly exists. One thinks of elements of Junot Díaz's *The Brief Wondrous Life of Oscar Wao* (2008) and of Helena María Viramontes's *Their Dogs Came with Them* (2007), and, of course, there is Ron Arias's *The Road to Tamazunchale* (1975) and Cecile Pineda's

Face (1985). Even in the most generous accounting, however, these experimental works constitute a numerical minority in Latinx fiction. The vast majority of stories fall under the rubric of realist or social realist fiction, often about life in the barrio, farm work, migration, and immigration. What I find compelling about *The People of Paper* is its combining of recognizable themes of Latinx literature with a formal project uncommon to Latinx letters. In the remainder of the chapter, I focus on what Plascencia refers to as both his "consciously reenacting what a Chicano is thought to be" and "the challenge" *The People of Paper* puts to "our conception of the Chicano-Latino novel" (Benavidez, "Salvador Plascencia," par. 41).

How Form Begets and Breaks Traditions

We might best begin with some basic formal questions: To what degree does *The People of Paper* operate according to its own internal discursive logic? To what degree does it depend on our knowledge of the "real world" to understand it? How does the novel's metafictional conceit relate to the questions of mimetic fidelity that haunt the criticism of Latinx fiction? What is this world into which Plascencia brings us, and to what end does he do so?

In the novel's "war for volition and against the commodification of sadness," there is much that is recognizable from our everyday lives and much that strictly conforms to the internal logic of *The People of Paper*. That is to say, there are observable phenomena to which one could make mimetic appeals, but there are equally (if not more so) phenomena that cannot be measured in terms of verisimilitude. They can only be read as being consistent or inconsistent with the world that Plascencia creates. Furthermore, they are not necessarily allegories either. This distinction between the "purely fictional" and the fictional that may resemble the world we inhabit is important insofar as it raises questions about the nature of fiction that cannot be answered by the tendency to worry over mimetic fidelity and whether representations are "authentic," "positive," or "negative."

Let me be more specific about these two representational fields in the novel. In the realm of world-making specific exclusively to *The People of Paper* and, therefore, obedient only to the internal logic of the novel, we have a number of salient features: (1) the war for volition and the narrative structure it creates, (2) characters who could not exist in the "real world" (e.g., Merced de Papel and the mechanical tortoises), and (3) acts that could only take place in a fictional universe (e.g., the conflagration caused by a

saint's halo or lead homes to prevent the narrator from peering into characters' lives). Of those features that could be seen as referencing a world outside
of the novel, we have (1) recognizable emotions (e.g., love, pain, remorse,
and so on), (2) references to actual things or people (e.g., the planet Saturn
and Rita Hayworth), and (3) an organization of daily life that resembles that
of our everyday world (e.g., the need to work, eat, sleep, and so on). The
goal, then, is to analyze how these representational fields come together to
tell us, or not, something about racial representation in fiction and to tell us
something about "our conception of the Chicano-Latino novel."

To write a novel that is a story about story, one that is obsessed with its
own narrativity, is to be engaged in a project that considers the very nature of fiction. Let us start our analysis with the novel's opening. It begins
with a prologue that strikes a biblical or mythical tone and provides a genesis story for the people of paper. Observe the tone and diction of the first
sentence: "She was made after the time of ribs and mud" (11). We have the
intrigue and grandiosity of a pronoun with no antecedent. Who is this *she*,
and why do we care about her? The noun phrase "the time" puts us in both
a vague realm because it offers no specific temporal measurement (e.g., no
year, no decade, and so on) and a supposedly known realm through its use
of the definite article—"*the* time." Accentuating this august phrasing is the
post-modifying prepositional phrase "of ribs and mud," which places us in
the realm of the mythological, in both its diction and allusions. "Of ribs"
clearly references God making Eve from Adam's rib and Adam from the
"mud," and conjures as well Prometheus's creation of people from clay. The
opening continues in this mythical manner. Plascencia, however, is not
after sheer stylistic imitation. He also plays with and pokes fun at the style.
As, when, in the second and third sentence, he writes, "By papal decree
there were to be no more people born of the ground or from the marrow
of bones. All would be created from the propulsions and mounts performed
underneath bedsheets—rare exception granted for immaculate conceptions"
(11). The papal decree sentence continues in the biblical vein, but using
the mock-mythical diction to refer to penal-vaginal sex as "propulsions and
mounts performed underneath bedsheets" alerts us that we have a playful
narrator, who is self-consciously aware of his narrative style. The remaining pages of the prologue proceed in this tone and offer the creation myth
of the first person of paper—Merced de Papel—and the story of her creator, the "origami surgeon" Antonio.

Thus, while we have a narrative world to which we can make intertextual ties to other books (e.g., the Bible) and to features and characteristics
of our contemporary world (e.g., monks, surgeons, medical journals, ori-

gami, and so on), it is also strictly a world of Plascencia's invention and which obeys its own logic. There is no such thing as a person of paper. Organs, capillaries, and veins cannot be folded from paper, yet in *The People of Paper* such beings "live." Indeed, as with Dr. Frankenstein's monster, Merced de Papel walks out of the "factory" in which she was created and "into the storm" (15). That last image is, of course, consistent with the sympathetic nature one associates with the nineteenth-century gothic novel and is yet another intertextual connection for this novel and the narrative conventions with which it works. Finally, in its function as prologue, it sets the tone and possibilities for the world the reader enters, and thereby assists in setting the readers' expectations and the conventions from which the novel will create its effects.

The prologue, in short, telegraphs not just that old chestnut that to enter the fictive realm requires the suspension of disbelief. We do that with every fictive creation we read. But this prologue—through the genesis story it tells—also counterintuitively literalizes the world-making capacity of fiction. Genesis stories, that is, are about the creation of the world. Fiction—notwithstanding its proliferating digital incarnations—is about creating through marks on paper. Merced is not simply Merced. She is Merced de Papel, Merced of Paper, and to a large extent she is created not just from any paper, but from the pages of books:

> Antonio split the spines of books, spilling leaves of Austen and Cervantes, sheets from Leviticus and Judges, all mixing with the pages of *The Book of Incandescent Light*. Then Antonio unrolled the wrapping paper and construction paper and began to cut at the cardboard and then fold.
>
> She was the first to be created: cardboard legs, cellophane appendix and paper breasts. Created not from the rib of man but from paper scraps. There was no all-powerful god who could part the rivers of Pison and Gihon, but instead a twice-retired old man with cuts across his fingers. (15)

Merced is the literal embodiment of the fictive act, and the Eve of her people. That fictive act involves, by necessity, the mixture of the mythical with the mundane. It is mythical to the extent that it employs the tropes of genesis stories, but mundane (i.e., of this world) in that there is neither an "all-powerful god" nor a biblical setting, nor rivers from the Garden of Eden—Pison and Gihon. Merced de Papel is not the creature of an omnipotent god living a celestial existence with a legion of angels in his service, but of an everyday man who once had two jobs and is susceptible, like

any other human, to life's indignities, including paper cuts. This literal-
ization of the fictive act—drawing our attention to Merced being made of
paper—can also be read allegorically.

Antonio can be read as an author. Authors—as does Antonio—bring
beings to life through their marks on paper. Indeed, the success of *The
People of Paper* depends on our reading this prologue literally *and* allegorically. As Robert Scholes reminds us, "The great allegories are never
entirely allegorical, just as the great realistic novels are never entirely
real" (*Fabulators* 99). That is certainly the case in this extraordinary novel,
which blends—perhaps even confuses—the literal and metaphorical or
allegorical. In addition, it should be noted that in this allegory of world-
making there is nothing especially Latinx undertaken—not in theme, not
in characterization, not in identity construction. Aside from a series of
names that are Latinx, the prologue is characterized best as one about the
nature of fiction, not about the nature specifically of Latinx fiction, which
brings us to the next critical point—the narrative structure of the remainder of the novel.

In one of the few extant treatments of *The People of Paper*, Ramón Saldívar
has written a brief, terrific analysis of some of the novel's formal play, particularly its use of *parabasis* and "the rupture of the illusion of the separation
between the fictional and the real worlds, as the audience is drawn into the
illusion at the same time that the illusion reveals itself as an illusion"
("Historical Fantasy" 579). However, notwithstanding reminders throughout his essay that the novel "does not allow us to return to the Real—
historical, political, magical, postmodern, or otherwise" (582), Saldívar
assiduously attempts to read the novel as a continuation of the critiques of
social injustice and alienation that characterized many novels from the
Chicana/o movement (ca. 1965–1975). He offers important qualifiers to his
argument such as: "In contrast to its historical forebears in ethnic fiction,
it attempts to claim sincerely the utopian vision of achieved freedom and
justice all the while *not* believing in their attainability" (582; emphasis in
original). He is attendant, that is, to all of the metafictional play in the
novel, but he insists, in a Marxist vein, on reading novels "as abstracts of
social relationships" (581). Allegory becomes his tool to execute this work.
He attempts to use the narrative arc that focuses on "the commodification
of sadness" as the allegorical conceit that signals "the centrality of alienation and reification in the daily lived, and felt, experience of the racialized worker protagonist" (582). The novel, however, affords him scant
textual evidence to substantiate his claim.[8] At one point, Saldívar paren-

thetically references "the life of poverty and exploitation of these rose and carnation harvesters" (583), but the novel tells us little about the workers' lives, their struggles, or back-breaking labor.[9] In his essay "From 'Latinidad' to 'Latinid@des,'" Paul Allatson notes that the novel's location in El Monte, California, "does evoke a 'real world' site and associated history of Mexican immigration and labor exploitation, but that, arguably, is as far as the novel gets in gesturing toward historical veracity and realism" (135). *The People of Paper* pays much greater attention to the war for volition, the war against Saturn, and the novel's various romances. The workers we hear most about are the lettuce workers (and all of the passages about them combined would take up less than a page or two). We do not, however, glimpse their working conditions. Rather, Plascencia portrays them in relation to feeling betrayed by Rita Hayworth.[10]

Let me assert further that the sadness in the novel is not about the commodification of labor, but about unrequited love—that between Federico de la Fe and Merced, and that between Saturn and Liz. It is impossible to read their love stories as a symptom of the economic mode of production or as connected to alienated social relations. Saldívar's attention to the novel's play with illusion and reality and its state of permanent *parabasis* is on point; however, the interpretation gets derailed when he tries to read the novel as a revelatory symptom of economic and social relations.

Let us turn again to form. As we leave the novel's prologue, the traditional physical format of the novel as one column, and often one narrative voice, shifts to multiple columns organized around multiple voices. This layout is crucial because it reinforces the conceit that the characters are in a battle for volition with the supposedly omniscient narrator—Saturn—and that their respective columns represent their voices and perspectives. Thus, the reader is challenged to put together a picture of the past and the war for volition from multiple testimonies—those of the numerous characters involved in the war and those of the omniscient narrator, who is anything but detached and whose omniscience, we shall see, comes into question. A story of rotating and competing voices is never a simple one. It places demands on what we can and do accept as the truth. The columnar structure—perhaps more than traditional novelistic structures—further affects how we experience space and time. Novels told from multiple perspectives are hardly new. One thinks of novels such as Samuel Richardson's *Clarissa*, Wilkie Collins's *The Moonstone*, and more recent exemplars such as William Faulkner's *The Sound and the Fury* and Iain Pears's *An Instance of the Fingerprint*, among many others, but there is something about the sheer material layout of Plascencia's novel in columns that affects how we experience the time and space of the novel.

Of Time, Tortoises, and Rita Hayworth

While the prologue—with its diction and genesis story—places the novel in a space of mythical time, the novel does not stay there. Nor, however, does it reside in any easily recognizable temporal frame. A number of literary theorists have discussed the construction of ontological worlds in fiction as distinct from the actual world. In his foundational study of postmodern fiction, Brian McHale, drawing on Thomas Pavel, notes, "[R]eaders do not evaluate the logical possibility of the propositions they find in literary texts in the light of the actual world . . . but rather abandon the actual world and adopt (temporarily) the *ontological perspective* of the literary work" (*Postmodernist Fiction* 33; emphasis in original). Nevertheless, fictional worlds are not wholly invented; they bear traces of the real world. Umberto Eco argues that this is so "because no world can be described exhaustively; instead of trying to describe a world 'from scratch,' it is much more feasible simply to 'borrow' some entities and properties from the ready-made world of reality" (McHale, *Postmodernist Fiction* 34–35). We should not judge the attempt to situate the novel temporally as a retreat to mimetic concerns. Rather, it is an attempt to understand the experience of the novel and to understand that that experience is affected by the spatial and temporal. Additionally, insofar as the ontological world of the novel crosses over into the ontological realm of the actual world, the clues from that world, too, help us discern the time, space, and experience of the novel.

There are clues from the real world that suggest we are in the twentieth century. In the first chapter of the book, Federico and Little Merced board a bus from Guadalajara, Jalisco, to Los Angeles, California. We know that we are not in the nineteenth century because, among other things, motorized buses did not exist in the nineteenth century and because both Napoleon and Nostradamus are treated as historical personages. Moreover, the novel offers more specific clues about the potential temporality of its ontological universe. It features Rita Hayworth as one of its minor characters, and given the specificity of references to her films and acting career, she does seem to be a representation of *the* Rita Hayworth, who lived from 1918–1987. In addition, since she is a speaking character in the present time of the novel (Plascencia 232, 235), we might be tempted to say that the present time of the novel is in the 1980s, after the height of her acting career, but before her death. There is, however, a wrinkle. While she does seem to be the Rita Hayworth of Hollywood fame, the narrator has fabricated a story of her origins. When he introduces her, he tells us that she was born "in a coastal town in Jalisco" (41–42) and then relates the seemingly significant story of how "at the age of six she sowed a plum orchard irrigated solely by salt water" (42). The Rita Hayworth from the actual world was born in Brooklyn to a father from Spain and a mother of Irish-English descent. So we cannot, in any reliable way, assess the time of the novel from Rita Hayworth's biography.

Chapter 3 of the book, in which Rita Hayworth is introduced, is of further interest because of its temporal play. The chapter rotates between three characters—Froggy El Veterano, Margarita (i.e., Rita Hayworth), and Julieta. That rotation continues until each character has three sections, each of which is narrated in third person, ostensibly by Saturn, and each represents a distinct time in the novel. First there is Froggy. Aside from the label—"Froggy El Veterano"—that heads each of his sections in this chapter, the character is referred to as Froggy. Moreover, in the remainder of the novel, his sections are labeled "Froggy," and he is one of the key fighters in the war for volition. Crucial here, and what can be hastily overlooked, is the label "El Veterano." It is key because in the three sections focused on him in this chapter, we are in a future time, relative to the present time of the novel—the time of Federico's migration to Los Angeles and his war against Saturn. The chapter opens, "Many years after the Saturn War and in the unwritten afterword of this book, Froggy survived to be a very old man" (41), and in his second section of the chapter, we are told, "one of the greatest wars against tyranny had been fought years before, a war against the future of this story—Federico de la Fe's war" (46). Second comes Margarita. It is still early enough in the novel that it is not that surprising to encounter a new character, but relative to the storyline that we know up until this point, she is an odd fit. The temporal space she occupies in this chapter is indeterminate. It spans her birth and, at the very least, her career through the making of *Trouble in Texas*, as well as through her five marriages. Third is Julieta, who represents a past and a future time. The past time entails her life in the town of El Derramadero, and the future time is when, as a transplant to El Monte, she meets Froggy and becomes a soldier in the war for volition. It is not unusual for novels to eschew a strict linear chronology in favor of flash forwards and flashbacks. What matters is how they do it and to what effect.

In *The People of Paper*, that effect, as witnessed in Chapter 3, is a layering one that generates feelings of disorientation and simultaneity. Rita

Hayworth would seem to offer a temporal mooring station, but that is taken away as soon as we know that she is and is not *the* Rita Hayworth. Moreover, as soon as the character of "Mechanic" introduces the story of mechanical tortoises into the equation (57) (tortoises who later speak in binary code [97]), we know we are no longer in the ontological universe of the actual world, but in the ontological world of the novel, which, given that tortoises speak, we may want to place in a future time or time parallel to our lived world in which such things might happen. In short, the temporal play of the novel underscores its narrative play, its emphasis on being a story about story. "Don't look to the real world to comprehend me," it would seem to enjoin us. "I exist only in the imagination."[11] In whose imagination, however, is a crucial struggle in the novel, as we see in the battle for the narrative's center.

Voice and the Struggle for the Center

In dramatic Bakhtinian fashion, *The People of Paper* is the heteroglossic novel *par excellence*. Staged as the novel's principal conceit is a battle for control of the narrative between centrifugal and centripetal voices. Bakhtin would call this a struggle for the ideological center, but I prefer not to stage this as an ideological struggle for fear that it will trigger a politically instrumental reading, one insufficiently attentive to the narrative and aesthetic complexities of the novel. Saturn is the novel's centripetal force. As the omniscient narrator, his challenge is to maintain control over the novel's voicing. Federico and the other characters battle to break Saturn's narrative hold and have not only their voices heard, but also their stories told in the way they wish. This explicit staging of the struggle between a narrator and his characters presents a perhaps insurmountable battle.

In reading novels, we know that we are encountering characters, not actual people. The more engaging a story, the more complex the characters, and the more we sympathize with the protagonist's plight—and the more we allow ourselves to get lost in the illusion of the story. We might even be reading the same book with a friend and say something like, "Can you believe what that horrible Heathcliff did? He's so despicable!" This kind of talk shows just how invested we can become in a particular fictional world. We frequently treat and talk about characters as we would about people we actually know. We forget, if only for a few fleeting moments, that there is an author who created these fictions. But a novel such as *The People of Paper* disallows immersion in its illusion, and I would add that it does not do so in a Brechtian manner to remind us of the political import of what is being staged.[12] Rather, Plascencia is drawing our attention to the very possibility of fiction itself. This is where the insurmountable obstacle enters.

It is nearly impossible to buy into the centripetal/centrifugal struggle between Saturn and the other characters because it *is staged* explicitly as a battle between a supposedly omniscient narrator and his characters. Moreover, in order for the battle to work within the logic of this narrative structure, Saturn's parts are written in a third-person voice, and the "soldiers" in the war for volition speak in the first person. The first-person voice for the other characters demonstrates that Saturn has not yet won control of the narrative. They are able to speak for themselves. That third-person-and-first-person structure, coupled with the staging of the battle between narrator and characters, reminds the reader that someone other than the narrator is writing the story. Thus, it is difficult to find oneself cheering for either Saturn or the other characters because one is always aware that there is a puppet master at a level above who is creating and orchestrating the action.

This is especially true when, in the sections labeled "Saturn," Saturn refers to himself in the third person. For instance, Saturn in his initial column in Chapter 4 begins, "The night Federico de la Fe dreamed of his wife Merced, he awoke to a soaked mattress and the faint smell of wood rot" (52). Everything is seemingly fine here. This sounds like typical omniscient narration in which Saturn is in charge of the story. Just two sentences later, however, we are told, "When awake, Federico de la Fe could dull the sadness and memory of his wife with fire, but he could not control the alignment of the planets or the heavy weight of Saturn while he slept" (52). One might be tempted to argue that the Saturn of this sentence is not the narrator, but rather the planet. Indeed, the novel often playfully maps narrator and planet onto one another. However, the reference to Saturn by Saturn in this passage is not an isolated instance. It occurs throughout the novel. Just a couple of pages later we have a Saturn column that announces, "On the second day of the campaign against Saturn" (54). My point here is twofold: (1) it is peculiar to know the name of an omniscient narrator—part of the conceit is that this person knows all and, thus, exists outside the realm of the story, speaking as if she were a god on high, not a named character—and (2) it is exceedingly odd to have an omniscient narrator refer to herself in the third person. Thus, we are forced to ask who is writing this story, making it difficult to believe that we are witnessing a battle between a narrator and his characters because it brings in an additional voice, namely, that of an author. It is a standard convention of criticism not to confuse narrator with author. As Gerard Genette reminds us in *Narrative Discourse*: "As to the narrating that produced the narrative

[*Recherche du temps perdu*], the art of Marcel recounting his past life, we will be careful from this point on not to confuse it with the act of Proust writing the *Recherche du temps perdu*" (28). Nevertheless, passages like the ones just cited from Saturn's columns force us into such confusion.

Plascencia, aware of this basic narrative tenet, pushes it into the foreground of the novel. In Chapter 8, Smiley—who is in favor of omniscience— learns that Saturn's "real name is Salvador Plascencia." We get a detailed exploration of this doubling as Smiley cuts a manhole-sized entrance into "the California sky" and pulls himself "into the house of Saturn" (103). The language in this chapter oscillates between referring to Saturn as author and narrator and thereby redoubles the collapse between Salvador Plascencia (whom we know to be the author of *The People of Paper*) and Saturn. Consider, for instance, the tension and collapse between these two roles in the two paragraphs that immediately follow Smiley's pulling himself into the house of Saturn:

> It should have been the moment when the creator acknowledges both the necessity of my existence and the reader's role as witness. But it was not the dignified meeting one might expect: the author sitting in his chair, wearing a starched dress shirt with a double-stitched collar, smoking hand-rolled tobacco, awaiting the visit because, after all, he is omniscient, foreseeing all surprises.
>
> But when I came to Saturn he was no longer in control. He did not have the foresight to see that I was coming, nor did he care. He had surrendered the story and his power as narrator. (103)

In that first paragraph, the language is almost exclusively that of Saturn as Salvador Plascencia. Though called "Saturn" here, he is labeled first as "the creator" and then as "the author," and Plascencia has a good bit of fun drawing a picture of his supposedly own writing environment, which borders on a stereotypical author's. In the last line of the paragraph, however, it reverts to language typically used to describe a narrator. I refer, of course, to the use of "omniscient." We think of narrators in terms of their closeness to and knowledge of a story because we understand them as an instrument in the story that is being conveyed, but one does not speak of omniscient authors. That's simply a redundancy. The author is the creator of the story. The author is the one who put the words on the page, who created the illusion before us. And in order to stay in the world of that illusion, we must leave the author out of the equation. If we think about the conveyance of the tale we are reading, we think in terms of the intermediary (i.e., the narrator) who relates the tale. Thus, this initial paragraph upon Smiley's entrance into Saturn's domain—fittingly housed in the sky, since Saturn is a planet and also because there is an inclination to associate omniscient narrators with gods and gods with the celestial realm—while using the label Saturn, refers to him as both author and narrator. In the subsequent paragraph, however, Smiley returns to characterizing him as the narrator, albeit one who has lost control of his tale. That, however, is at least consistent with the logic of the novel as being about a war for volition.

Both the maintenance and collapsing of the distinction between author and narrator needs sorting out. It is too regular and conscious of a feature simply to be written off as a mistake. For instance, it occurs again and repeatedly in Cameroon's postcards and letters. Cameroon, whom we have understood to be Saturn's love interest, addresses the postcards and letters she writes by turns to Saturn and to Sal (208, 215, 216, 218). Similarly, the novel early on describes Liz as Saturn's love interest: "But despite the warnings of his great-grandfather, Saturn fell for a woman who descended not only from a tawny family of Gypsies but from Ticuananse blood as well. Her name, which is cited on the dedication page of this book [author's dedicate novels, not narrators], was Elizabeth of Helen, but was abridged to simply Liz" (107; see also 117–119). But in Chapter 14, in which Liz is the narrator, it is clear that she is Plascencia's (former) love interest and that she attributes actions that the novel would have us understand to be Saturn's to Plascencia:

> But, Sal, I will not be your Rita Hayworth.
> I loved you, I loved you very much, but things changed. You went away to fight de la Fe and then there was someone else who was not from Monte [his name is scratched out in black ink whenever mentioned], who could not speak a word of Spanish, and who had never heard of EMF or tasted the tripe of menudo. And I fell in love with him. And because of this you want to cast me not only as the woman who hurt you but also as the woman who turned her back on Monte, as the sellout. (137–138)

What are we to make of these oscillations between (these confusions of) author and narrator? It is not a question to which there is a definitive answer, nor should we necessarily strive for one. Rather, what merits investigation is the effect of this oscillation and confusion.

In his study of postmodern fiction, Brian McHale writes instructively on the intrusion of the author into his novels:

> No longer content with invisibly exercising his freedom to create worlds, the artist now makes his freedom visible by thrusting himself into the foreground of his work. He represents himself in the act of

making his fictional world—or unmaking it. . . . There is a catch of
course: the artist represented in the act of creation or destruction is
himself inevitably a fiction. The *real* artist always occupies an ontological level superior to that of his projected, fictional self, and
therefore *doubly* superior to the fictional world. . . . There is a possibility here of infinite regress, puppet-master behind puppet-master *ad
infinitum*. The romantic godlike poet is, to revert to theological
discourse, both immanent and transcendent, both *inside* his heterocosm and *above* it, simultaneously present and absent.

But if the fictional world now acquires a visible maker, its own
status must inevitably change, too: it has become less the mirror of
nature, more an *artifact*, visibly a *made* thing. As a corollary, then, to
the artist's paradoxical self-representation, the artwork itself comes to
be presented *as* an artwork. (30; emphases in original)

No doubt, the intrusion of the author into his or her fiction is a regular
feature of postmodern fiction. One could think of any number of examples to support this claim. Paul Auster's appearance in his novel *City of Glass*
comes readily to mind, and that example is consistent with the trajectory
laid out by McHale. Auster, that is, becomes a fiction within his own fiction, while Paul Auster, the man who wrote the novel, still remains at a
remove (a doubly superior one) from *The City of Glass*.[13] In that particular
example, and in the many others like it, we do not, however, have Paul Auster or the novel's characters confusing Auster with the narrator. There is
something slightly different happening in *The People of Paper*. As with the
postmodern fiction McHale is writing about, *The People of Paper* is also an-
nouncing itself as "a visibly made thing," presenting itself as an artwork,
not a mimetic illusion. But I think there is also something unique in the
Saturn and Salvador oscillations and confusions, and it is tied to the convention of omniscience.

Omniscience and the Matter of Knowing to Tell

In *The People of Paper* the possibility of omniscience, as well as the effect of
omniscience, comes into play. By the "possibility of omniscience," I refer to
the conditions necessary for there to exist a being who is all-knowing. Aside
from those who place faith in omniscient and omnipotent gods, there is no
occasion in our daily lives in which we believe in such a being. We do not
even accord those whom we recognize as veritable geniuses the attribute of
omniscience. Narrators, however, often strike the pose of omniscience, and
readers are asked to accept that possibility. We indulge the illusion. Con-

joined to the possibility of omniscience is the effect of omniscience, for *The People of Paper* asks us to consider what the outcomes of omniscience are, not for the reader, but for the characters. What does it mean to have this unifying centripetal voice (otherwise known as Saturn) telling the story? Who is he to know this story? What does he know? Does he know enough to tell it "fairly"? Fiction does not give us the possibility, as does history, of reading multiple accounts of an event or series of events to assess their validity and the accuracy of their recounting.[14] A fiction exists, as mentioned earlier, in the imagination. We have only the fiction itself to make sense of the events, and the multi-voiced *People of Paper* offers us the opportunity to hear the story from multiple perspectives, but not in a fashion innocent of the very narrative conventions that make its existence possible.

When we have a third-person omniscient narrator, rarely does the narrator call attention to their all-knowingness because it would mean not recounting the events of the story being told, but rather speaking of her powers, which would mean an awkward and impossible shift to first person or a casting of herself in third person, which, as mentioned earlier, is precisely what Saturn does beginning in Chapter 7:[15]

> Saturn can see the roofs of El Monte, the surrounding ring of ash, the two-ton trucks that pull in empty and drive away heavy with carnations. The movement of people crossing streets, hoeing weeds, and crouching down in furrows. The tortoise that pokes feet and head from its metal shell and slowly crawls away escaping by the back door, down the stoop, and into the flower fields. Sights usually reserved for hovering crows and crop dusters.
>
> Saturn's power is of piercing strength, able to penetrate asbestos and wood shingles, tar paper, plywood, the darkness of the attic where yellowing cardboard boxes are kept, the painted plastered drywall, the spinning lead blades of the ceiling fan that Saturn carefully eludes (after first banging himself against the whirling vanes). (84)

I will come to the odd third-person references and their connection to the author/narrator conflation later in this section, but my point here is two-fold: (1) narration such as this announces the conditions and extents of its possibility and (2) it sets in place how this omniscience forces the characters to feel surveilled, which, in meta-fashion, draws to our attention that the characters know they are characters in a story. It is not received as detached, omniscient reporting. Consider, for instance, Little Merced's and Sandra's thoughts from their respective columns, which follow the one above. Little Merced: "My father had launched a war against a force that I could not see but I could now *feel*, and somehow it had left traces of its presence" (85; emphasis added). Sandra, who has left her love interest, Froggy, contemplates returning to him: "And Froggy would be happy and I would be happy too. But there are forces that don't let you turn back and undo things, because to do so would be to deny what is already in motion, to unwrite and erase passages, to shorten the arc of the story you don't own" (85). Those "forces" are those of Saturn, and as she emphasizes at the close of her column, if she could undo "the arc of the story," then "there would be no reason for me to fight this war" (85).

This hyper-attention to the act and effects of omniscience continues throughout the novel; they are in many ways *the* novel, and I think the effect of this attention results in a metaphysical examination of the nature of fiction and the reading experience. It reads as a rejoinder not to fall into the illusion of omniscience, not to believe that because someone may know everything that she is impartial, or that she does not have a vested interest in the story she is telling. Omniscient narrators are not reporting a series of facts from on high. What they tell us shapes how we feel and think about characters and what the characters themselves get to feel and think. *The People of Paper* asks us to consider not just the conventional question of reliable and unreliable narration, but also that of interested and disinterested narration.

We might want to believe in narrative disinterestedness, but this novel suggests otherwise. Take for instance this passage from Saturn recounting the poisoning from which the characters are suffering because they tried (upon Federico's instructions) to block Saturn's prying eyes with the use of lead houses: "Saturn lacked the decency to look away, the ability to empathize with Federico de la Fe and his daughter and their need to be alone and unseen. Instead, Saturn focused on the vomit on Federico de la Fe's lap . . . and then onto Little Merced . . . , Saturn listening to everything that they said" (186). Lest we feel this is only an indictment and examination of narrating, it quickly turns to implicating the reader. For in this very scene, Little Merced learns that for years Federico has been secretly burning himself as a strategy to combat the sadness he feels over losing Merced—his love and the mother of Little Merced. Consequently, she lashes out at the readers' voyeurism: "She began to feel her own resentment, not only toward Saturn, but also against those who stared down at the page, against those who followed sentences into her father's room and into his bed, watching as he pressed matches to his skin, perhaps even laughing and saying to themselves, 'Get over it, old man—it is only a woman'" (186).

Yet the illusion of a narrator at war with his characters is itself ruptured by the very illusion we are reading. Not all of the members of the EMF feel a war with Saturn is wise, Smiley chief among them. As Chapter 8 opens, the characters have successfully—through the use of lead houses and the thinking of irrelevant, repetitious thoughts—blocked Saturn from their lives. Smiley, whom we understand to be in favor of being watched over, who doesn't "want to look up at the sky and think that nothing is up there," points out the central contradiction in the very idea of a war for volition: "I knew that the defeat of Saturn would bring our own end, that everything would conclude with its crash" (101). From within the narrative of the war with Saturn, Smiley ruptures the illusion. The characters need a narrator to tell their story, much as a story needs readers. Decades ago, Jean-Paul Sartre argued that without readers, a book is merely black and white marks on a page.[16] Even if we were to allow that a story and characters could exist without its narrator, we would have a mass of textual confusion. The centripetal force of Saturn's voice is what gives the story coherence. The centrifugal forces cannot win without reconfiguring the narrative around a new centripetal force, a new center. When the characters do seem to succeed at pushing "Saturn further and further to the margin" (208), Smiley tells us "the order had been upset, lost in a *melee* of voices that for years wanted their freedom" (217). Plascencia captures this dilemma through the layout of the text. We find in Chapter 24, not the heretofore orderly use of columns, but a scattered and irregularly laid-out set of pages. Additionally, we see not only blackout used to represent Baby Nostradamus's thoughts, but here and there blackout over sections of Little Merced's thoughts. She has begun to learn, that is, Baby Nostradamus's blocking technique. The upshot of all of this is, again, a foregrounding of the possibility and effects of omniscience, or a lack thereof, which brings us to Baby Nostradamus.

Aside from the author/narrator conflation, Baby Nostradamus represents the single greatest challenge to the concept of narrative voice in the novel. The very idea of an omniscient narrator is that she knows all, yet from the very first appearance of Baby Nostradamus (23), Saturn proves unable to see his thoughts. Thus, the ontological world of the narrative is called into question because our supposedly all-knowing narrator has blind spots. Not only does Saturn not know Baby Nostradamus's thoughts, but Baby Nostradamus is also cast as knowing more than Saturn—another wrinkle in the ontological world of *The People of Paper*. In Chapter 16, we are told, "Though at times forgetful, Saturn knew most of what was contained within the covers of this book . . . But Saturn had never been able to penetrate the black of the Baby Nostradamus" (160). And if it were not enough that these revelations cast Saturn's omniscience, and thereby authority, into doubt, the narrator suggests that the Baby Nostradamus is not confined to the ontological universe of the novel (an impossibility). He relates that the Baby Nostradamus's "knowledge extended beyond the plot and details of this book, reaching not only into the future but beyond it, circling fully around, intersecting with the past and resting wherever he wished" (160). We need not be versed in narrative theory to know that fictional characters cannot access our actual world. To imagine that they could would be to treat characters as people, not the invention of an author at a keyboard. Let us, however, stick to the logic of the narrative, which is vexing enough. While the opening pages of Chapter 16 speak of Baby Nostradamus's omniscience, the narrator realizes that in order for a character like Baby Nostradamus not to completely capsize the narrative, constraints must be placed on the exercise of his knowledge:

> Because of the Baby Nostradamus's great powers, supplemental laws governed his abilities, further limiting his actions. The Baby Nostradamus had the power to undercut Saturn by prematurely disclosing information and sabotaging the whole of the novel. Ending everything here by simply listing the character fates: announcing who would win the war, revealing whether Merced would return to Federico de la Fe or whether Liz's diaspora would eventually bring her back to Saturn. (167)

Given all of this information about Baby Nostradamus, it seems impossible to respect the ontological consistency of *The People of Paper*. We have a group of characters at war with an omniscient narrator, whom we have just learned is exceeded in his knowledge by one of the very characters in the war against him. This is a logical impossibility.

Furthermore, Chapter 16 presents additional problems regarding narrative voice that return us to the aforementioned narrator/author oscillation and confusion. Who is narrating Baby Nostradamus's sections of this chapter? We know that Saturn is incapable of seeing into Baby Nostradamus's thoughts, so it cannot be Saturn. If it were Baby Nostradamus himself, it would make more sense for him to speak in the first person, unless, as with the Saturn sections, the possibility exists that he enjoys the affectation of speaking of himself in the third person. I think that is neither the case in the Saturn sections, nor in the Baby Nostradamus sections in Chapter 16. Rather, I contend, the author Salvador Plascencia is challenging the very idea that there exists a distinction between author and narrator in third-person novels. Perhaps one wants to suggest that this is a matter of narrative regress and that what we are reading between the covers of the novel we bought called *The People of Paper* is another novel called *The People of Paper* narrated not by Saturn, but by a truly removed omniscient narrator, whose name (as is typical with omniscient narrators) we do not know.

If, however, Saturn is not the omniscient narrator, but simply another character in the story, then the whole conceit of the novel becomes ridiculous because Federico and the EMF are fighting a war against the wrong person. In that scenario, Saturn would be just another helpless character in an omnisciently narrated novel. Instead, I believe, all of the evidence I presented in this chapter about the confusion of author and narrator supports my contention that Plascencia is challenging narrative conventions of the absolute distinction between author and narrator. And in this challenge is the "something different" that I suggested is occurring in *The People of Paper*, as opposed to other metafictional novels such as Italo Calvino's *If on a Winter's Night a Traveler*, Paul Auster's *City of Glass*, and so on. If all of these novels present themselves as drawing attention to their narrativity, *The People of Paper* seems to take it a step further and suggest that even the laws that govern the ontological world of a given novel (the heterocosm) are violable. It is a difference in degree more than kind, but it challenges how we think of narrative, narrative voice, and the construction of possible worlds. *The People of Paper* is a meditation on the very nature of fiction. If Brecht's epic theatre asked us to think about real-world problems through fictive acts without getting lost in their illusion, and if much metafiction and post-structuralist theory employ narrative to have us consider the textual and discursive nature of the world, *The People of Paper* asks us to reflect on the conventions fiction employs to create its illusions, not to give us some connection to the world outside of the text, but to have us consider the very construction of the text.

One of the salubrious benefits of Plascencia's absorption in the act of narrativity is that it abjures any hasty mimetic assessments, for it reveals itself to be engaged in nothing more or less than a reckoning with the construction of a fictive world. By so insistently engaging the act of fictive world-making, it reminds us that all fiction—including fiction which purposefully conceals its illusion-making—is best measured by its own aesthetic logic and not by whether it faithfully, accurately, positively, negatively, and least of all authentically holds a mirror to the world. Novels such as *The People of Paper* ask us to engage carefully and intimately with the fictional worlds *they* construct. To continue analyzing the literature we have heretofore labeled *Latinx* through a taxonomy built around fictional genres, I turn next to the short story and the narrative acts it employs to generate intimacy and distance.

CHAPTER 3

From Where I Stand: The Intimacy and Distance of *We* and *You* in the Short Story

Despite its deep roots in nineteenth-century U.S. fiction and its proliferation ever since, in both U.S. letters generally and Latinx literature in particular, the short story remains treated as a minor form.[1] Critics and the publishing world still privilege the novel. Editors and agents maintain that they have a far easier time selling novels than collections of short stories.[2] In this vein, Junot Díaz, in his introduction to *The Best American Short Stories 2016*, writes, "I hate the endless shade thrown at the short story—whether from publishers or editors or writers who talk the form down" (xii). Yet later in the introduction, he, too, confesses to having to be converted to the form. It occurred when the first story he submitted as an MFA student was gutted in workshop. He then dove into the form, determined to excel. "It dawned on me finally," he writes, "that this was no intermediate form, a step en route to the novel, but an extraordinary tradition in its own right, not easily mastered but rich in rewards. I started yammering on to my friends about the form's surprising complexity, its power, its mutability—how structurally instructive it was" (xvi). The short story is indeed a complex and nuanced form. It has flourished in Latinx letters, and a principle of equity demands that we meet it on its own terms.[3] I am especially interested in analyzing rare forms of storytelling, namely, stories focalized in first-person plural (*we*) and second-person singular (*you*).[4] What particularly interests me about these narrative perspectives is the affective textures they create in terms of intimacy and distance. I analyze these affective dimensions in exemplary short stories by Manuel Muñoz, Patricia Engel, and Ana Menéndez.

Reading with Feeling

The now decades-old affective fallacy notwithstanding, form and affect cannot be divorced. They are mutually reinforcing phenomena. I hasten to point out that the subtitle of Stanley Fish's article "Literature in the Reader" is "Affective Stylistics." Though written well before the advent of affect studies and though not, to the best of my knowledge, cited by any of the major theoreticians in that field, what it shares in common with affect studies is the way the reader is affected by what she reads and how her responses are equally, if not more, important than the information presented in the text. Meaning is made through the reader. In an affective stylistics, "the focus of attention is shifted from the spatial context of a page and its observable regularities to the temporal context of a mind and its experiences" (Fish, *Text in This Class* 91). I emphasize the formal dimensions of the literature somewhat more heavily than Fish, but what we share is a desire to know how the text comes to mean, and what a word, sentence, or paragraph does. In this chapter, I examine the affective dimensions of intimacy and the formal features a select group of fictional texts employs to render that intimacy legible.[5]

By *intimate* I mean closeness, tenderness, knowingness, and a sense of confidence between reader and narrator. *Intimacy* is a state or condition with numerous conflicting and complex affects and emotions. In particular, I engage what we might call close acts of fiction. These fictions break with typical first- and third-person narration, and opt instead for the more irregular use of *we* and *you*. Though, by no means, a unique act in the writing of fiction, these focalizations are still rare enough that they capture the reader's attention, unsettle her, and raise questions as to their causes and effects. I want to think about the intimate, and perhaps coercive, acts narrators perform in wrangling the reader into their stories. What does it do, for instance, to use that intimate first-person plural gesture of *we* to denote narrator and reader? What does it do to narrate a first-person self *I* through the second-person pronoun *you*? What happens when characters are never named, but instead labeled exclusively *you* and *I*?

These intimate acts of narration depend not only on an "informed reader," but on the conversion of that reader into a sympathetic one. Fish defines the informed reader as follows:

> The informed reader is someone who (1) is a competent speaker of the language out of which the text is built up; (2) is in full possession of the "semantic knowledge that a mature . . . listener brings to his task of comprehension." This includes the knowledge (that is, the experience, both as a producer and comprehender) of lexical sets, collocation probabilities, idioms, professional and other dialects, etc.; (3) has *literary* competence. (*Literature in the Reader* 145; ellipses and emphasis in original)

In addition to this linguistic and semantic competence, the reader brings with her certain political and social beliefs that influence the making of meaning. If the text is not an idealized locus of meaning, the reader, even the informed reader, is not a uniform entity. Fish explains the variety of readings of texts and the legitimacy of those readings based on the criteria of the interpretive community from which the reader hails, but he never explicitly, to the best of my knowledge, talks about the specific influence of the ideological baggage a reader brings with her to the text. Nevertheless, he does note that an interpretive community's perspective is "interested rather than neutral" (*Text in This Class* 14).

The predominant way of interpreting Latinx literature (notable exceptions notwithstanding) has been from a leftist perspective. Influenced by such readings, we, critics, can forget that there are readers out there who do not approach this body of fiction in the same way we do. We still lack (as the field of literary studies as a whole does) ethnographies of readers that might tell us how a diverse (in every sense of that word) range of people respond to texts.[6] I am not proposing such an undertaking here. Regardless, in a chapter such as this, where I am analyzing the intimate aspects of fiction, it warrants pointing out that if the intimacy between reader and narrator is to take hold, you need not only what has been traditionally called a sympathetic character, but also a sympathetic reader. Indeed, the very idea of a sympathetic character depends on a reader who sympathizes and empathizes with the character's plight.

One can imagine that not all readers share the same sympathies. Paula M. L. Moya captures this notion deftly in her recent book *The Social Imperative: Race, Close Reading, and Contemporary Literary Criticism*. She argues there for the adoption of social psychology schemas in interpreting literature. She correctly maintains, "Key to the impact a text will have on a reader is the manner and extent to which *that* text activates for *that* reader a set of cognitive-affective structures social psychologists refer to as schemas" (15; emphasis in original).[7] In the case of "Monkey, *Sí*,"—the first story I analyze in the next section—I can imagine that there would be homophobic readers not at all sympathetic to the story of the unrequited love between Tomás and Nestor. These readers come at these texts, in Moya's critical vocabulary, with a different set of schemas.[8] The affect these readers register might be one of disgust and repulsion.[9] Even readers who share one's worldview might fall out on different sides of "Monkey, *Sí*." It is a complicated story. Whereas readerly dispositions influence meaning-making in all stories, they become particularly pronounced in stories of affections and intimacies. I turn now to Manuel Muñoz's "Monkey, *Sí*"; Ana Menéndez's "Why We Left"; and Patricia Engel's "Green."[10]

Translating Affections

Muñoz stands at the forefront of a new generation of Chicanx writers. He received his undergraduate degree from Harvard and his MFA from Cornell University, where he studied with the eminent Chicana author Helena María Viramontes, who also trained H. G. Carrillo and overlapped for a semester with Junot Díaz. In 2003, Muñoz published his first collection of short stories, *Zigzagger*. *The Faith Healer of Olive Avenue*, his second collection of short stories, came out in 2007, and in 2011, Muñoz published his first novel, *What You See in the Dark*. His stories, particularly those in *Zigzagger*—from which "Monkey, *Sí*" comes—often defy the traditional understanding of narrative as composed of a beginning, middle, and an end.[11] His fictions regularly present a picture of a conflict or trace the outlines of a character without arriving at a conclusion or resolving the tension at play in the story. Even in his fictions that adhere to a more traditional narrative emplotment, Muñoz eschews tidy conclusions, uncomplicated representations, and a flattening out of nuance. He is gifted at generating affective textures full of rich, complex emotional depth. Indeed, it is to these affective, emotional terrains that I want to direct our attention.

Manuel Muñoz's "Monkey, *Sí*" is a curious story. On the one hand, it is the tale of Nestor's unrequited love for Tomás and how that quest results in Nestor's violent rape by two strangers. On the other hand, it is a story ever aware of itself *as* story, a story that asks us to consider how to construct a story and why. The story is not curious, however, in terms of its content, but in the way that, given its horribly *painful* content, it achieves a surprising level of intimacy. It is an intimacy that establishes itself between narrator and reader while paradoxically being a story about an intense lack of intimacy between Nestor and Tomás. Furthermore, as the story draws intimate lines of connection to the reader through its formal features, it also simultaneously highlights the distance among the reader, narrator, and story. Thus, in working through my reading of the story, I want to focus on intimate moments of connection and tenderness as well as ways in which distance (physical and emotional) is manufactured and maintained. I attempt—to borrow a phrase from the story—to translate the story's affections by analyzing its first-person plural narration, its numerous meta-fictional intrusions, and the connection between sentiment and culture.

Certainly among the first things one notices when reading "Monkey, *Sí*" is its focalization through the subject pronoun *we*. It draws attention because it is a narrative device not frequently used. There are a number of things to observe about this *we*. The first is that its referent is ambiguous. It, at times, feels like an arch, royal *we*, and that is certainly in keeping with the narrator's tone of voice and his vivid presence in the story. At other times, however, it feels like an inclusive *we*, a perhaps in-group *we*. Those in the know—the story seems to say—can be included in this *we*. To be in the know is to know something about gay life, to know something about how fiction operates, and to be sympathetic to and empathetic with the proper characters. The narrator uses *we* to draw the reader close to him, to pull us into his confidences, to build a shared sympathy for and empathy with Nestor. It is not a manipulative inclusivity, but rather one that suggests we are allies. We are included in this first-person plural gesture, that is, not to get us to see things the narrator's way. It is not an act of moral persuasion. Rather, the narrator believes *a priori* that we share his values, beliefs, and sympathies.

There are not always bright line distinctions between the *we* as an arch, royal *we* and as a more inclusive plural *we*. I begin with the arch. Throughout the story, the narrator maintains a strong presence with a distinct personality. We are not, that is, in the detached world of omniscient narration. This is the world of a raconteur recounting to and with you a tragic story, as if we were seated around a table at a club and he were holding court. Perhaps more to the point, this royal *we* is a voice of judgment that presumes we share his affective responses and emotional concerns. The knowingness of the narrator is extended as compliment to us by the very use of *we*.

Consider, for instance, the scene in which two older men preying on Nestor at a gay bar in San Francisco—the bar outside of which they will rape him—have just drugged his drink. The narrator remarks, "[W]e know that Nestor shouldn't drink that drink (Alice! Dorothy!) but the anger blooming in his chest will cause him to see one of the men and think he is a good-looking man. (We hate to admit that the men are good-looking.) We know, even through their clothes, that they are slick as seals and hard" (174). The content of the two parentheticals signals that this is a royal *we* speaking. Here, the royal *we* tone is a blend of an arch, camp sensibility with a genuine pathos for poor Nestor. It is a mock royal *we* that goes over the top with its tone to make a serious point. You can see the arched eyebrow, the pursed lips, and even hear the *tsk* in the narrator's voice as he shares the knowledge that Nestor shouldn't drink that drink, emphasizing that point with a campy reference to *Alice in Wonderland* and *The Wizard of Oz*. The second parenthetical—(We hate to admit that the men are good-looking.)—and use of *we* operate in a similarly affective way. They register a playfully incriminating guilt, as if in what is about to be a violent scene, the narrator should not distract himself with such details. However, he also recognizes that such seemingly superficial particulars are important to the story, for Nestor—who is portrayed throughout the story as overlooked by Tomás and particularly in this bar scene in which Tomás has abandoned him to pursue another man—needs to feel he is the object of someone's attention and affection. The campiness of the mock royal *we* in this scene, conjoined with the narrator's deep concern for Nestor, draws us to the narrator and forges an intimate storytelling connection with him.

On the other hand, the inclusive, first-person plural use of *we* casts us as knowing as the narrator, as he intends to draw us into the various scenes of the narrative with him. Early in the story, for instance, Nestor, Tomás, and a group of friends walk down the street. The narrator remarks, "We can see them, from a distance, as a group of friends. We know that a group of friends walking together to the one bar in town cannot line up side by side as they do on television. . . . Later, if we like, we can get as close to Nestor as we want when we listen to Tomás tell him about why the two were walking on either side of him" (168–169). The *we*'s here suggest that we know this story, that we are part of it. The inclusive *we* accords us desire and volition. We can do what we like. We can will ourselves closer to the conversation between Nestor and Tomás, if that's what we want to hear. We are not passive "narratees." We are empowered narrators.

This strategy of intimately connecting us to the narrator through the use of the first-person plural is reinforced by the strategy of telling the story nearly exclusively through summation, not dramatization. Even in the most affectively moving scene—Nestor's rape—we do not witness the characters interacting with one another; rather we, along with the narrator, recount what has happened. We even, at times, consider what to recount: "Do we want to see it [the rape] happening? (We know what's happening.) Do we want to enter Nestor's haze as this goes on? Or would we be better off (in the way that none of us ever wants to see the accident but wants to see the glitter of glass) seeing how Nestor will be found?" (175).

This brings me to another narrative technique I want to consider vis-à-vis the generation of intimacy. The creation of a fictive world typically depends on rendering a universe so realistic that you forget you are in an illusion. You fall under the spell of the enchanting storyteller. You are transported to another world full of complex, intriguing lives, lives that you recognize, that you come to believe in. You know the characters as if they were your acquaintances, friends, and enemies. Such finely drawn characters and worlds are responsible for eliciting a range of emotional responses in readers. It is why you sympathize, for instance, with the farm-workers in Tomás Rivera's . . . *And the Earth Did Not Devour Him* and why you loathe Vevoda in J. J. Abrams and Doug Dorst's novel *S*. In contrast, stories that regularly remind you—through a range of techniques—that you are reading a story shatter this illusion, as we saw, for instance, in *The People of Paper*. By drawing attention to their fictionality, such stories make it potentially more difficult to elicit emotional and affective responses, for they appeal to the reader's ratiocinative side in lieu of the emotive one. Interestingly, however, "Monkey, *Sí*" manages to do both. It makes us aware of the ontological universe it constructs, but that does not vitiate our emotional response to the story or undermine our feelings of intimacy with and for both the narrator and Nestor. "Monkey, *Sí*," breaks the narrative illusion of Nestor and Tomás and yet paradoxically also maintains it. It calls attention to the fact that we are in a fictive universe, yet it keeps us rapt (and wrapped) in the emotional lives of the characters.

It should be noted that this illusion-breaking happens quite frequently in the story and is not merely a trick tossed in at the end (more on the highly self-aware ending in a moment). The illusion-breaking is there from the beginning and is fundamental to the narrative. We are a mere fifteen lines into the story when the narrator notes,

> But it never gets cold here, because it is Fresno. Why Fresno? A good question, but others are already in line. And this roster of names [the opening paragraph of the story is exclusively a roster of names]—are these friends of Tomás? Tricks? A list of lovers that only shows how flighty a character Tomás will turn out to be? Do we already know that Nestor will lose out by the end of the story (and in life, because we have mentioned that he is dark skinned and small and these men don't like either)? (167–168)

Whereas in a more conventional story, the narrator would begin by introducing the principal characters, enticing you into the story, and casting a narrative spell on you, our narrator draws attention to the story's fictive elements, namely, its setting and its opening gambit. Moreover, he does not coyly hint at what is to come, but rather forecasts it through a bit of racial predestination—Nestor is doomed because he is dark-skinned. If this outcome seems not carved in stone because it is suggested as a question, the narrator eradicates that ambiguity a mere five lines later with the declarative assertion, "Nestor will come close to death, by his own doing, but we already know he'll survive it and live (unfortunately) in continued unhappiness" (168). The figurative fourth wall is demolished. The questions that build the fourth paragraph of the story make us well aware that we are in the midst of the construction of a fictive ontological universe, but the narrator also keeps us affectively tied to the story. We may know that things will not end well for Nestor, but we do not yet know why. Our curiosity is piqued. At the close of section 1 (the story is composed of fourteen sections), additional intrigue is created with the inviting interrogative: "What has Tomás to do with any of this?" (168). This question plays on our emotions and our narrative curiosity because we should want to know the answer and because we know from a prior paragraph that Nestor is in love with Tomás.

Furthermore, if we think of reading and therefore meaning-making as a temporal sequence, how we get from one word, one sentence, one paragraph, one section to the next matters. What follows this initial rupturing of narrative illusion is a section that pulls us fully back into the affective register of the story. The story heightens its intimacy through a twofold narrative strategy. It momentarily suspends the use of *we* in favor of a more traditional third-person narration and pulls us into the visceral causes for Nestor's attraction to Tomás. It moves, that is, from an abstract, cerebral plane of narration to a physical plane of intimacy: "Nestor likes Tomás because of what he wears. He wears muscle shirts and open short-sleeves, unbuttoned, even to work, and Nestor thinks that no one complains because Tomás smiles with straight teeth and teases the women. All in good nature because Tomás has no hair on his chest breaking through the white cotton of his shirt . . ." (168). This expository summation is deft. It offers a sense of Tomás's physicality and Nestor's attraction to it. Across all fourteen sections, the story continues in this back-and-forth between rupturing the narrative illusion and heightening it, moving between a first-person plural narration and a third-person one, and in all of these narrative moves, Muñoz takes an unlikely candidate for an intimate tale—one of violence, rape, and unrequited love—and renders it intimate, triggering a range of affective responses.

I close my analysis of "Monkey, *Sí*" by contending that the story both rejects the sentimental and embraces it. More specifically, it oscillates between embracing a particularized racial cultural sensibility and rejecting a generalized gay sensibility. Twice in the story, the narrator puzzles over what music might be fitting as a soundtrack for various scenes. The first scene is the rape of Nestor, and using a first-person inclusive voice, he asks if we want a soundtrack, and if so, what would we like to hear. He rejects Elton John because he is "too much a sentimentalist" and because "(. . . Nestor and Tomás and all the rest are not children of opera and show tunes, but Mexican *ranchera* in the mornings.) So we will imagine Lola Beltrán and Amalia Mendoza, the one who cries at the end of every song she sings" (175). We can have sentiment, but it needs be the tragic sentiment of a Mexican diva, a Mexican chanteuse. And, again at the close of the story, as the narrator considers what music to send us out on, he rejects a "generalized" gay cultural sensibility: "Not opera and (God, no) not Judy Garland. Not here," in favor of "trumpets with a Mexican flair (yes, Mexican)" (182).

However, in the final paragraph of the story—which immediately follows the lines about the trumpets with a Mexican flair—the privileging of the particular over the general grows complicated, as does the intimacy that I have argued inheres between narrator and reader. For in this closing paragraph, the narrator—through the inclusive use of we—shows us dividing (if not fully divided) over the choice of the Mexican trumpets and over stereotypical expectations that "some of us" have when reading stories with Latinx characters:

> It isn't fitting. We are splitting and not agreeing because Mexican trumpets are too specific. His name is Nestor and some of us think he should levitate or endure something spiritual like that to close this story, floating right through the ceiling, sprouting wings. His name is Nestor, and don't stories with names like that need to have levitation and a good deal of magic? No, not this one. It won't. It can't. Leave him be, eating his cereal. Some of us will stay with him. Others of us won't (so go to Tomás, or Tommy, because, he lets people call him that now). (182)

In addition to underscoring the troubling of the particular and the general, these lines show us splitting not just over readerly expectations but dividing our affections, which the story has been working hard to translate (and render communicable and understandable). The assumed solidarity of the *we* ruptures over whether we elect to follow Nestor or Tomás. And the use of the imperative "Leave him be" suggests that there is now a "you" among the readers, a "you" that grammatically cannot be part of the *we*. I still maintain that this is an intimate tale for all of the reasons I have heretofore pointed out, but the closing of the story suggests the complications entailed in that intimacy. Closeness does not preclude division.

"Monkey, *Si*" only invokes a *you* briefly in its closing. *We* is the staple of its narrative. I thus turn now to Patricia Engel, who uses *you* to great dramatic effect in her story "Green."

You as I

Patricia Engel, the daughter of Colombian parents, was raised in New Jersey. She holds an undergraduate degree in French and Art History from New York University and an MFA from Florida International University. Engel's debut collection of linked stories, *Vida*, won her wide critical acclaim. Junot Díaz's front-cover blurb calls it "the debut I have been waiting for." Among numerous nominations and awards, *Vida* was a finalist for the PEN/Hemingway Award for Debut Fiction, a Barnes and Noble Discover Great New Writers selection, and a *New York Times* Editors' Choice, and it was named Best Book of the Year by NPR, Barnes and Noble, *Latina* magazine, and *Los Angeles Weekly*. She has since published two novels: *It's Not Love, It's Just Paris* (2013) and *The Veins of the Ocean* (2016).

Like the writers examined throughout *Latinx Literature Unbound* and many others beyond this study, Engel maintains a complex relationship to the label *Latina*. When asked in a 2011 interview for the literary magazine *Saw Palm* how she feels about being labeled a Latina writer, she responded,

> The "Latina" label wasn't yet popular when I was growing up. We were Hispanics or Spanish, at best, but of course we didn't think of ourselves as Hispanic or Spanish—because we weren't from Hispaniola or Spain—but as Colombian, or even more commonly, as Paisa (from the region of Antioquia) so you get an idea of how disconnected we were from what we were called. I think the need to designate literature the way they do for food in the supermarket aisles is sort of a recent trend and one that I try not to give too much importance. (Díaz, "Next Literary Superstar," par. 7)

These ideas of connection and disconnection, homeland and exile, run throughout Engel's engaging body of work.[12] I will be examining the story "Green" from her book *Vida*.

Vida is a collection of nine interlinked stories that follow the narrator Sabina Rios from her childhood to roughly her thirties. As such, it is in many ways her coming-of-age narrative. It tells the story, among other things, of Sabina and her family's immigration to the United States and what it means to settle here, to change homelands, and to be racialized. I focus on the story "Green," for it makes use of a rare narrative point of view, namely, second person. Moreover, this particular *you* is not an address to the reader, is not a rupture of the fourth wall, as we saw in "Monkey, *Sí.*" Rather *you*, here, is a stand-in for *I.* As with the other eight stories in the collection that are told in the first person from Sabina's perspective, "Green," too, is focalized through Sabina, but Engel uses *you* in place of *I.* I examine how this narrative gesture creates both intimacy and distance.

Engel heightens the dramatic impulse and affective texture of her story by narrating in the second-person voice. In its starkest outline, "Green" is the story of how Maureen Reilly, a girl who tortured and humiliated Sabina in school, died from an eating disorder. It is, of course, much more than that. From the opening, we know the story's dramatic questions and, thus, what we are reading toward. We might render the questions as "Why does Sabina, now in her twenties, care about the death of her school nemesis Maureen?" and "What, if any, lasting effect has Maureen's torture had on Sabina?" All well-crafted stories reveal their dramatic questions early and, thus, generate the intrigue necessary for us to want to keep reading.

However, "Green" goes beyond its starkest plot outline and its dramatic questions. It intensifies, that is, the reading experience through its choice of point of view. Let us register the effect of this narrative choice by examining the opening sentence of the story. I present it first as Engel wrote it, and then I convert it into first-person narration, which is how every other story in the collection is told:

> Your mom just called to tell you that Maureen, the girl who tortured you from kindergarten to high school, who single-handedly made it so that you were never welcome in Girl Scouts, soccer, or yearbook, is dead. ("Green" 47)

> My mom just called to tell me that Maureen, the girl who tortured me from kindergarten to high school, who single-handedly made it so that I was never welcome in Girl Scouts, soccer, or yearbook, is dead.

The first-person voice places us much closer to Sabina. When told from this perspective, we can feel her pain and perhaps pleasure more clearly, and this is not even the most painful and moving sentence of the story. By contrast, in second person, Sabina, and by extension the reader, becomes more detached from the story. It is as if she is observing (like a scientist), not living, her own life. This is not the invocation of *you* as a fourth-wall break that generates a conviviality with the narrator. This is placing *I* under the microscope by naming it *you*. Let us go from this opening and the tone and distance it creates into a deeper analysis of the story.

The use of *you* creates observational distance, but it can create its own peculiar form of intimacy, not the closeness of first-person narration, but a closeness nonetheless. For instance, even at the close of the story's opening paragraph, we can still feel the childhood sting that Maureen's racism and stereotyping hold over the twenty-something Sabina: "Maureen, who said that your skin was the color of diarrhea, that your Colombian dad dealt drugs, that boys didn't like you because you looked like their maids, is finally, finally dead" (47). In that use of "finally, finally dead," we hear not the voice of an adult, but that of a child. The doubling of "finally" is childlike, for it imagines the need to repeat the adverb, as if not to allow Maureen to return from the grave, to make doubly sure she is dead. This subtle move brings us into Sabina's state of mind, and in showing us the durable effect of Maureen's words, it cuts down the distance we feel between ourselves and Sabina. The use of *you* will oscillate between distant and intimate throughout the story by way of narrative moves such as "finally, finally." For the author, the trick of the second-person narration is to figure out how to use it to create the distance you desire, but also not preclude the closeness necessary for readers to sympathize with and even root for the characters.

Given the topic of the story—the death of a young woman due to an eating disorder—and given the epidemic proportions of eating disorders among girls and women and the rising figures among boys and men, one might expect a heartbreaking story about Maureen's death, but this is not a story of heartbreak, at least not in the way Sabina presents herself.[13] Throughout the collection, Sabina is unflinching and wonderfully unsentimental in her self-portrayal. She presents herself replete with contradictions and complexities. The news of Maureen's death, which serves as the catalyst for the story, pulls us back to two different moments in Sabina's life—her school days and the last time she saw Maureen (i.e., when Maureen asked her to get together). These moments afford Sabina the opportunity to reflect on how the past ramifies into her present, and the story closes on how Sabina might behave in a projected future time.

On the one hand, Sabina, as an adult, wants to forget about Maureen and be cavalier about everything in the past. We learn that a few years preceding Maureen's death that Sabina and her family saw Maureen at midnight mass. When Maureen waves to her, Sabina informs us, "You tried not to look at her decaying body, tried to be matter-of-fact about it when your family talked about the sight of her during the car ride home" (49). On the other hand, she is unable to simply forget the past, "try" though she might. Ultimately, the story is one about Sabina's understanding of the world as an unjust, cruel place. Or as Sabina reflects about why Maureen asked her to meet up, "[Y]ou thought maybe the world was becoming a place of justice and Maureen was looking to repent for her cruelty" (50–51). But Maureen is not looking to repent. She is looking for help. She knows that Sabina suffered from an eating disorder in high school and believes, therefore, that Sabina can help her "stop."

Engel herself has described the story as one about pity and forgiveness. In a 2010 interview for the literary magazine *Gulf Stream*, Susan Falco asserts that the second-person narration "sort of demands the reader's empathy" and then asks Engel what led her to make that decision. Engel replies, "In 'Green,' Sabina is really engaged in battle with herself, trying to rise above her wounds to pity her abuser, but she fails, and in failing, she understands herself a bit more. It's the lesson that forgiveness doesn't always come served up on a plate and one cannot rely on it."

What interests me about this theme is how Engel sets it up in the story. Sabina is not uniformly unforgiving. Unless we are dealing with some type of fairy tale or Christian allegory, characters should not be wholly heroic or wholly demonic, for such characterization breaks the illusion of the narrative, draining it of nuance and art. Sabina is able to pity Maureen in one regard, namely, as a "wounded woman." After Sabina sees Maureen at that midnight mass, we learn that the only news or gossip that Sabina has had of Maureen in recent years is that Maureen's high school boyfriend "impregnated and married her former best friend" (49–50). Sabina says, "You even felt pity for Maureen. You'd just been cheated on for the first time and felt the pain of wounded women everywhere" (50). *Pity* is a peculiar word because, depending on the context, it can mean feeling sorry for someone in a tender way or in a contemptuous way. Moreover, unlike *sympathy* or *compassion*, *pity* places the speaker in an elevated position to the person receiving the pity. Since Sabina casts Maureen's situation here in the same light as the infidelity to which she was subject, we understand that the pity comes from a place of tenderness, not contempt. Or, if not tenderness, at least solidarity, since she aligns them both as wounded women.

Engel expertly gives us this information immediately in the paragraph just before Sabina goes to meet Maureen, which she does because her mom guilts her into it (50). The juxtaposition of how Sabina responds to Maureen as a "wounded woman" with how she will respond to Maureen's confession that she has "a problem with food" (50) works to help us understand the complexity of Sabina's character and the difficulties of forgiveness. As the scene first unfolds, we witness a restrained Sabina. When Maureen wonders if Sabina knows about her eating disorder, Sabina tells us both what she said and what she didn't say. By giving us both, Sabina reveals herself, from the observational, distant perspective of second-person narration, as a temperate character:

> You said you had a vague idea. Didn't say it'd been all over the town wires for years already, how she dropped out of some crap college to get treatment, was working a few hours a week gift-wrapping at a local children's clothing store. Not to mention the road map of fat veins that looked like they were trying to break out of her face. (50)

In other words, Sabina does not rub her knowledge of Maureen's eating disorder in her face. Neither, however, does she paint herself as saintly. To say that she "had a vague idea" is kind, but Sabina also lets us in on the fact that she harbors a number of wicked thoughts about Maureen, perhaps even relishes Maureen's fallen state. That she holds them back, however, shows growth in her character. In the last interaction between the two characters, right after high school graduation, we see a quite different Sabina. We experience a Sabina who responds in kind to Maureen's abuse:

> She called you a shit-skinned whore in your white dress, miniature red roses in your French twist. She'd only just started losing weight and you shouted back that she was a fat albino midget no diet would ever save, something you will always regret. (48)

That graduation scene juxtaposed to the scene at the diner with the confession of the eating disorder and Sabina's response allows us an evolving portrait of Sabina, as does her retrospective assessment that she "will always regret" having said those words. But two telling moments at the story's conclusion disallow a fully heroic, sentimental reading of Sabina's growth into a forgiving character, someone capable of always turning the other cheek.

The first comes in the exchange at the diner when Maureen asks Sabina how she was able to stop. We learn that Sabina herself went to therapy and benefited from the experience. More important, Sabina tells us "You gave Maureen all of your processed therapy talk" (56). Thus, we get a character willing to share her life lessons with someone who had brutalized her as a child. This makes her incredibly sympathetic. Sabina does not, however, close there. She reveals that she could have continued with the advice, could have imparted tough love wisdom as her brother did with her, but she does not. In fact, the Sabina she reveals to us, the reader, in three successive paragraphs is a complex character equal parts callous, hurt, and perhaps even a little vindictive:

> But you held back. Told yourself it wasn't your problem.
> Instead you said you had to be on your way, that you had to catch the next train back to the city. Made it sound like you had a really exciting life waiting for you.
>   Silly to think of it now but before you left each other that day, you still hoped, in that strange space of reminiscing and advice-giving, that Maureen would ask you to forgive her for hurting you. (57)

The use of *you* here works to good effect. We, as readers, need the distance and detachment it provides from Sabina. If this were narrated in first-person it would be too close to Sabina and thereby perhaps make her come off as too callous, too evil. To see her hold back information that might help the human being across from her—a human being described in sundry ways as desiccated, as a shell of a person—would be too much. Even in the *you* voice, it is a little hard to watch as she attempts to make Maureen envious of her fabricated "exciting life."[14] The last thing I want to note is Sabina's use of "silly to think of it now." That retrospective assessment is wonderfully ambiguous. Is it silly to think of it now because in retrospect she can see that Maureen was never going to ask for forgiveness, that Maureen was there only to seek Sabina's assistance? Or is it perhaps silly to think of it now because Sabina is years removed from that meeting and should have moved on with her life? In short, Maureen is dead now, so why bother thinking over not having received and apology from her.

This then brings me to the second and final moment at the story's conclusion that, as I mentioned earlier, disallows a fully heroic or sentimental reading of Sabina. So unflinching is one of the sentences in the penultimate paragraph that perhaps the second-person narration works to Sabina's own benefit, protects her from the brutal characterization of herself. In this final section, which is after her meeting with Maureen (we do not know exactly how long), Sabina relates that she left that meeting at the diner telling Maureen "to write or call whenever she wanted, said you'd always be there for her if she needed a friend" (57). Sabina does not disclose her motives. We do not know, that is, whether this was said out of obligation or if Sabina really meant for Maureen to reach out. But then comes the unflinching sentence that I mentioned perhaps served Sabina in its second-person narration. We discover that Maureen did write. Sabina says, "When another letter did come, you read it quickly, tossed it into the trash, and never thought of Maureen again" (57). That is a steely-eyed self-assessment that can tell us, in the space of a paragraph, that she encouraged Maureen to reach out, but that when she did, Sabina paid the gesture scarcely any attention and tossed it off as so much rubbish. Still, we do not close on that note. In that dialectical push and pull that we experience throughout the story, we end with, if not a forgiveness of her abuser, at least a bit of intimate, self-acceptance:

> Your plan was to forget. But you did think of her, often, while wishing you could cull your memory to craft a provisional mercy. You never managed. Told yourself, In time. In time. (57)

Sabina does not give us a heroic self who is able to forgive someone who, indeed, should have been seeking Sabina's forgiveness, nor does she give us a self-loathing character angry for being able to offer mercy to her abuser. Rather we get a character full of contradictions and nuance. I maintain that, in light of the racist brutality Sabina experienced at Maureen's hands, that characterization and self-assessment is possible only for Sabina (and for readers as well) with the distance that the second-person narration allows. I turn now to a more standard yet intriguing use of second-person in Ana Menéndez's short story "Why We Left."

The Intimacy and Distance of Loneliness

Ana Menéndez is the daughter of Cuban exiles who fled to Los Angeles in the 1960s before settling in Miami. Since 1991, she has worked as a journalist in the United States and abroad, most recently as a prize-winning columnist for the *Miami Herald*. As a reporter, she has written about Cuba, Haiti, Kashmir, Afghanistan, and India, where she was based for three years. She is also a former Fulbright Scholar to Egypt. She holds a BA in English from Florida International University. She received her MFA from New York University's creative writing program, where she was a *New York Times* fellow. She is the author of four books of fiction: *In Cuba I Was a German Shepherd*, which was a 2001 *New York Times* Notable Book of the Year and whose title story won a Pushcart Prize; *Loving Che* (2004); *The Last War* (2009), chosen by *Publishers Weekly* as one of the top 100 books of the year; and *Adios, Happy Homeland!* (2011).

Menéndez's story "Why We Left" is an apt, perhaps perfect, comple-
ment to both Manuel Muñoz's "Monkey, *Sí*" and Patricia Engel's "Green"
because it makes a distinct yet connected use of the pronouns *we* and
you. In its, at times, lyric rendering of the *I* in the story, it also serves as an
ideal set up for the following chapter in this study, in which I take up the
lyric self and the radical singularity of the *I*, but more on that in a moment.
"Why We Left" comes from her collection *In Cuba I Was a German
Shepherd*, which details the lives of characters in the wake of the Cuban
revolution. Many of the characters speak of the loss of homeland; they
deal with the plight of living in exile, of having been a regal German
Shepherd in Cuba, but only a degraded mutt in the United States; they
wrestle with the complications of family, and a persistent theme throughout is memory—its nostalgia, its capacity to misremember, and the illusions
it creates. In a collection of exquisite stories, "Why We Left," however, stands
out as special for a number of formal reasons, and those formal matters, especially the use of pronouns, are what I aim to tackle in this section.

From its very title, Menéndez plants a number of dramatic questions in
the reader's mind: Who is the *we*? From where have they left? And why
have they left? We, readers, know, that is, what we are reading toward as
we embark on our narrative journey. We get answers to these questions, but
they are either not as direct as we might imagine, or they are not, given
the context in which the story appears, what we might expect. Let me begin with the *we*.

The *we* here is not the unique *we* of "Monkey, *Sí*." It is, rather, the common use of *we*, a pronoun that indicates a group of at least two people, one
of whom is *I*. That is precisely what we have in the story "Why We Left"—a
specific *you* and a specific *I* who constitute the group *we*. More specifically,
we have a couple. However, for a story that announces its coupledom from
the start, what we get throughout the story is, more often than not, the
individual *you* and the individual *I*. Throughout the entire story, *we* is used
only ten times. Should you think that not infrequent, contrast it with the
use of *you* and *I*. On the first page of the story alone, *you* is used seven times
and *I* is used eight times, nearly matching in just one page the use of *we*,
and those pronouns, then, eclipse the use of *we* were we to count their to-
tal usage in the entire story. I highlight this not because I am fond of
counting pronoun use, but because the pronominal imbalance highlights
an important theme in the story, namely, the division of the couple in general and the pronounced emotional isolation, solitude, and loneliness of
the *I*, the narrator. Moreover, we never come to know them as uniquely
named individuals; we experience them only as *you* and *I*, which I main-

tain underscores the chilly, emotionally collapsed, yet affectively intense, texture of the story. This is not the *you* cast as *I* of Engel's "Green." This is the separation of a *we* into *you* and *I*, as in you are over there and I am here, apart from you.

So why this emotional despair, this loneliness, this solitude? Given the context in which the story appears, one might reasonably think that it has to do with the hardship of exile, of adjusting to life in a new country. We know from the start that things are amiss, that the two characters are living in a city that neither one likes, that it is much colder than they are used to, and that they cannot stay warm, even in their home. We learn of emotional troubles in the relationship, but we do not find out until halfway through the story that the despair and the troubles have seemingly nothing to do with the homeland or exile. We find out that they have left Miami, not Cuba, because they have lost a child. It seems to have been a miscarriage. This, then, becomes the catalyst for emphasizing division rather than union. It is the reason why it is so important that the story relies more heavily on *you* and *I*, rather than *we*. No, not all miscarriages divide couples, fictional or otherwise, but this story is trying to underscore that emotional separation, and it achieves it, in part, through its pronominal choice and emphasis.

Consider, for instance, the very opening of the story. In this narrative whose title has announced it as a story of *we*, the reader is introduced not to a couple, but to a *you* and an *I*:

> You sit on the floor sorting nickels and dimes into straight little piles when I walk in. You look up and let one nickel drop. The pile collapses sideways as if reacting to bad news. You straighten it. I close the door behind me, watch that it doesn't slam. You bend your head and go on sorting, making meaningful metal villages out of your odd change. (77)

In addition to the utter lack of a *we* in this paragraph, a number of important narrative choices have been made. There is absolutely no direct, or even reported, dialogue, which is consistent with the rest of story. It is largely an interior story. We stay, that is, in the head of the *I*. It is not just that there is no dialogue. It is that there is no dialogue when one might expect it. The *I* has just returned home, and is not greeted or spoken to at all by the partner.[15] They simply look up and go on sorting their coins. Thus, from the opening paragraph, which sets the tone for the story, we know we are in a world of emotional isolation. Moreover, and tellingly, the narrator even ascribes feelings to inanimate objects—coins, "as if reacting to bad news." These coins become an avoidance strategy for the *you*, at least as we receive the story from the narrator. For not only is the partner's attention directed away from the narrator and toward the coins in this scene, but that divide will recur in the story.

We hear a few pages later, for instance, "By February your piles of change reach the ceiling, metal columns that keep the roof from caving in. You count in your sleep. You put pennies in your breakfast cereal. We walk through the icy house wrapped in our separate blankets. You stop eating and count dimes by firelight" (79–80). The partner is seemingly more interested in and obsessed with their coins than with the narrator. This is drawn into powerful relief not just by the description of coin stacks which exceed the bounds of the real (i.e., coins stacked presumably eight to ten feet high), but by the revealing use of *we* stitched in between a series of sentences that begin with *you*. As I have noted, *we* is a pronoun rarely used in the story, and it particularly stands out here because as the sentence unfolds temporally, the reader might expect a bit of relief from the couple's isolation. We see them in the first eight words of the sentence walking in the house together, but then that unity is stripped from the sentence with the final three words, "our separate blankets." There is no collective *we* here.

A felicitous way to analyze this division is to consider further the formal dimensions of crafting a story. In a work of fiction, a character wants something, and in pursuing what they want they encounter a series of conflicts—internal and external. These conflicts persist, as does the story, until the character gets or does not get what they desire. In "Why We Left," we have a narrator who wants a more emotionally available partner and a relationship full of the love they once had, wants to return to Miami, and wants to recover from the loss of her son. We see the transition from loving relationship to emotional collapse after the first section break (which occurs on the opening page) in the story. Menéndez masterfully achieves this emotional transition by juxtaposing a paragraph of love and one of dissolution. In the first paragraph, we hear how the *you* quoted Yeats on their first date and how the narrator could not stop reading Yeats for a week, nor could she sleep because she was so obsessed with him. Indeed, the narration asks that we see the narrator collapse into the Irish identity of Yeats and that of the narrator: "My brown hair fell out and fine red strands grew in its place. I looked like a sister of yours. My dark skin sank into itself, leaving freckles where it entered the bone" (78). Here is a union, here is a *we*, if the story ever had one. Indeed, the short paragraph closes with a proposal of marriage.

Menéndez, however, then brings us away from intimacy and toward distance and division in the next two short paragraphs. We learn that the narrator makes lists and leaves them stuffed in the partner's clothes and drawers for them to find. Consider how the narrator syntactically establishes both the cause for her list writing and the separation. She uses a parallel syntactic structure—tellingly a fragment—that connects the cause to the partner's refusal to communicate, and the parallel structure also emphasizes the divide between the *you* and the *I*: "The less you say, the more I write: elephant grass, manatee swamps, that restaurant on Eighth Street afloat in mirrors like the sea" (78). Moreover, we see in the list-making the narrator's desire to return to Miami. Each of the items in the list is an emblematic feature of Miami, with Eighth Street referencing in particular Miami's Little Havana.

The more pronounced the distance and isolation becomes, the more the narrator's story breaks with realism. Her quest to get what she wants brings her into a space where there are impossible feats of nature. She returns one December night, her face "wet with melted snow," to tell her partner that she's "found a forest where hibiscus bloom from the slender limbs of birches. I say the snow shrinks from them as if they were on fire" (79). A few pages later, we learn that an ancient palm in this forest speaks to her, even sings her a song. Indeed, so special is this palm tree, I would argue, that it is the only character given a line of direct dialogue, and it is important to note what the dialogue is about. The palm tree is telling her of a tree that grows straight and slender with two branches emerging from the trunk, lifted to the sky like two grateful arms: "She stands taller than the rest," the palm said, "and everyone hates her because her uppermost leaves are green with happiness" (83).[16] The tree merits attention because it has two grateful arms unified in a solid trunk, and it is full of happiness. The tree has everything that the *you* and the *I* do not.

The two final scenes I wish to explore deal with the forest and the emotional rupture as they relate to the narrator's quest, the narrator's desires. Following the aforementioned scene with the talking palm and the singularly happy tree, the narrator brings that lyrical world, that world beyond the faculty of logical reasoning, into stark contrast with the quotidian world of her relationship. Doing so makes more pronounced the distance between the *you* and the *I*. The passage I am about to cite comes after the forest, which is important for the temporal unfolding of the story. It is the partner's response to the question the narrator posed two and a half pages earlier. She asked if the partner remembered why they left:

You say, We lost a baby. That is why we left. Our baby is gone. You say it as if it were something that you read in a book. As if you could never

believe that the leaves that fall in the forest glow blue at night, that
hibiscus can grow in the snow, that palm trees remember. You pretend
you don't know that our baby lived within me. When I felt him turn, it
was like that first touch in the dark, like a single caress you remember
for years. (83; [*sic* no quotations marks])

What she can have in the forest is a communion with nature, a connection with entities that understand her. While we comprehend through the
story, through episodes with the coins, for example, that the partner is also
suffering, the narrator does not perceive it as such. She perceives the partner as detached, as coldly logical in describing the death as "something that
you read in a book." The narrator, however, needs this lyrical interpretation of the world to make sense of the loss of their baby.

While I want to steer clear of an overly sentimental reading of this story,
the final scene returns us to the forest and to a, perhaps, reunited couple.
The couple here looks a lot like the couple described on the first date
with the quoting of Yeats, with the folding into one another, with the character becoming like her partner in hair and flesh. We still live in the pronominal land of the *you* and the *I*, but it is a distance with a difference. Let
me explain. In the final scene, the narrator retreats once again to the forest,
standing naked this time on the last day of winter. The ancient palm is once
again talking to her, comforting her. The narrator hears "the song of old
days," even hears "the colors of Miami" (84). But she also falls unconscious
in the forest, and this is how the partner finds her. They try to shake her
awake, and it is in the revival efforts that we see the narrator elect to use
language similar to that of the first date. She describes the resuscitation as,
"And then I feel your breath, hot and wet in my lungs" (85). Then she
notes of the buzz of insects that she hears: "It is so beautiful that I begin
to weep in your voice, your breath leaving me in bursts of song" (85). We
have a corporal union in these poetic descriptions of mouth-to-mouth resuscitation. They seem not only like the couple on their first date, but also
like the two grateful branches united in the trunk of that exemplary tree.
The insects, like one of the forest trees, are important because both the
insects and the trees are described as having children (79 and 80). Then
the last line of the story takes us one step closer to the union of the characters, for in it we see the *I* care for the *you*. We have, that is, a reciprocal
caring for the other, even if we still lack a *we*: "Shh, I say, and put a finger to
your lips. Don't cry" (85).

In each of the stories analyzed in this chapter, we have a unique rendering of affective intimacy and distance. From where the narrator stands,

from the pronominal choice of narration, that is, we get a range of complex emotional textures as each of the narrators navigates a traumatic life experience—rape, eating disorders, and a miscarriage. I hope to have shown, through a critical approach that treats reading as an event unfolding across time with each word, sentence, paragraph, and so on, that these authors and narrators have employed a number of noteworthy techniques to allow us to become intimate with and distant from their characters. I have paid particularly close attention to the rare focalizations the stories employ—first-person plural and second-person singular. I have illustrated how these focalizations create a unique narrative voice that generates a dramatically different reading experience than if the authors had opted for the more usual narrative perspectives of either first-person or third-person singular. In the following chapter, I shift away from an analysis of *we* and *you*, and turn instead to the radical singularity of the lyric.

CHAPTER 4

The Lyric, or, a Radical Singularity in Latinx Verse

Rich attention has been paid to narrative traditions and political tendencies in Latinx poetry. I think of Juan Bruce-Novoa's *Chicano Poetry: Response to Chaos*; José Limón's reading of the anxiety of influence in Chicano poetry; María Herrera-Sobek's work on the corrido; Marta Sanchez's analysis of emerging voices in Chicana poetry; Rafael Pérez-Torres's masterful study of postcoloniality, postmodernity, and Chicano poetry; Urayoán Noel's historical and cultural studies analysis of Nuyorican Poetry; and Michael Dowdy's examination of Latina/o poetry, neoliberalism, and globalization, among many others. Furthermore, in her fine overview essay "Latin@ Poetics," Norma Elia Cantú notes that "the collective reach of the work [Latina/o poetry] surfaces in the unifying themes of solidarity, the search for linguistic freedom, and the political struggles on human and civil rights issues" (153). While acknowledging the important work of these foundational studies and Cantú's insightful assessment of trends in Latina/o poetry, I want to pick up the needle and move it to a different track on the album of Latinx poetry, to a tune to which we listen less regularly. I want to focus on poetry that cannot be readily paraphrased as having a message or making a political statement. I want to examine poems that do not easily accord with what we understand Latinx literature to be and that do not in some readily recognizable way represent a known Latinx worldview. The lyric poetry I want to look at strikes a dissonant chord with the tradition of narrative-driven Latinx poetry.

It is not the aim of this project to redefine or re-theorize lyric poetry. Let us, however, at least have a working definition at hand. Stephen Burt defines lyric poetry as "short pieces of language (spoken, or sung, or written, or all three) in which the psyche finds the language and sounds to fit its own internal states; through that language we can imagine that we know what it is like to be a particular person, or kind of person, or else what it is like to be ourselves" (x–xi). Additionally, in *Dickinson's Misery: A Theory of Lyric Reading*, Virginia Jackson deftly argues that the lyric is a form that we have created through our critical reading practices. In summarizing her book's argument, she notes that "from the mid-nineteenth through the beginning of the twenty-first century, to be lyric is to be read as lyric—and to be read as lyric is to be printed and framed as lyric" (6). She shows us "how poems become lyric in history. Once we decided that [Emily] Dickinson wrote poems (or once that decision is made for us), and once we decide that most poems are lyrics (or once that decision is made for us), we (by definition) lose sight of the historical process of lyric reading that is the subject of this book. Precisely because lyrics can only exist theoretically, they are made historically" (10–11).[1] Taking up this notion of the lyric and closer to home for the concerns of this project, John Alba Cutler, in his terrific reading of Sandra Cisneros's poetry, demonstrates how Cisneros swerves away from both Jackson's understanding of lyric poetry and Adorno's claims about the alienated bourgeois subject striving for wholeness in the face of alienated modern life. Cutler acutely observes that "Cisneros is not a 'bourgeois subject' in any simple sense, and she grounds her poetry in the particulars of local history. In other words, lyric poetry is not a boundary-crossing mechanism for Cisneros but a form for giving voice to experiences rooted in material history" (Cutler, *Ends of Assimilation* 120). In his fine analysis, Cutler argues persuasively that Cisneros's lyric poetry "offers a counter-discourse to culture-of-poverty theory" and that it works against "the internal policing of Malinche discourse" (121). The Latinx lyric poetry that I take up in this chapter interests me precisely because it is not easily rooted in Latinx material history and thereby asks us again to assess the Latinx literature rubric under which we often do our critical work.

Building on the aforementioned understandings of lyric poetry, I examine the understudied radical singularity we witness in much Latinx lyric verse, a condition distinct from that of the narrative tradition during and after the cultural nationalist movements of the 1960s and 1970s. The radical singularity I study frees writers from the burden of representation and cultural ambassadorship. To understand the texture, affect, emotion, and nuance of the radically singular lyric is a complex matter. As a suggestive illustration of how this radical singularity operates, I analyze the work of three exemplary lyric poets—Eduardo Corral, Rosa Alcalá, and Amanda Calderon.

On Making Meaning

Poetry is a genre that is notoriously difficult and even elusive at times. In order to best understand how the lyric's radical singularity functions, and because a secondary thrust of *Latinx Literature Unbound* is an argument about how we read, I pause to consider how we make meaning from poetry. Let us look first at three different types of lines. First, there are lines (even in lyric poetry) that make immediate sense. That is, they cause no interpretive difficulty. For instance, the first line of Rane Arroyo's poem "The Book of Names" reads: "I was to be named Alejandro" (57). We might (and even should) wonder why this act of naming is drawn to our attention and what its significance is, but at the level of sentence, it is readily understood. Second, there are lines that at first make sense but that become more challenging as we continue reading. Consider, for example, the opening three lines of Rosa Alcalá's "The Fortune Teller's Insurance Policy": "A boy falls down the stairs / and yells uncle / to the man he'll become" (41). The first two lines present no challenges to our linguistic talents, but line three complicates their possible meaning. Third, there are lines that refuse meaning, in any ordinary sense of that word. Consider the opening of Eduardo Corral's "*La Pelona*: Mixed Media: Ester Hernández: 1980": "fist of ice skin trellis pagan rubble whistling ash" (*Slow Lightning* 15). The line lacks a governing syntax to aid us in discerning the relationship among its nine words. There is also no punctuation to help us understand the syntagmatic relationship. If someone were to run into you on the street and utter those nine words, you would give them a puzzled look to indicate that you did not understand what they were saying. One might sum up my scenarios as Stephen Burt, in an essay on reading poetry, does: "Poetry constitutes a second language within any spoken or written (natural) language; a second language containing its own mutually incomprehensible dialects, to be acquired by visiting the place or the milieu in which they become the norm" (*Close Calls with Nonsense* 360–361). The challenge, then, is to visit that place often enough to become fluent in those seemingly incomprehensible dialects.

Because those dialects can be difficult to master, there can be a tendency in criticism to paraphrase the narrative of a poem, to deal not with its poetic features, but to treat it as if it were so much prose that could be summarized. Take, for instance, the two shortest poems from Martín Espada's *Imagine the Angels of Bread*:

When the Leather Is a Whip
At night,
with my wife
sitting on the bed,
I turn from her
to unbuckle
my belt
so she won't see her
father
unbuckling
his belt (65)

Governor Wilson of California Talks in His Sleep
The only
aliens
we like
are the ones
on Star Trek,
'cause
they all
speak
English (90)

For the critic only interested in *what* a poem says (the critic who treats poetry like prose), these poems are simply enough paraphrased. She might tell us that the first one is about a husband concerned about not triggering his wife's history of physical abuse and that the second one is about Governor Wilson's xenophobia. Not all poems, however, are easily paraphrased. Indeed, many of them resist narrative and grammatical meaning.

Furthermore, while content is significant, we cannot talk of poetry devoid of its poetic features. No one analysis of a poem can treat all of its poetic features, but we need to be attentive to them, to analyze how they abet the poem's meaning. Otherwise, critics may just as well, for instance, type Espada's poems out as one continuous prose sentence.[2] On the other hand, if Espada did so, we would still be compelled (and should be prepared) to discuss that layout and its significance to the poem's meaning. For the sentences still appear in a book of poetry, and we are, therefore, bound to read them as poems. In short, the context in which a poem appears is part of its meaning-making. I will not develop a reading of Espada's poems, for they are not the focus of this chapter. I offer them rather as tools for understanding the importance of reading poetry as poetry, not as prose. Finally, I want to close this section with a brief passage from Edward Hirsch that aptly captures the work we must do to get at the work a poem does on us and the work we do with it, how we get at its affective registers, its presence, its subject, and the other features which make it a poem. I offer the passage as an idea upon which to ruminate as we move through this chapter:

> I have the idea that a certain kind of exemplary poem teaches you how to read it. It carries its own encoded instructions, enacting its subject, pointing to its own operation. It enacts what it is about—a made thing that indicates the nature of its own making. Poems communicate before they are understood and the structure operates on, or inside, the reader even as the words infiltrate the consciousness. The form is the shape of the poem's understanding, its way of being in the world, and it is the form that structures our experience. (*How to Read a Poem* 31)

Eduardo Corral—The Familiar Made Strange

In 2012, Eduardo Corral's *Slow Lightning* won the Yale Series of Younger Poets Prize, the oldest annual literary prize in the United States. In his introduction to *Slow Lightning*, the award-winning poet Carl Phillips explains Corral thus: "Like [Robert] Hayden, Corral resists reductivism. Gay, Chicano, 'Illegal-American,' that's all just language, and part of Corral's point is that language, like sex, is fluid and dangerous and thrilling, now a cage, now a window out. In Corral's refusal to think in reductive terms lies his great authority" (xv).[3] For Phillips to declare that it's "all just language" is not to miss the material force of language. That lesson—in short, the idea that language is constitutive, not merely representative—has been written on our critical DNA since the linguistic turn of the late 1960s and 1970s. The salient point in Phillips's assessment is that language has the potential to be many things. It is fluid and changing, and one would do well to refuse the traps of singular, absolutist thinking.

It is also important to bear in mind how Corral conceives of his own poetic voice and the traditions into which it fits. He often describes himself as the love child of Federico García Lorca and Robert Hayden.[4] Given his writing style, the "politics" of his poetry, and the fact that Corral is an openly gay poet, it is not difficult to understand why he imagines himself as the offspring of these two great poets. Lorca is believed to have been killed by Franco's Nationalist forces during the Spanish Civil War (1936–1939) for his homosexuality and his liberal political views. Hayden, who published poetry from the 1940s to the 1970s, gained international recognition in the 1960s. His desire for an art free of propaganda and one that championed innovation and experimentation placed him in conflict with the Black Power movement. "Many of [the Black Power adherents]," writes Arnold Rampersad, "openly rejected both Hayden's ideas and his art as outmoded, at best, and a form of racial treachery, at worst" (201). In a May 16, 2012 interview with Michael Klein for *Ploughshares*, Corral describes Hayden's influence on his work:

> *Slow Lightning* is an homage to Robert Hayden. I borrow from his poems—I steal, I riff. His thumbprints are all over my book. Hayden taught me only the poem matters. My background and my beliefs will pulse through my lines, but the poem has to exist without me, it has to breathe on its own. In other words, he taught me the supreme importance of craft. He also taught me a poet of color doesn't need to explain his art to anyone—not even to his community. This realization was a breakthrough for me: it freed me from worrying if I was too Latino or not Latino enough. It freed me to write the poems I needed to write.[5]

Craft has often received short shrift in the analysis of Latinx literature. Indeed, that Corral's answer pivots from talking about the importance of craft to that of community and the burden of representation tellingly reveals how the latter has often trumped the former. It is, of course, a false dichotomy. Should one choose to write about themes important to the community, there is no reason it could not be done with a supreme concern for craft, nor does an attention to craft mean one cannot attend to community.[6]

Furthermore, Corral encourages an approach to writing that is wide open to influence, that is catholic in its textual referentiality. There are a whole host of writers and artists decorating the pages of *Slow Lightning*—some through direct intertextual reference, others through dedications or the titles of poems, and others still named as the influence for the style or content of a given poem. A map of this constellation of writers and artists would include Tino Rodríguez, Julio Galán, Gloria Anzaldúa, Ester Hernández, Javier O. Huerta, Bei Dao, Jean Valentine, Jorge Luis Borges, Juan Gabriel, Ana Castillo, Frida Kahlo, Diego Rivera, Joseph Beuys, María Meléndez, José Montoya, René Cardona, Lorna Dee Cervantes, Gwendolyn Brooks, Ronald Johnson, Arthur Russel, Gabriel Orozco, John Olivares Espinoza, and Félix González-Torres. The range of writers and artists are consistent with the advice Corral once offered, in an interview, to young writers of color: "Dear Young Chicano/a Poet, The literary life is hard work. . . . Your *abuela* is not special. Read the world. Open your mental veins. Synthesize. Absorb Hamlet. Read the African American canon" (*Border Triptych*).[7] Corral was being instructively provocative in dismissing the uniqueness that Latinx writers may feel inheres in their *abuela* (grandmother). Though Corral's provocation may discomfort some, he raises an important point.

There is a tendency in all writing to rely on the familiar, the known, and the knowable. We have all heard the adage "Write what you know." Taken to extremes, however, the known becomes the type, even the stereotype, and begins to narrowly define groups. In the introduction to *The Racial Imaginary*, Beth Loffreda and Claudia Rankine observe, "It should . . . not be assumed that it is easy or natural to write scenarios or characters whose race matches (whatever that might mean) one's own. This is the trap that writers of color in particular still must negotiate; it's the place where 'write what you know' becomes plantational in effect" (17). This plantation effect is tied to what I have been emphasizing throughout *Latinx Literature Unbound* as the tendency of publishers, editors, agents, even some readers and critics to insist that "ethnic" writers write in a way that "authentically" represents their group. Some writers are happy to write in this way and do it well, but others push against such strictures.[8] In pushing against these strictures, Corral repeatedly makes the familiar strange in his poetry and, in so doing, compels us to rethink what we believe we know.

We find, in this rendering the familiar strange, what José Muñoz would likely characterize as "astonishment," a quality he speaks of in *Cruising Utopia* as "help[ing] one surpass the limitations of an alienating presentness and allow[ing] one to see a different time and place" (5). There is something uniquely queer in Corral's rendering the familiar strange, of not getting bogged down in the specialness of his *abuela*. Muñoz reminds us that "Queerness is always in the horizon," and that is what gives it its value (11). It is futurity and hope. I maintain that in their looking awry at the world, in their making the familiar strange, in their astonishment, and in their refusal of our usual classifications, Corral's poems and Corral himself look out to the horizon which Muñoz saw in queerness, the "not-yet-here," and its rich "potentialities."

To draw this argument into sharper relief, I examine the internal frame poems of *Slow Lightning*. Both are titled "Acquired Immune Deficiency Syndrome." Were the titles to be removed from the poems, one would be hard-pressed, however, to identify them as poems about AIDS. They carry, that is, none of the recognizable markers or tropes of AIDS literature. Unlike much AIDS literature, which is set in hospitals, hospices, and cities, the first of Corral's AIDS poems is set in a sylvan environment, a nod, if anything, to the pastoral tradition. The second is set in a more generically familiar urban, or at least domestic, environment, but it, too, enlists the service of animals of the forest, specifically deer and mules. In the first poem, there is no mention of another human being, let alone a lover, but in the second, the speaker "at a quarter to midnight" awakens "panicked" next to his "lover" in bed. The poem opens as follows:

> At a quarter to midnight,
> blue beetles crawling
>   along the minute hand
> of the wall clock,
>   I awaken, panicked,
>   next to my lover,

The relative realism of that stanza contrasts sharply with the more surreal opening stanza of the first AIDS poem:

> I approach a harp
>   abandoned
> in a harvested field.
>   A deer leaps
> out of the brush
>   and follows me

The relatively realistic first stanza of the second poem, however, quickly gives way to the surrealistic world of the first, a surrealism that becomes more pronounced in the ensuing six stanzas.

In addition to the surrealistic imagery that characterizes much of both poems, there is also the disorienting effect—especially in the first poem—of not knowing anything about the temporality of the poems, or their "when." Given the history of AIDS in the United States, we can reasonably conjecture that they occur sometime between the late 1970s and the present, but we cannot get more specific than that. This temporal dislocation contributes to the hallucinogenic quality of both poems, which I now reproduce in their entirety, since we will need access to them for our continued analysis.

ACQUIRED IMMUNE DEFICIENCY SYNDROME
I approach a harp
    abandoned
in a harvested field.
    A deer leaps
out of the brush
    and follows me

in the rain, a scarlet
    snake wound
in its dark antlers.
    My fingers
curled around a shard
    of glass—

it's like holding the hand
    of a child.
I'll cut the harp strings
    for my mandolin,
use the frame as a window
    in a chapel
yet to be built. I'll scrape

    off its blue
lacquer, melt the flakes
    down with
a candle and ladle
    and paint
the inner curve
    of my soup bowl.

The deer passes me.
    I lower my head,
stick out my tongue
    to taste

the honey smeared
    on its hind leg.

In the field's center
    I crouch near
a boulder engraved
    with a number
and stare at a gazelle's
    blue ghost,
the rain falling through it. (4–5)

ACQUIRED IMMUNE DEFICIENCY SYNDROME
    At a quarter to midnight,
blue beetles crawling
    along the minute hand
of the wall clock,
    I awaken, panicked,
        next to my lover,

  a caramel-hued cello asleep
on embroidered linen.
    A light bulb blazes,
burns out,
  a doe's flash of white tail
    that instructs

    the fawn to follow its mother
in flight. I hurry down
    a hallway, through a door,
into a pasture
    where mules are grazing
      Moonlight

  floats in the air like coarse cloth,
silver-speckled
    & woven on the looms
of mirrors. Once
    I tore into the torso of my cello
    & discovered

  its heart: a pair of horse shoes
caked with red clay.

The mules surround me:
necks bent,
    nostrils pluming out different lengths
    of breath

    I toss off my robe. A mule
curls its tongue around
        my erection. I throw
my head back,
    & stare at the slowest lightning
    the stars. (71–72)

It would seem impossible to make either poem mean, in the sense of ascribing a narrative to them. Yes, there may be a sequencing of events, but they do not generate a coherent story. We could, of course, take refuge in Archibald MacLeish's maxim that "A poem should not mean/ But be."[9] Both poems in their "being," however, create an effect. They have an uncanny affective resonance that unsettles what another poet might have rendered as familiar domestic and sylvan scenes. Corral, however, does not go that route. Rather he interests himself here and in the entire collection with making the familiar strange.

In that regard, these two poems compel us to rethink what we think we know. The first AIDS poem combines a sense of wonder (perhaps delirium) with one of purpose. The images of this fablistic forest—the deer with a snake in its antler, a large string instrument somehow abandoned in the forest—do not strike the speaker as curiosities, or, at least, he does not present them as such. Rather, he surprisingly shifts to the future tense to tell us to what instrumental ends he will put the harp he has found—he'll cut and repurpose the harp strings for his mandolin, the harp's frame is to become a window in a chapel, and its lacquer is to become a sealant for his soup bowl. Such gestures convert a seemingly absurd or surreal world into a banal, quotidian one. The persona registers no surprise at the scene in which he finds himself. Indeed, in the final two stanzas he continues in this surreal-as-real fashion as he converts a honey-besmeared deer into a culinary treat and a gazelle's ghostly apparition into a cause for solemn observation. A world that approximates that of a fairy tale is treated pragmatically, as if without wonder.

We might consider as a productive point of comparison and contrast the pragmatic way in which Marie Howe talks about what the living do, after her brother dies from complications related to AIDS. Indeed, the title poem from her collection *What the Living Do* is a catalog of the mundane, quotidian things we do in the course of any given day and the ache created in doing these things in the absence of her brother:

> For weeks now, driving, or dropping a bag of groceries in the street, the bag breaking,
>
> I've been thinking: This is what the living do. And yesterday, hurrying along those
> wobbly bricks in the Cambridge sidewalk, spilling my coffee down my wrist and sleeve,
>
> I thought it again, and again later, when buying a hairbrush: This is it. Parking. Slamming the car door shut in the cold. What you called *that yearning.* (89; emphasis in original)

No references in this excerpt (or in the entire poem for that matter) orient us toward understanding this as a poem about HIV/AIDS, but read in the context of the whole collection, we understand that this poem is part of the elegy for her brother's death. We could also take as another productive point of comparison and contrast poems from Rafael Campo's collection *What the Body Told.* Poems such as "Her Final Show," "For You All Beauty," "The 10,000th AIDS Death in San Francisco," and "Prescription," for instance, deal explicitly with a realist referentiality. We hear about Kaposi sarcoma, "drag queens dead of AIDS," (25), "By AIDS, so beautiful and true" (56). The poems are filled with the familiar hospital beds, illnesses, and nurses consistent with a realist poetics.

Returning to Corral's first AIDS poem, the imagery—field, deer, brush, boulder, and gazelle—keeps us squarely centered in his sylvan scene, and we are asked to observe, to let its images run over us. Our readerly instincts tempt us to make the poem accord with its title, perhaps even to read the poem as an extended metaphor for AIDS. It is a not an unreasonable instinct, but it is a perhaps impossible quest. The poem asks us, I contend, to sit with its haunting images—its snake-wound antlers, its honey-smeared hind leg, its eerie blue ghost—and to register the mood they create. The mood will vary from reader to reader, but that is not the point. The point is that we need not constrain ourselves to what the lines of these poems "mean" per se, but what they do. Rachel Blau DuPlessis puts it more elegantly, more poetically: "Poetry is not argument or image exclusively but an approach to knowing that dissolves into a variety of sensations or touches multiple scales of feeling" (*Blue Studios* 5). These poems' scales of feeling create a haunting, eerie, otherworldly mood. They render a spectacular world mundane. They make the haunting banal, as if we are surrounded by it, just as much as we are by the recognizably quotidian—trees, cars, streets, houses, and so on. Indeed, the haunting of the AIDS epidemic rendered the world terrifying and the disease another unthinkable feature of our mundane existence.

Like the first, Corral's second AIDS poem also employs a combination of the wondrous and the practical. And because of their governing role as the internal frame poems, they incline us to note the structuring and hermeneutic role that the real and surreal—or perhaps the surreal made practical—will play in the collection. Whereas the first AIDS poem takes place entirely in a peculiar sylvan universe, as if that perhaps is the only world, the second AIDS poem importantly conjoins those two ontological universes. That is to say, in the second AIDS poem, the persona journeys from a world recognizable as our own—one that keeps time like ours ("midnight" and "minute hands"), and one that has cellos, lovers, and linens—into one as peculiar as that of the first AIDS poem. There is a path, that is, from our mundane world into the surreal world of the forest. The way to that forest is notably through following a doe's tail, an image that unites the two poems and lends them a touch of symmetry.

As Alice famously followed a rabbit down a hole, our anonymous persona follows a deer out of his mundane world of clock, lover, and bed into a suddenly indeterminate space. In the midst of the third stanza, he hurries down "a hallway" (the indefinite article renders it not *the* hallway of his home) and through "a door" (similarly indefinite) not into another space of his home or even *a* home, but into a pasture full of mules and moonlight. The closing of the fourth stanza and opening of the fifth return us to the second stanza's metaphor of lover as cello, but it is not a fully realized anthropomorphization of the cello, for its heart is not the beating heart of a human nor even the sound holes of the cello as analog to a human heart. Rather, we have a heart made of "horse shoes" [*sic*], which, while at a peculiar remove from cello as lover, do return us to our pastoral scene. And in that pastoral scene we, again, have the familiar rendered strange—an act of oral sex not between two humans, but the speaker and a mule. That act closes the poem and returns us to the paradoxically slow lightning, which unites this collection of poems.

Meaning, however, cannot be forced upon this poem. Or, perhaps in keeping with Fish's model of an affective stylistics, the meaning of a word, a sentence, a paragraph, a stanza, and so on is in what it does to and with the "informed reader." The meaning is in the experience of reading. While Fish's method could be applied to any reading experience, it is especially good at dealing with lines that are not attempting to convey a thought or

a meaning in any conventional sense. His affective stylistics is not necessarily invested in figuring out the logical utterance of a sentence, but rather
in registering its effects ("Literature in the Reader" 134–135). "In an experiential analysis," Fish writes, "the sharp distinction between sense and
nonsense, with the attendant value judgments and the talk about truth content, is blurred, because the place where sense is made or not made is in
the reader's mind rather than the printed page or the space between the
covers of a book" (134).[10] Thus, we simply have to sit with the imagery of
both of these AIDS poems and register their effects. The effects they create influence not only our experience of these two poems themselves, but
in them we note many of the themes, the language, and the images that
characterize the collection as a whole—light, musical instruments, attention to sex and sexuality, the use of the ampersand, attention to body parts
(especially sexual organs and the smalls of backs), and the real and the surreal. This familiar made strange becomes the strange and complex presence of presence in the poetry of Rosa Alcalá.

Rosa Alcalá—The Presence of Presence

What mirror reflects as whole
a slip of truth. And the business
of breaking it into lines,
this privileged
art.[11]

Rosa Alcalá is the author of a limited-edition chapbook, *Some Maritime
Disasters This Century* (2003), and two books of poetry: *Undocumentaries*
(2010) and *The Lust of Unsentimental Waters* (2012).[12] In his introduction to
The Wind Shifts: New Latino Poetry, Francisco Aragón writes of Alcalá's experimental poem "The Sixth Avenue Go-Go Lounge" (one of six included
in the anthology) that "its generous use of white space, the short line or
phrase, and the lack of an immediately recognizable narrative or plot, represents a facet of Latino poetry that remains underexplored and underap-
preciated with both the Latino literary community and the more established
(read 'academic') circles of the avant-garde" (8). Alcalá teaches in the bilingual creative writing program at the University of Texas at El Paso and
has translated works by Cecilia Vicuña, Lila Zemborain, Lourdes Vázquez,
and other poets. While keeping all of her work in context, my focus in this
section will be on poems from *Undocumentaries* and *The Lust of Unsentimental Waters. Undocumentaries* is divided into five sections—"Undocumentary,"

"A Girl Like Me," "Footage of the Past," "Weak at the Laptop," and "American Recycler"—and contains forty-eight poems.[13] *The Lust of Unsentimental Waters* consists of three untitled sections. Like *Slow Lightning*, there are narrative poems to be found in both collections, but the emphasis is on free verse lyric.

Both Glyn Maxwell and Allen Grossman have spoken of the importance and creation of presence in poetry. Maxwell writes, "I imagine it is possible to write a poem that does not coherently express the presence of a human creature, but I don't believe such a thing could survive time better than its maker" (*On Poetry* 30). Allen Grossman's assessment of *presence* perfectly complements Maxwell's. Grossman avers, "In poetry language has gone strange. The strangeness in poetic language arises from the presence of the *eidos*, the presence of presence" (*Sighted Singer* 232).[14] Thus, in thinking about the lyric's radical singularity and the effects it achieves, I want to approach it through the optic of presence, for there is a tantalizing, protean, and complex presence alive in Alcalá's work.

The presence of presence is not divorced from Alcalá's mirror and truth in the epigraph for this section. Presence in poetry has to do with the conjuring of a feeling, a moment in time, a thought that the poet captures so vividly, so tenaciously, so movingly that we feel ourselves as if there in the poem. It creates a truth, and yet I feel discomfited by that word. When people feel they have found a truth, they doggedly hold onto it. They get it between their teeth and refuse to let go. In a world characterized by uncertainty, it is not odd to want the comfort of truth, but it becomes troubling when unthinkingly embraced, when the truth becomes something somehow beyond critique, beyond questioning. And yet look more closely at the Alcalá epigraph. It begins with *what*, but it is not a question. It is not "What mirror reflects as whole a slip of truth?" We get a period, not a question mark, after *truth*. While the line may enjoy its ambiguity, the period makes the utterance much closer to "What mirror reflects as whole [is but] a slip of truth." Alcalá's placing of *whole* at line's end draws attention to *whole*, but the whole figure we may think we see in the mirror is undercut by the subsequent line's opening, *a slip*. What we get is not the whole truth but a detail, a sliver, a slice, *a slip*. And as the remaining, self-reflexive lines of the stanza make clear, it is the art of poetry to break this truth into lines so that even if we get only a detail or a slip, we see and feel its presence. In fact, because we are not overwhelmed with its wholeness, we are more likely to register its presence. This is not a dogmatic holding onto truth, but an awareness that in the art of poetry, a poet selects the vivid detail and breaks the lines just so, in order that the reader can see and feel. Alcalá's self-awareness undercuts the dogmatism of truth-telling, and she does so without vitiating the lives, the moments, or the ideas in her poetry. To bring Grossman into the equation, I contend that Alcalá's is a language gone strange to create a presence we see and feel.

In this particular poem, mimicry is the making present, the making felt, of a working-class childhood. Indeed, the thread that runs through the collection is the making present of that which too often goes unnoticed or gets relegated to the sidelines, hence the title of the collection, *Undocumentaries*. That slip of the undocumented lives we see in "Mimicry" is captured by a communion dress, a car, and a factory: "There's a girl there / with her communion dress / against the Chevy's celestial / blue. The Sun Chemical factory / imparts a special / glow." (48). Those perfectly picked details bring us into the life of the poem, mimic in a positive sense the undocumented lives the collection brings forward. As Alcalá poignantly reminds us in the final three lines of her poem "Autobiography," "Factory is both fact / and act, and mere letters from face / and story." (50). Alcalá teases *factory* apart to bring us into the facts and acts that constitute the subjects of undocumentaries. Moreover, the line-ending *face* emphasizes the workers' humanity and individuality, and the masterful line break then singles out *and story*, reminding us of all the stories that make up the lives of the factory workers. Alcalá is "creating footage of the past," as the title of the section from which these poems come is called. She limns "what can't be told" (14). She renders the absent present.

Moreover, I want to underscore that the presence created in Alcalá's poems—that radical singularity that underwrites this chapter—is markedly different from the narrative poetry that characterizes much Latinx verse. I pause to highlight this distinction not to privilege one form over the other, but to draw the distinction to your attention so that we might better understand the work being done in both styles and particularly so that we might begin to better understand the radical singularity of the lyric, which heretofore has received scant attention. Consider, for instance, the narrative vein in which a poet like Luis J. Rodriguez writes—also aptly capturing the presence of many undocumentaries—as a productive counterpoint to the way Alcalá creates presence. Here are some representative lines from Rodriguez's poem "Carrying My Tools," which appeared in his 1991 collection *The Concrete River*:

Any good craftsman carries his tools.
Years ago, they were always at the ready.
In the car. In a knapsack.

Claw hammers, crisscrossed heads,
32 ouncers. Wrenches in all sizes,
sometimes with oil caked on the teeth.

. . .

Millwrights also carried dial indicators,
Micrometers—the precision kind.
They were cherished like a fine car,
a bottle of rare wine,
or a moment of truth. (89)

This selection accurately represents the narrative Latinx verse with which
we are familiar. It is certainly poetic, and the language of tools it employs
poetically renders the presence of the workplace. The narrative tradition
it represents, however, is not as elusive or as singular as the lyric with
which Corral, Calderon, and Alcalá work. I draw your attention to these
lines (I could have chosen any number of lines from the corpus of Latinx
poetry) so you will have them in your ear, as a tool for understanding
the different work Alcalá's poetry does. To understand the presence created by the language gone strange, one needs to understand the tradition
it has gone strange against. I should also note that it is precisely the
lyric's language gone strange that often generates a strong dislike of contemporary poetry. It frustrates because it does not always make itself
easily accessible.[15]

With all of that in mind, I turn now to Alcalá's poem "A Girl Leaves
the Croft." It, too, is a poem about workers, working women in particular
and the disdain with which they have been treated historically. As Alcalá's
notes to *Undocumentaries* indicate, the poem gains some of its inspiration
from Wanda Fraiken Neff's study *Victorian Working Women: An Historical
and Literary Study of Women in British Industries and Professions (1832–1850).*
The title of the poem alerts us to a certain temporal oddity. I refer to its
use of the word *croft*, which means farmland and derives from Old English.
The latest use recorded in the *Oxford English Dictionary* is 1884. The *OED*
entry profile indicates a heavy use of the term in the late nineteenth century,
with it all but flattening out in the twentieth and twenty-first centuries. It
is certainly not a term of common parlance and thereby draws attention
to itself. Beyond the title, the poem will continue to navigate a curious,
shifting temporal space and, thus, a peculiar presence. I think we should
ask to what effect, to what end.

The poem opens in a space of small-scale (i.e., cottage), preindustrial
labor (including a reference to William Wordsworth's sonnet "Nuns Fret

Not at Their Convent's Narrow Room") and employs the antiquated use of capitalizing personified nouns (e.g., *Beauty*). The first stanza runs as follows:

> Cottage work, the spinner at the door. A halo of sun a tidy room
> behind her. "Maids at the wheel . . . /Sit blithe and happy." Such
> chastity in the pre-electric. Or, in the moldy flax
> under the finger, causing Beauty's allergic reaction. (27)

The effect of the stanza is to create a space of contented, sexless, female workers—halo of sun, tidy room, blithe and happy, and so on. An innocent first reading of this stanza might perhaps allow the most naïve of readers to think we are entering a poem of laboring bliss, but even that reader would be quickly disabused of her innocence. The following two-line stanza makes our complicity clear: "We're all framed in this/who-dun-it." The line break at the demonstrative pronoun *this* performs double duty. It emphasizes the first stanza that, at first, seems to be its antecedent, but as we read across the enjambed line, we see it also modifies *who-dun-it*. What makes that double duty interesting is that the pronoun highlights what seems to be a condition, but resolves into a mystery, which must be solved. We are to attend to the female gendering of labor and sex and to be skeptical/critical of its origin and legacy.[16] The poem's temporal play, however, underscores that this is not a poem exclusively about nineteenth-century spinners.

By the third and fourth stanzas, we have jumped into a mythical, fairy-tale world of set-upon and vilified women. We get vague hints of Rapunzel and Sleeping Beauty. The Rapunzel allusions include "hair to be thrown from a window" and "A witch holds stolen braids." This is not, however, a simplistic recuperative poem in which women are made heroes and men are shown to be in need of rescue or to be simply self-interested humans. Consistent with the assertion that "We're all framed in this," the poem continues in its implication of this never defined *we* and *us*. First, it casts us as fools: "A witch holds stolen braids,/singing out to the fool (which is us)." Then, like the prince from Rapunzel, who in his failed attempt to save Rapunzel from the witch falls from the tower into a bush of thorns, we, too, are blinded to wander the woods in solitude: "Or we are thrown into/a bush, blinded by thorns, and woods/our only friend" (27). Are we fools because we have put such stock in fairy tales? Are the gender roles and gender expectations these stories create complicit in the gender inequalities that riddle our world?

Certainly, the fourth stanza in its use of rhetorical questions and double entendre would seem to answer my aforementioned questions affirmatively:

What's more important? The wheel or the distaff, or, finally,
the prick? (27)

The stanza continues with the archaic language of the poem's title. Similar to Alcalá's opting for *croft* over *farmland*, she opts here for *distaff* over
the more prosaic *spindle*, keeping us in an enchanted realm, which is, of
course, redoubled by the allusion here to Sleeping Beauty, who would fall
into her deep sleep because of the machinations of an evil fairy who poisoned the distaff of the wheel at which she would spin. A recuperative reading would want again to point out the gendered expectations and gender
roles fairy tales create, but there is another possible reading—still consistent with this gender recuperation, but potentially more interesting. Metonymically the *wheel* and *distaff* represent the women laborers, and
conjoined with the double entendre play of *prick*, we are simultaneously
asked two—admittedly rhetorical (for the answer is known in advance)
questions: (1) What is more important, the women laborers or this fairy
tale you hold in mind of poor Sleeping Beauty who has been poisoned by
being pricked? (2) What is more important, these women laborers or the
prince/male metonymically represented by his genitalia, his prick?

Continuing with the poem's temporal play, Alcalá moves out of this
mythical time and returns us again to the material world of female workers
in the nineteenth century and does so with an almost fairy-tale or comic
book conjunctive adverb, *later*. That is, we leap from the unspecified fairy-
tale time of Rapunzel and Sleeping Beauty in the third and fourth stanzas
to, in the fifth stanza, some indeterminate time after the fairy tales but
before the present moment in which we find ourselves reading. Furthermore, we enter that time in dramatic fashion: "Later, a girl leaves the croft
and is scalped" (27). We are back to the eponymous girl of the poem and
her farmland, but now we learn of her fate, and this is perhaps the mystery
(really not one, but rather the machinations of capital and the extent it will
go to maximize its profits, heedless of the fragility of its workers' lives), the
"who-dun-it" in which we are framed. We might finish the opening line of
the stanza thinking that an individual has scalped her. Given the racist
mythography that has depicted Native Americans as savages responsible
for scalping their victims,[17] some readers may expect them to be the agent
of this passive verb construction. It turns out, however, that she's been
scalped by "an unboxed machine." These early machines of the industrial
age lacked the safety mechanisms of later machinery.

Both the fifth and sixth stanzas take us far away from the supposed contented wheel spinners of the first stanza and the fairy-tale world of the

third and fourth stanzas. They bring us, rather, into a material world in which workers are clearly disdained, not looked after, and treated as so much expendable labor. Note the intensity of the language in these stanzas. Right after we are told of the scalping, the speaker tells us "What savages/these Englishmen," ostensibly the owners of the factories and the managerial class. The speaker turns the language of civilization and barbarity against itself. Continuing in this forceful diction, the sixth stanza closes as follows: "Either way, the lot [the Calico workers]:/'ignorant, prejudiced and sensual.'" (27). According to Alcalá's notes, that last bit of spoken dialogue comes from Leonard Horner, a Scottish manufacturer and one of the first English factory inspectors. It represents his assessment of workers' character.[18] These stanzas give us a brutal material work world, no "halo of sun" or "tidy room." From here we move to the final stanza.

In a poem that inhabits a curious temporality and presence, this final stanza may be the most curious of all and simultaneously the one that emphasizes the documentary quality of the collection and its interest in photography:

> Which leads us to a kind of photography. Like a loose coif
> and white stockings held at the thighs by two
> unrepentant bows. Who produced these pillars
> of the community? This is art in the age of ribbon
> production. She stands so still
> for the image:
>
> A flash of pussy. The Industrial Age. (28)

It is curious because it is simultaneously nebulous and luminescent. Its opacity or cloudiness resides in what the poem declines to reveal or make clear. The *she* can no longer be the girl who left the croft. She's been scalped. We are compelled to ask who is she? How old is she? Is *she* a stand-in for all women? Who are the pillars of the community, about whom the speaker inquires? Is this an ironic swipe at the men who present themselves as gentlemen, yet exploit women for their visual and sexual pleasure? Are the stocking-clad legs being lucidly referred to as the pillars of the community?

Yet despite this vagueness, there is also a crystal-clear image at the center of this stanza. One can conjure up the image of a female subject with a white coif (hat) about her head, perhaps looking a bit like a shepherdess (a Bo Peep figure consistent with the earlier fairy-tale figures, except sexualized) and wearing stockings held up by bows on the thigh. The image is present and clear. The camera here, however, is perhaps not being used in the fashion imagined in the collection's title poem, as an instrument to document undocumented lives. Is it perhaps an instrument of exploitation? Clear here also is the purposeful play on Walter Benjamin's 1930s essay "The Work of Art in the Age of Mechanical Reproduction," in which, among other things, he worried over the aura of the work of art in an age in which it was no longer a singular object. Photographers, that is, could produce numerous images from one negative. It was no longer a singular painting, say, robust with a creative aura, a secular holiness. In Alcalá's stanza, this is art in an age of ribbon production, an age that puts women on display. Coming after a series of stanzas about the exploitation of women, I think one must be inclined to read this as yet another way in which women are exploited. Indeed, the final line of the poem paratactically links a photo of "pussy" to the Industrial Age. The strong punctuation after each phrase joins them in solidarity. Indeed, it is almost as if the "flash of pussy" itself is what reveals (or what calls forth) the Industrial Age, as if a magician pushing back a velvet curtain to reveal her surprise. It is both a nebulous and fully consistent ending to a poem invested in exploring the world of women workers. It strives for a representative documentary of women's work while also maintaining a lyric singularity.

I want to conclude this section on Alcalá's poetry not with a close analysis of another poem, but with some essential observations about her collection *The Lust of Unsentimental Waters*. There is an interest throughout *Unsentimental Waters* in what can be seen, said, presented and represented. In that regard, it is a collection very much invested in the key tenets of post-structuralism and the now famous linguistic/cultural turn of the late 1960s and 1970s. The philosophical concerns of the various post-structuralisms, that is, animate *Unsentimental Waters*. Indeed, the very first poem of the collection is called "The Thing" and opens "The thing becomes the thing/because of some speaking habit" (9). One does not hear here echoes of Plato's ideal forms or the thingness of the thing, but rather the thing's representation in language and language being what constitutes the thing. Felicitously, then, the collection closes with a brief one-stanza poem called "Swell" whose concern is what one does when confronted with such anti-foundational, linguistic shortfall and contingency: "To say nothing,/too, is a tactic, a test/of animal proportions" (73).

Between the opening poem, "Thing," and the closing poem, "Swell," we get images, titles, lines that productively resonate with this opening and closing. In "Safe Distance," for instance, we hear "This poem acts/as if the world/exists" (23). The first stanza of "This Way of Talking" runs "What can call itself/language tonight?" (59). Later, through the use of quotation marks, it calls attention to the signifying capacity

of the words *house, harm, hell,* and *here* (60). "Some Maritime Disasters
This Century" regularly presents us with illogical propositions: "British
insurance actuaries have placed sex/as the least reliable form of trans-
portation" and "I would not have been able to use my legs/ as salt der-
vishes" and also "My ovaries were tested for patience" (53). Then there
are the numerous titles that concern themselves with language, the signifying act, and representation: "Without the Ties of Realistic Representation," "The Poetics of Silence," "The Translator's Blues," "How
Language Spanks Us," "This Way of Talking," "Historia de la lengua
española: A Ghazal" (written, by the way, entirely in English, despite its
mostly Spanish title), and "Atopia of Bliss" (a phrase taken from Roland
Barthes's *The Pleasure of the Text,* one of the bibles of poststructuralist
thought about textuality). All of this attention to the linguistic act cannot but draw attention to what Grossman referred to as the "presence of
presence" in Alcalá's poetry.

   I take leave of this analysis of Alcalá's poetry to investigate the work of
Amanda Calderon. The singularity, the astonishment, the presence of presence characteristic of Corral's and Alcalá's work is, of course, also manifest in Calderon's work. We do not find in her poetry a reproduction of a
recognizable Latinidad. Rather what we see in her poems is an intensifica-
tion of radical singularity and astonishment.

Amanda Calderon—An Otherworldly Aesthetic

The youngest of the writers in this chapter, Calderon is quickly establishing herself as a poet with a unique voice and an acute talent at versifica-
tion. She received her BA from Brown University in History in 2004. She
holds an MA in English Literature from Fordham University and received
her MFA in poetry from New York University in 2013, where she completed her thesis under the direction of Matthew Roher. In 2012, she was
a fellow at the Norman Mailer Writers Colony, and in 2014, she was an
Emerging Poets Fellow at Poets House in New York City. Her poems have
already appeared in such prestigious magazines as *Poetry, Poets and Writers, Kenyon Review,* and *Words without Borders.* She is currently completing
her first manuscript, which is tentatively titled, *A History of the East as the
West.* The manuscript consists of two parts: (1) an imagined history of the
Mongols discovery of America two hundred years before Columbus and
(2) a section called "Nuclear Semiotics," which is interested in how to convey danger across eons. How do you alert humans ten thousand years
in the future, for instance, about the dangers of nuclear waste we have

buried in the earth? What language system might they have? Will ours
be comprehensible to them?[19] Both her unpublished manuscript and her
published poems manifest an otherworldly aesthetic, and it is this aesthetic
that I am interested in examining.

In Calderon's poems, we often never know temporally quite *when* we
are; geographically we often never know quite where. "For Tourists and
Armies" is perhaps the exception to that generalization. We know we are
in France, and it is likely the present day or some time in the not too distant past. However, in poems like "Werewolf on the Moon," "Composite
Tiger," "The Khan's Wife," and "Just Before the Ape," there has been "an
aesthetic transformation of the world."[20] We are not, that is, in a world that
obeys the laws of the universe we know. In "Just Before the Ape" we hear of
an ape that has gone blind in a rather peculiar fashion: "the pupil from
one migrates to the other." The final stanza closes the poem with this curious pairing: "Miniature whale in a miniature sea. The ape presses two
pupils up against the glass. If she scoops it / out & holds it in her palm too
long, the whale succumbs to gravity. Its bone sags into its tenderest / organ." Then in "Composite Tiger" we have a beast whose foot was as wide
as a cinema: "Each toe was the head / of your national bird, sprung from
the mouth / of a jackal." "Werewolf on the Moon" bears many recognizable features of our world. It opens, for instance, with an unnamed trophy
hunter: "You want to touch big animals, / animals not touched by your
peers." The figure sounds like a character in a Hemingway short story, and
this hunter, we learn, once shot the endangered Amur tiger in Ussuri State
Nature Reserve. Additionally, the poem is populated with similarly recognizable geographic locales (principally in or around Russia) easily found
on any map—Franz Josef Land, Primorsky Krai, Tumen, among others.
But the very title that ostensibly gives an organizational rubric, if you will,
to the poem conjoins the world we seemingly know to the supernatural
world of the werewolf. In similar fashion, "The Khan's Wife" joins a world
we know with a folkloric one, and we, moreover, are addressed as knowing subjects in this universe: "You know the story where the woman / has
a tiger for a husband," and a few stanzas later "Remember the story: It
crawled from a ten-thousand-years- / old vault // Like a heavy robe from a
steel trunk." These poems represent an imagination on fire. These poems
reorient how we see, and, even in the defamiliarized worlds Calderon creates, we are moved to feel deeply.

With that overview in place, I want to slow down and dig deeper into
Calderon's otherworldly creations, for it is a radically singular and exciting
world that she produces in her verse. In order to generate a close analysis,

I will focus on two poems, "Just Before the Ape" and "Composite Tiger." I reproduce them in full so that we may have them ready at hand:

Just Before the Ape

Just before the ape goes blind, the pupil from one migrates to the other.

We cannot say if one side mists & the other, overpopulated, goes doubly sharp. We cannot say if the pupil passes across or through its counterpart. If distinct interpretations are superimposed.

If the ape perceives only half a field in this condition. Half a room & half the aquaria therein.

If the misplaced pupil mangles the fish, or if the world delivers mangled fish.

Miniature whale in a miniature sea. The ape presses two pupils up against the glass. If she scoops it out & holds it in her palm too long, the whale succumbs to gravity. Its bone sags into the tenderest organ.

Composite Tiger

It was so wide you thought it was a cinema.
It was his foot. Each toe was the head
of your national bird, sprouting from the mouth
of a jackal. Each thick leg,
a jackal's wily torso, tail
tickling the ribs and hooking the thighs
of a farmer tucked in the neck,
clutching his goat—man and beast agape.
It played a newsreel across its spine:
decorated horses on the march. They come upon
a writhing blue elephant
the size of a man, its trunk
locked with the tusks of a wild boar sloshing
about the belly on its back.
A bitter war. Everyone suffered.
Here, the sky grows red with embarrassment.
Life's work is to lie in wait.

Juxtaposing these two poems illustrates one of the salient features of "Just Before the Ape," namely, the length of its lines. It looks on the page much like prose. In the opening of this chapter, I drew on Glyn Maxwell to note that the poet must make good use not only of the black marks but the white space of the page. Calderon does that masterfully here. Each new line is justified to the left. There is no drifting across the page or hanging indents or other layout features that poets take advantage of when playing with the juxtaposition of long and short lines. Moreover, each of the clauses and sentences (and, for a poem, there are an exceptional number of complete sentences) ends in a full stop, just as if it were prose. It is not only that the lines look like prose, but they do so, I contend, to augment the feel of this poem as a scientific report.

Adding to the report feel of the poem is the use of the first-person plural subject pronoun *we*. *We* is often used in academic writing to give it the feel of objectivity, as if we are receiving the knowledge from a detached, unbiased observer. What is so fascinating about the *we* in "Just Before the Ape," however, is that it conjoins the scientific feel with a poetic resonance through its use of anaphora. Controlling the middle of poem, the "we cannot say if" structure repeats itself explicitly twice and an additional four times implicitly. The repetition lends a lovely cadence to the detached academic style being imitated here. The final element that cements the feel of scientific prose is the poem's diction. Consider some of the words Calderon employs in relating the tale of the ape who goes blind. A pupil *migrates* in the opening line. The second stanza includes *overpopulated, counterpart, interpretations,* and *superimposed.* The third stanza underscores the scientific effect with *half a field in this condition* and *half the aquaria therein.* It is not that a poet cannot use any word they see fit in writing a poem. It is that certain words feel as if they belong to certain discourses (in this case a scientific discourse), and, when they migrate from one to the other, they heighten our curiosity.

Created through the look of the lines, the repeated use of full stops, the diction, and the use of *we*, the scientific report feel gains interest when we concentrate on the "meaning" of these lines, as we would be inclined to do when reading a report. The "content" of the lines, that is, are at odds with any "real" report. Pupils cannot migrate from eye to the other. While it may be true, as the second and third stanzas suggest, that we cannot know how this ape that is going blind perceives the world phenomenologically, we certainly know pupils do not get misplaced, nor do they mangle fish. And miniature whales are not scooped from fish tanks by apes, nor do they have just one bone. My interpretive gesture is not to set the score right on what is and is not possible. We do not (or at least we should not), as I suggested earlier, read poems for veracity. As William Carlos Williams wrote in "Asphodel, That Greeny Flower," "It is difficult to get the news from poems / yet men die miserably every day / for lack of what is found there."

Poems may not give us the news, but they give us equally important material for sustaining our lives as we amble through this world and attempt to make sense of it and ourselves. Thus, what I mean to highlight here is not the "objective" truth of the poem or its lack thereof, but rather the fruitful tension and the resonance that emerges from the tension between its scientific look and its otherworldly, emotional center. Though none of the poem is verifiably true, it still moves us. We still feel the pain of this ape going blind. I would argue, moreover, that the final stanza accentuates our connection and underscores our capacity for empathy. For in this last stanza, we witness a desperate ape staring longingly at a whale in an aquarium, seeking perhaps companionship with this other curious creature, a whale—the largest mammal rendered miniature. Yet if our hero ape holds her desired companion "in her palm too long," she dies. Calderon, however, does not just opt for the prosaic *dies*, she selects *succumbs* and closes that potential death with the powerfully gripping "tenderest/organ." The line break draws attention to that vulnerability and possible death. This otherworldly animality comes out as well in "Composite Tiger."

While my juxtaposition of the two poems calls attention to the length of the lines in "Just Before the Ape," it equally draws attention to the shorter lines and more poetic look of "Composite Tiger." The latter is both a description of this tiger made up from a range of elements and, in its final three lines, a seeming reflection on a world not unlike our own, one full of war and suffering. But let us begin at the beginning.

The speaker of the poem addresses an unidentified *you*, unfamiliar to us, readers, but clearly familiar to the speaker. Indeed, the speaker seems to be explaining this tiger to the addressee, and therefore the poem suggests the speaker is the wiser of the two. The opening line of the poem shows us the addressee mistaking the foot of the tiger for something altogether different, a cinema. It is the speaker who clarifies that it is the foot of the tiger. Indeed, the tiger is so unfathomable that that is why the addressee, like Dante, needs a Virgil to guide them. Given the harsh scene of the poem, the enormous dimensions of the tiger, it may not be foolish to suggest that the addressee is being guided through the rings of hell and tutored in the ways of life. The tiger seems to have menaced the addressee's land. The very description of the foot suggests so: "Each toe was the head/of your national bird,/sprung from the mouth/of a jackal." In addition, the tiger's tail is so large that it has grabbed a farmer by the thighs who in turn clutches his goat in his arms, as the tiger holds them in his tail suspended over his neck. The tiger haunts the land, and we witness him traipse through a ravaged space of the addressee's country, a space where a blue elephant has been reduced to the size of a man and finds itself sloshing on the ground in battle with a boar. Everything about these opening fourteen lines highlights the martial and dystopic nature of this poetic world. The decorated horses featured on a newsreel running across the tiger's spine constitute the one image of pomp and gallantry. Through the knowing reader's head runs a trove of images from the nightly news of victorious armies marching on conquered or liberated towns.

In the poem's final three lines, we leave the description of the tiger and the ravaged country. In these lines, we are back to the knowing speaker offering wise, empathetic advice to the distraught addressee, the one who has seen their country destroyed. We go from the two terse end-stopped phrases of the fifteenth line: "A bitter war. Everyone suffered." which can sound cold, perhaps even justifying the idea to the addressee that it was not only their people who suffered, but also the victors, to a more ruminative diction and syntax, a perhaps philosophical pose in the face of destruction. The penultimate line moves us out from the narrow confines of the speaker and addressee to suggest that even the universe (i.e., the sky) is in dismay. The plight here is bigger than the tiger, the speaker, the addressee, and the country. The final line, then, brings us back home to the tiger, whose behavior is perhaps a site of instruction. We know not what for, but we must wait, and, like the tiger, be patient and strike at the right moment. Again, as with "Just Before the Ape," we are in an otherworldly universe, but the poem nevertheless moves us. We recognize the beast of violence, the tragedy of war. We know how the poem comes to mean and how it makes us feel.

Each of the three poets examined in this chapter moves away from many of the familiar themes in the canon of Latinx poetry—the struggle for social justice, the battle for recognition, the call for solidarity, and the like. In making the familiar strange, in attending to a presence of presence, and in generating an otherworldly aesthetic, Corral, Alcalá, and Calderon help us see an altogether different construction of the world, one not consistently in line with the Latinidades we have come to know. Their poems speak not to, of, or for the community, or even of a self in relation to a community, but rather they bring forth a radically singular self—or as Allen Grossman puts it in his discussion of the lyric, "A poem has the same singularity as a self" (*Sighted Singer* 235). Indeed, these poets in their lyric writing have freed themselves from a burden of cultural representation. Moreover, in making the familiar strange, they compel us to see things from new angles from different vantage points. That new seeing is in keeping with the project of *Latinx Literature Unbound* to scrutinize first principles about the critical work we do and the taxonomies under which we do it. The poetry of Corral, Alcalá, and Calderon unbinds us from common conceptions we might have about the Latinx canon. Again, in the José

Muñozian sense, these poems astonish. They "help one surpass the limitations of an alienating presentness and allow one to see a different time and place" (*Cruising Utopia* 5). They afford us the opportunity to see our creative and critical projects anew.

Conclusion: Thinking beyond Limits

Latinx Literature Unbound has been driven by an excitement about literature, reading, and writing. I have spent over two decades of my life studying
the literature we call *Latinx*. Thus, it is with the love of an amateur and
the dedication of a professional that I approach this topic. I have endeavored
to respect the very craft of creative writing and to understand better the
many techniques fiction writers and poets use to bring their imagined
worlds into being. I hope my own critical reflections have matched the
efforts and insights of these writers. I desire that we critics create a world
of scholarly plenitude in which fiction writers and poets might thrive in all
of their nuance and complexity.

In addition to unbinding the literature which we have come to label
Latinx from the identity and thematic strictures that govern it (more on
that in a moment), I have also argued for an attention to form—genre in
particular—and for slow reading. Such reading is itself, to borrow Stanley
Fish's phrase, an event. It follows the temporal unfolding of sentences,
paragraphs, stanzas, and so on, appraising what this word, image, phrase,
etc. does. I have taken careful and deliberate strides in asking us to consider
how writers like Danny Santiago, Brando Skyhorse, and Eduardo Halfon

confound, and thereby make more complex, the criteria we use to define Latinx literature. In a purposeful turn to genre as a historically durable form, I have examined how metafictions such as Salvador Plascencia's *The People of Paper* build their own ontological universes and, thus, teach us important lessons about mimetic fidelity, author, and narrator. These lessons, I believe, provide instructive guidelines for how we make meaning from reading. In turning to the writings of Manuel Muñoz, Patricia Engel, and Ana Menéndez, I have demonstrated the close tie between narrative point of view and intimacy and distance in the short story. The rare first-person plural and second-person singular focalizations of these stories bring into sharp relief the affective exchange between reader and narrator. Finally, I shifted our attention away from narrative poems and asked us to consider the radically singular presence created in the lyric poetry of Eduardo Corral, Rosa Alcalá, and Amanda Calderon. I believe my readings make manifest the positive critical returns we can expect from a neo-formalist approach to reading. Furthermore, my hope is that each of these chapters has individually and collectively helped us unbind Latinx literature from the preconceptions that often govern its definitional criteria, its marketing, its readership, and its criticism. On that note, I want to return once more to the questions that animate this project and to point to possible future directions for the study of the literature we have come to call *Latinx*.

Two basic questions served as the catalyst for this study: (1) What, if anything, does it meaningfully tell us to label a single work or a corpus of literature *Latinx literature*? and (2) If it tells us something meaningful, what is that and can it be used to generate a poetics of *Latinx literature* that would help us better understand the literature so named? Pursuing those two questions has meant unbinding Latinx literature from a number of the preconceptions we employ to classify and analyze it. In defining Latinx literature, we too often lean on the author's identity—an identity we imagine is readily legible and knowable. Consequently, we take an author's complex identity and flatten it out into one of the neat boxes the census offers.

There are many consequences attendant to such a narrow view on race. It can lead to purity tests—in Bruce-Novoa's stinging phrasing, a *prueba de sangre*—about Latinx identity and authorship. It results in masking, brushing aside, or completely ignoring the multiple racial ways a person is formed. As long as we rely on the racial taxonomies passed down by the government, there is no way around that cordoning off because those monolithic signifiers will never be able to attend to the complex subjects colligated beneath them. Let me reiterate that I fully understand that strategically essentializing racial and ethnic identities has been and will continue to be useful in furthering causes for social justice and building political coalitions. Such strategic essentialisms are not, however, helpful for illuminating the literature we study. Given the heterogeneity within even one subcommunity, say Cuban American, how could we possibly expect the umbrella—thereby even more varied—rubric *Latinx* to tell us something meaningful about the literature. As Cristina Beltrán observes, "Rather than striving to uncover the unitary core that binds Latinos, scholars and advocates should embrace, rather than resist or deny, the instability and incompleteness of the category 'Latino.' Such an approach does not mean abandoning the pragmatic political needs of subjects positioned as Latino in our society. Nor does it mean denying the racism and discrimination that Latinos have experienced as a group" ("Crossings and Correspondence" 482). Leaning less heavily on the identity category in creating literary taxonomies and moving away from a unitary notion of Latinx identities would help us better understand the literary output of subjects identified and self-identified as Latinx and would open up broader avenues for writing about this literature.[1]

A related consequence of relying on the author's identity, is that it has resulted in readers, critics, and the publishing industry expecting Latinx authors to write on themes that are imagined to be "authentically" Latinx. Such themes do not guarantee that the literature is going to be outstanding, but it assures it will be identifiable as Latinx. By the same token, I do not mean to say that what is familiarly Latinx cannot be great art. There are works on these recognizable themes that are aesthetically exceptional. Tomás Rivera's novel about migrant farmworkers, . . . *Y no se lo tragó la tierra/ . . . And the Earth Did Not Devour Him*; Cristina García's novel about exile and homeland, *Dreaming in Cuban*; Junot Díaz's Pulitzer Prize–winning novel about Dominicans on and off the island, *The Brief Wondrous Life of Oscar Wao*, among many others, come readily to mind.

My critique, then, is not of what results from writers employing such readily recognizable themes. Rather I am concerned about the expectation that Latinx authors write solely on such recognizable topics. It has a two-fold deleterious effect: (1) it influences what many critics are willing to examine in their studies of Latinx literature, and (2) it unnecessarily encourages, rewards, and possibly constrains Latinx authors to write about what agents, editors, and publishers believe the market desires from Latinx writers. Many authors will want to take up these familiar themes, and they should. Some, however, do so because they have been told by an agent to make their writing more "ethnic," or they police themselves into writing what they know will be deemed acceptable. Ricardo L. Ortíz certainly has this troubling logic of a preconceived authentic fit in mind when he writes, "I am also interested in demonstrating the manner in which Cuban American culture, certainly since 1980 but especially in the post-Cold War era, has freed itself of the geographical isolation of South Florida. Most of the writers I study [in *Cultural Erotics in Cuban America*] were never based in Miami, and thus they fight to attain a kind of visibility as writers from a minority culture *without falling back on the kinds of stereotypes that would most easily lend them that visibility*" (279; emphasis added). We need to resist the imposition of demands for "authentic" topics because it presupposes a homogenous, even at times provincial, understanding of the dynamic peoples and cultures that fall under the umbrella term *Latinx*.

Furthermore, Latinx critics have not often taken up Latinx writers who do not write on recognizable themes, and I feel we are missing an opportunity here. Take, for instance, the author Manuel Gonzales. He is decidedly Latino, but his exciting book *The Miniature Wife and Other Stories* (2014) does not traffic in what we might deem Latinx themes. His stories have to do with zombies, hijacked airplanes, miniature wives, unicorns—basically anything other than "traditional" Latinx themes. He is one of the most novel and exciting writers working today; yet, given the extant definitional criteria, we cannot discuss him under the rubric *Latinx literature*. Some may contend that is fine. Other critics can take up his work. However, I believe that does a disservice to his writing and even to one of the principal tenets that has long driven Latinx literary criticism, namely, according attention to writers who have typically been overlooked because of structural racism in canon formation and in the world of mainstream, New York publishing houses.

A related limiting factor is that not only are there necessary identity and thematic criteria to meet, there are also, for many critics, progressive political criteria to which a writer should conform. Although in the preceding chapters, I have not hit that note as strongly as some of the others, I have been subtly trying to unbind Latinx literature from politically instrumental criticism. This criticism believes that art should be used to effect political change. While I believe that literature can effect change, the claims marshaled on behalf of literature as a political instrument are often attended by little evidence to support them. It is often as if the critic's claim, alone, makes the work politically salient. Here I would caution moderation. Of greater concern is that politically minded critics often only engage works that satisfy their politics, wherever those happen to fall on the political spectrum. We do not serve the literature well if we only attend to authors who serve our political ends and if we only value the work to the extent that we see it being political. Rich literary works present life in all of its complexity. They do not flatten it out into a world of political sloganeering. Or, as the prominent contemporary writer Teju Cole notes, "I am a novelist. I traffic in subtleties, and my goal in writing a novel is to leave the reader not knowing what to think. A good novel shouldn't have a point" ("White-Savior Industrial Complex" n.p.). I believe we must always strive to interpret cultural formations robustly. While complete objectivity is a fiction, we should proceed with as much critical disinterest as possible and try to apprehend what is actually happening before us on the page.

So what can the label *Latinx literature* do, and what are we critics to do as we move forward? Here, I want to make a distinction between institutional and intellectual projects and potentialities, which may also at times overlap. At a pragmatic institutional level, the label can give us a tool for developing courses and writing syllabi. Given that much of this literature will not be taught with regularity or depth in nonspecialized courses, there is a need to work with the necessary fiction of the label, to offer courses, for instance, on Latinx literature. In this regard, it is not at all unlike the need to galvanize strategically around *Latinx* to effect necessary political and social change. As an intellectual project, however, the future directions can and, I think, must be somewhat different from where we have been since the field developed its particularities around Chicana/o and Puerto Rican/Nuyorican literature and where we have been headed since the 1980s and 1990s under the broader organizing rubric of Latinx literature.

As I contended throughout this study, the system we use to group and organize literature matters because it is through that system that the horizon of meanings is set. To return to Jonathan Culler, "[T]he literary work is dependent for its meaning and effects on a system of possibilities, which need to be described" (*Literary in Theory* 8). As a category, *Latinx literature* describes one system of possibilities, and it has certainly generated a host of significant interpretations for the literature so described. I, however, think that system of possibilities has perhaps limited what we might know about the various texts we label as *Latinx*. We can certainly continue down that path, for it has generated much fine scholarship. We could, however, also stand to move down some other ones. I offer the following provisional suggestions.

I am asking scholars, myself included, to take a breath and not dive right into our usual ways of proceeding, to stand back and think about the categories we employ and the insights they afford and preclude. I am simply trying to come up with a generative way to approach the literature that allows us to measure fully its art and craft. I believe we should let our scholarly projects and arguments drive the principle of selection for the texts we choose to analyze. If identity figures in, that is, of course, fine, maybe even necessary, but let us not always use it as the first principle of selection. For the purposes of this project's arguments, I have restricted the authors I examined to ones we would identify as Latinx. I thought it was necessary in making an argument about unbinding Latinx literature to first demonstrate in the introduction and in the chapter, "Brown Like Me?," what the identity category *Latinx* and its attendant recognizable themes afforded and precluded. Then in the remaining body chapters I aimed to show how an attention to genre might help us read Latinx literature otherwise. I believed those were necessary first steps to support the broader claims of *Latinx Literature Unbound*. My hope for my future work is to move into broader comparative projects that take advantage of the plentitude of exciting contemporary writing. For instance, one guiding principle I would like to carry forward is to think about literature as existing in an interlocking network.[2]

In particular, I find myself especially interested in a group of Boston-based writers who identify themselves as the Back Porch Collective.[3] These writers include Jonathan Escoffery, Shuba Sunder, Sarah Colwill-Brown, Stacy Mattingly, Ani Gjika, Dariel Suarez, and Tara Skurtu. Hailing "from places as far flung as Albania, Britain, Cuba, India, and Atlanta," these writers fashion themselves as an international writing collective with ties to the United States and abroad. I find them an inspiring and exciting collective on their own merit. However, what interests me in light of my arguments in *Latinx Literature Unbound* is that building a research project around them offers the opportunity to take a writer such as Dariel Suarez (who was born in Cuba and came to the United States when he was fourteen) and place his work in conversation with a number of other non-Latinx writers. Such a project lets me engage both Suarez's connections to and investments in Cuba (to date, all of his stories and his novel in progress take place in Cuba) and also the international and thematic overlaps in his work with writers from a host of different countries. While we have seen Latinx writers analyzed hemispherically in brilliant works by José David Saldívar, Kirsten Silva Gruesz, and Marissa K. López, among others, there has yet to be such a capacious international understanding of Latinx writing, as the one I propose carrying out in a study of the Back Porch Collective.

A host of other projects might emerge from this new critical imaginary that is attentive to the category *Latinx* but also seeks to unbind it from being too heavily dependent on identity and theme. Instead of seeing Latino writers like, say, Manuel Gonzales and Eric Garcia, who do not employ recognizable themes, being turned away, I can imagine an interpretive landscape that puts them in conversation with authors like Helen Oyeyemi, Karen Russell, and Amelia Gray, who similarly exceed the boundaries of the real to write in a surreal or fable-like style, and in even in conversation with Junot Díaz's apocalyptic stories, such as "Monstro."[4] This is not a usual lineup for analyzing Latinx literature. Another welcome addition would be a book that studied the interethnic embodiments and connections of Latinx writers similar to Caroline Rody's *The Interethnic Imagination*, which explores interethnicity in Asian American literature, or like Vijay Prashad's analysis of Afro-Asian linkages in his *Everybody Was Kung Fu Fighting*. I can envision a rich study of literary rewritings that would include Ernesto Quiñonez's *Bodega Dreams*, which is an adaptation of *The Great Gatsby*; J. M. Coetzee's *Foe*, which rewrites *Robinson Crusoe*; Zadie Smith's *On Beauty*, which reworks *Howard's End*; and Margot Livesey's *The Flight of Gemma Hardy*, a retelling of *Jane Eyre*, among other possibilities. Yes, we can and should keep Latinx writers in conversation with one another, but we do not need a critical call for that to happen. That work, including my own, is proceeding along admirably and excitingly. May those projects continue to flourish. I am making the modest proposal that we cast our critical nets into less explored waters as well, and it is my hope that *Latinx Literature Unbound* will generate some of the necessary enthusiasm to do so.

ACKNOWLEDGMENTS

Never is there simply one mind behind a book. Though only my name appears on the spine, the writing of *Latinx Literature Unbound* was anything but a solo project. I have benefited tremendously from the support of family, friends, colleagues, and various institutions in the writing of this book. I am delighted to have the chance to thank them.

My parents remain inspirations for all that I do. I couldn't have asked for more caring and loving ones. Gumaro and Sophie, I thank you for your encouragement, example, and unflinching support. I am also grateful to my sister, Tina, and my brothers, John and David, as well as my nieces, Stacy and Stephanie, for their love and good cheer.

Brown University, where I have spent the past thirteen years of my career, has been a terrific place to work. I would like to thank the university and Kevin McLaughlin, the Dean of Faculty, for a sabbatical leave that allowed me to advance the research and writing of this project and for a Faculty Development Grant. I am also grateful to Liza Cariaga-Lo, Vice President of Academic Development, Diversity, and Inclusion, for her support, both behind the scenes and face-to-face.

Two other institutions at Brown have been crucial to completing this project: the Cogut Center for the Humanities and the Center for the Study of Race and Ethnicity in America (CSREA). Tricia Rose, Director of the CSREA, invited me to share an overview of *Latinx Literature Unbound* as part of the Center's series "What Am I Thinking About Now?" It was engaging to share my work with colleagues and students and have a chance to address their comments and concerns. The Cogut Center generously awarded me a fellowship to work on the manuscript, where I had the opportunity to share my ideas and hear about the other fellows' projects. I am especially grateful to Leela Ghandi and Patricia Ybarra for attending my seminar in which I presented a portion of Chapter 2. Their feedback and that of the other fellows strengthened my arguments.

My colleague and friend Matthew Guterl deserves special mention. He has been a singular support and guiding light. He generously read early versions of the opening two chapters and offered his characteristically insightful feedback. He's always there to listen and push. Similarly, my friend Jacques Khalip has always been there to offer support and advice. I am wonderfully grateful to the inimitable force of friendship that is known as Sandra Latcha. Tremendous is she. For radical love, friendship, and inspiration, David Kyuman Kim stands out. Beth Piatote is a constant source of intellectual inspiration and unconditional friendship.

It has been an honor to work with and learn from my most recent colleagues in Latina/o Studies at Brown, Leticia Alvarado and Monica Martinez. Further, I want to thank all of my colleagues and graduate students in American Studies, Ethnic Studies, and English for their good cheer, support, and the regular opportunities to bounce ideas off of them.

Although Shawn Michelle Smith and I have only once had the good fortune of being at the same institution at the same time (a too brief year), she remains a dedicated interlocutor, friend, and supporter, and wow, can her insights blow you out of the water and lift you up. Pier Dominguez, whose dissertation I had the pleasure and honor of co-directing, has grown to be one of my best friends and writing companions. We have had an endless stream of conversations that greatly improved this book. He has also been a terrific writing friend, which is to say we have sat across many a café table with our laptops out and headphones on, keeping each other company. I would also like to thank Timothy Bewes for a rather long lunch conversation early on in the writing of *Latinx Literature Unbound*, where he helped me think through the organizational structure of the book and some of its foundational arguments. I am ever grateful to Michelle Clayton who enthusiastically brought up Eduardo Halfon at a party one evening.

I thank Raúl Coronado for generously reading early versions of two chapters and then taking the time to have an extended Skype session with me. Raúl was wonderfully generous with his time and insights. Two years ago, at the inaugural meeting of the Latina/o Studies Association, I had the good fortune of meeting Elda Maria Roman. We had a wonderful back-and-forth about our books, and have continued to do so ever since. Our conversations have energized me and strengthened my writing.

As I presented a number of ideas that appear in this book in my classes and seminars, my undergraduate and graduate students have been graciously receptive. The conceiving and writing of *Latinx Literature Unbound* benefited from their keen insights and feedback. I am especially grateful to the students who have been in my classes on Latinx literature and Latinx cultural theory. It was my great honor, on three occasions, to co-teach my survey of contemporary Latinx literature with Pia Sahni.

Refereeing a book manuscript is an act of great generosity and professional commitment. I benefited tremendously from the care and rigor with which the anonymous referees for Fordham University Press read my manuscript. I thank them for their time and for helping me make *Latinx Literature Unbound* a stronger book.

It has been a privilege and an honor to have Richard Morrison as my editor. His incredible editorial vision, guidance, and support have profited my work in no small way. Working with him and his assistant, John Garza, was a delight. I am grateful as well to Eric Newman and all of the wonderful people at Fordham University Press, many whom I may not know by name but who were instrumental in helping bring *Latinx Literature Unbound* into the world.

Even in a list of acknowledgments as detailed as this, I have, no doubt, inadvertently left out folks who deserve my gratitude. Please consider that an unintentional oversight, not an ungrateful heart. And know that I'm wonderfully appreciative of your support.

Finally, I gratefully acknowledge the following authors, agents, and publishers for granting permission to use the copyrighted material listed below.

"Governor Wilson of California Talks in His Sleep," "When the Leather is a Whip," from *Imagine the Angels of Bread* by Martín Espada. Copyright © 1996 by Martín Espada. Used by permission of W. W. Norton & Company, Inc.

"What the Living Do," from *What the Living Do* by Marie Howe. Copyright © 1997 by Marie Howe. Used by permission of W. W. Norton & Company, Inc.

Rosa Alcalá for her poems "Mimicry" and "A Girl Leaves the Croft," both from *Undocumentaries* (2010) and "Swell" from *The Lust of Unsentimental Waters* (2012). Both volumes published by Shearsman Books.

Ana Castillo for her poem "I Ask the Impossible" from *I Ask the Impossible*, published by Anchor Books, 2001.

Amanda Calderon for her poems "Composite Tiger," first published in the *Kenyon Review*, 37.2, March/April 2015; and "Just Before the Ape," first published at Poetshouse.org.

Eduardo Corral for his poem "Acquired Immune Deficiency Syndrome [I approach a harp]," which first appeared in the *Indiana Review*, 24.1, Summer 2002; and for his poem "Acquired Immune Deficiency Syndrome [At a quarter to midnight]," which first appeared in *Quarterly West*.

"Carrying My Tools" from *The Concrete River* Copyright © 1991 by Luis J. Rodriguez. Published by Curbstone Press. By permission of Susan Bergholz Literary Services, New York, NY and Lamy, NM. All rights reserved.

INTRODUCTION: WHAT WE TALK ABOUT WHEN WE TALK
ABOUT LATINX LITERATURE

1. There are competing umbrella terms used to identify Latinx people and communities. Currently, the three most common are Latina/o, Latin@, and Latinx. I will be using Latinx because I appreciate the gender fluidity and complex gender spectrum it denotes. For the plural, I will use Latina/os. However, when engaging the work of other scholars who use differing terms, I will adopt their language for the sake of clarity. Also, to avoid anachronism as much as possible, I will not rewrite past usages with the present nomenclature. For example, I will avoid calling the Chicano movement the Chicanx movement.

2. I reprint the poem, which originally appeared in issue 26 (1991–1992) of the *Berkeley Poetry Review*, for your perusal:

I ask the impossible: love me forever.
Love me when all desire is gone.
Love me with the single-mindedness of a monk.
When the world in its entirety,
and all that you hold sacred, advise you
against it: love me still more.
When rage fills you and has no name: love me.
When each step from your door to your job tires you—
love me; and from job to home again.

Love me when you're bored—
when every woman you see is more beautiful than the last,
or more pathetic, love me as you always have:
not as admirer or judge, but with
the compassion you save for yourself
in your solitude.

Love me as you relish your loneliness,
the anticipation of your death,

mysteries of the flesh, as it tears and mends.
Love me as your most treasured childhood memory—
and if there is none to recall—
imagine one, place me there with you.
Love me withered as you love me new.

Love me as if *I* were forever—
and I will make the impossible
a simple act,
by loving you, loving you as I do.

3. It bears noting, and yet goes beyond the scope of this project, that *Latinx* is often treated by turns as a racial *and* ethnic category. The critical literature on the distinctions between race and ethnicity is often hard pressed to distinguish between the two categories. Either way, however, whether you consider Latinx a race or an ethnicity or recognize that it often operates as both, my argument still holds.

4. Indeed, as Ramón Saldívar remarks of Salvador Plascencia's *The People of Paper* and Junot Diaz's *The Brief Wondrous Life of Oscar Wao*, both "share more with the form and aesthetics of Mark Z. Danielewski, Dave Eggers, Jonathan Franzen, Michael Chabon, Jonathan Lethem, Alex Shakar, or David Foster Wallace than with those of other Latino writers, and either Gabriel García Márquez or Toni Morrison." Of all the extant scholarship on Latinx literature, Saldívar's recent essay—"Historical Fantasy, Speculative Realism, and Postrace Aesthetics in Contemporary American Fiction" (*American Literary History* 23.3 [Fall 2011]: 574–599)—comes the closest to the direction that *Latinx Literature Unbound* is headed, though Saldívar and I have decided differences over the relationship between race and aesthetics.

5. See such works as José Aranda's *When We Arrive: A New Literary History of Mexican America* (Tucson: University of Arizona Press, 2003); Raúl Coronado's *A World Not to Come: A History of Latino Writing and Print Culture* (Cambridge, Mass.: Harvard University Press, 2013); Elena Machado Sáez and Raphael Dalleo's *The Latina/o Canon and the Emergence of Post-Sixties Literature* (New York: Palgrave Macmillan, 2007); and all of the scholars working with the *Recovering the U.S. Hispanic Literary Heritage* project.

6. For representative transnational and hemispheric approaches to understanding and reorienting conceptions of Latinx and Latin American literature, please see Kirsten Silva Gruesz's *Ambassadors of Culture: The Transamerican Origins of Latino Writing* (Princeton, N.J.: Princeton University Press, 2001); Marissa K. López's *Chicano Nations: The Hemispheric Origins of Mexican American Literature* (New York: New York University Press, 2011); Ramón Saldívar's *The Borderlands of Culture: Américo Paredes*

and the Transnational Imaginary (Durham, N.C.: Duke University Press, 2006); José David Saldívar's *Transamericanity: Subaltern Modernities, Global Coloniality, and the Cultures of Greater Mexico* (Durham, N.C.: Duke University Press, 2012); and Juan Poblete's edited volume *Critical Latin American and Latino Studies* (Minneapolis: University of Minnesota Press, 2003).

7. As regards thematic approaches, consider such work as Lázaro Lima's *The Latino Body: Crisis Identities in American Literary and Cultural Memory* (New York: New York University Press, 2007), María DeGuzmán's *Buenas Noches, American Culture: Latina/o Aesthetics of Night* (Bloomington: Indiana University Press, 2012); and Mary Pat Brady's *Extinct Land, Temporal Geographies: Chicana Literature and the Urgency of Space* (Durham, N.C.: Duke University Press, 2002). As to the generic focus, please see Frederick Luis Aldama's *Your Brain on Latino Comics: From Gus Arriola to Los Bros Hernandez* (Austin: University of Texas Press, 2005) and Susan Baker Sotelo's *Chicano Detective Fiction: A Critical Study of Five Novelists* (Jefferson, N.C.: McFarland and Co., 2005) and my *Brown Gumshoes: Detective Fiction and the Search for Chicana/o Identity* (Austin: University of Texas Press, 2005).

8. A representative sample of queer, feminist, and gendered appraisals would include Sandra K. Soto's *Reading Chican@ Like a Queer: The De-Mastery of Desire* (Austin: University of Texas Press, 2011); Michael Hames-García and Ernesto Martínez's *Gay Latino Studies: A Critical Reader* (Durham, N.C.: Duke University Press, 2011); Theresa Delgadillo's *Spiritual Mestizaje: Religion, Gender, Race, and Nation in Contemporary Chicana Narrative* (Durham, N.C.: Duke University Press, 2011); Juana Maria Rodriguez's *Queer Latinidad: Identity Practices, Discursive Spaces* (New York: New York University Press, 2003); José Quiroga's *Tropics of Desire: Interventions from Queer Latino America* (New York: New York University Press, 2000); and Ellen McCracken's *New Latina Narrative: The Feminine Space of Postmodern Ethnicity* (Tucson: University of Arizona Press, 1999).

9. As a label, *Chicana/o* is still used today and is applied fairly indiscriminately to any piece of literature written by someone of Mexican American ancestry, regardless of whether her politics align with those of the Chicana/o movement of the 1960s and 1970s. In a recent essay on Nuyorican literature that makes note of the shift from *Nuyorican* to *Latino* to describe the literary output of stateside Puerto Ricans, Frances Aparicio similarly observes, "In the wake of the vogue of multiculturalism of the 1980s and 1990s, . . . many writers—novelists in particular—found considerable mainstream success by offering up their culturally specific experiences to eager audiences who flattened them into a generically exotic 'Latino' category" ("Loisaida Literature" 982).

10. He also goes on to show that even the supposed common denominators (i.e., "Spanish heritage, Latin American historical roots, miscegenation, minority status in the United States as immigrants and a common language") used to group these populations highlight their very differences. See Bruce-Novoa, *Retrospace: Collected Essays on Chicano Literature* (Houston: Arte Público, 1990), 28–32.

11. The production and publication of the anthology was hotly contested, not because of the authors included or the parameters of the anthology, but because of its general editorship under Ilan Stavans, whom some characterize as an interloper.

12. I will hold in abeyance whether the nation is an appropriate scale for organizing and analyzing a body of literature. For some illustrative treatments of the nation and literature, see Benedict Anderson's *Imagined Communities: Reflections on the Origin and Spread of Nationalism* (London: Verso, 1991); Homi K. Bhabha's edited volume *Nation and Narration* (New York: Routledge, 1990); Michael Gardiner's *The Constitution of English Literature: The State, the Nation and the Canon* (London and New York: Bloomsbury, 2012); and Caroline Levander's *Where Is American Literature?* (Malden, Mass. and Oxford: Wiley-Blackwell, 2013).

13. This phrasing calls to mind E. M. Forster's discussion in *Aspects of the Novel* (New York: Mariner Books, 1985) of flat and round characters, whose richness or lack thereof could be measured through aesthetic criteria of evaluation.

14. In her exemplary review essay "What Was Latino Literature?" (*PMLA* 127.2 [March 2012]: 335–341), Kirsten Silva Gruesz highlights the anthology's central contradiction between periodicity and canonicity. She notes that "the *NALL* occupies the unusual position of presenting an authoritative canon for a body of literature that doesn't yet have a literary history" (336). She continues, "to some degree this is a chicken-and-egg question: periodicity and canonicity have in most cases evolved alongside each other. But in the case of Latino literature, all we have is an egg" (336). It bears noting here that my project is not engaged in writing a history of Latinx literature. Rather, although historically minded, I am asking a basic theoretical and first-principle question about the very nomenclature and taxonomy under which, in recent decades, we have been carrying out our critical work.

15. See also Lisa Sánchez González's *Boricua Literature: A Literary History of the Puerto Rican Diaspora* (New York: New York University Press, 2001), which dedicates a chapter to Williams.

16. For the shaping role that marketing forces have placed in the creation of *Latinidad*, see Arlene Dávila's influential book *Latinos, Inc.: The Marketing*

and Marking of a People (Berkeley and Los Angeles: University of California Press, 2001).

17. Two additional passages from Chabram-Dernersesian's essay "Refashioning the Transnational Connection" bear noting. After charting a series of examples that speak to the intersections among various Latinx groups, she writes, "I offer these examples as a way of demonstrating the complex relations that are to be negotiated among those people that the government documents loosely refer to as Hispanic, Spanish or Latino, *as if they all shared the same social, cultural, and ethnic characteristics and social interests*, and as if they all sought natural coalitions with one another" (275; emphasis added). And a little later in the essay, she asserts, "Encountering the new ethnicities that frame Chicana/o can also be border crossings in the positive sense. Now that these ethnicities are intersecting Chicana/os in a variety of ways, we have the opportunity to reconfigure *una relación* with our *América, desde adentro*/from the inside, *desde afuera*/from the outside, *de otra manera*/in a different way, and *we have the opportunity to problematize the pan-ethnic Latino essentialist identity that proposes an undifferentiated collectivity*. . . . Without a linguistic path to guide the strategic relations with Latino and to articulate a much-needed changing transnational project of Chicana/o, *this configuration, Latino, can offer little more than a dose of brown brotherhood, and this is a highly questionable effect*" (283; emphasis added). (Angie Chabram-Dernersesian, "'Chicana! Rican? No, Chicana Riqueña!'": Refashioning the Transnational Connection" in *Between Women and Nation: Nationalisms, Transnational Feminisms, and the State*, ed. Caren Kaplan et al. [Durham, N.C.: Duke University Press, 1999]).

18. I had the opportunity to hear Muñoz give a number of talks from his "feeling brown" project and to discuss its ideas with him. My hope is that in his personal archives there is enough of a manuscript for a book to be published posthumously.

19. See Vijay Prashad's *Everybody Was Kung Fu Fighting: Afro-Asian Connections and the Myth of Cultural Purity* (Boston: Beacon Press, 2002), esp. xi–xii and 65–66.

20. Yet in the subsequent paragraph, he observes, "The category Latino/a is an academic one. . . . any definitions that rest on talk of a shared **latinidad**—language, culture, history—are just that: academic, intellectual or interpretive demarcations that in many ways artificially cut into and across social reality" (xv).

21. For a send-up of this phenomenon, see Percival Everett's novel *Erasure* (Minneapolis: Graywolf, 2001).

22. The wealth of this material exceeds the scale of this project and certainly that of a note, but let me suggest a few sources in addition to the

cursory overview I give above. In terms of American letters, the national
model has been under scrutiny for over two decades. The reader interested
in the genesis of this debate can turn to Carolyn Porter's lengthy review
essay "What We Know That We Don't Know: Remapping American
Literary Studies," *ALH* 6.3 (Fall 1994): 467–526. Donald E. Pease and the
many others in the "New Americanist" movement have also done important
work in considering the complexities of national boundaries and what lies
beyond and troubles them. Key volumes in that regard include Pease's edited
volumes *National Identities and Post-Americanist Narratives* and *Revisionary
Interventions into the Americanist Canon* (Durham, N.C.: Duke University
Press, 1994) as well as Pease and Amy Kaplan's edited volume *Cultures of
United States Imperialism* (Durham, N.C.: Duke University Press, 1994).
Amy Kaplan's *The Anarchy of Empire in the Making of U.S. Culture*
(Cambridge, Mass.: Harvard University Press, 2005) has also been a bulwark
in these debates about the national and the global.

   23. While my project to unbind what we have heretofore called "Latinx
literature" from, among other things, its recognizable themes and its heavy
lean on authorial identity, is an ambitious one, it cannot match Dimock's
impressive use of "deep time" as the appropriate scale for thinking about
literature. Indeed, I can think of no other literary project about scale that is
as expansive as Dimock's. Her book, *Through Other Continents: American
Literature Across Deep Time* (Princeton, N.J.: Princeton University Press,
2006) "is an attempt to rethink the shape of literature against the history
and habitat of the human species, against the 'deep time' of the planet earth
as described by two scientific disciplines, geology and astronomy. The former
works with a geological record of some 600 million years, and the latter
with a record still more staggering, 14 billion light-years. The humanities
have no time frame of comparable length. What we do have are written
records going back five or six thousand years, and oral, musical, and visual
material going back further. Since American authors have made a point of
engaging this material, drawing on it and incorporating it in their own
writings, the least we can do, as scholars and readers, is to do likewise. These
old records and their modern transpositions give us a 'deep time' in human
terms" (6).

   24. Paul Giles, in critiquing Dimock, gives further proof to the nation-
based reliance in the study of American literature. He writes, "It is possible,
though, that Dimock's argument appears more original than it actually is
because her thematic focus is on American literature, a subject that, since
the days of V. L. Parrington and F. O. Matthiessen, has traditionally tried to
explain itself in academic terms by framing literary texts within national
contexts" (571). See also Giles, rev. of *Through Other Continents: American*

Literature Across Deep Time, Modern Language Quarterly (December 2008): 569–572.

25. Limón notes the paucity of sustained studies of critical regionalism and points us to the then two extant monographs on the matter: Cheryl Temple Herr's *Critical Regionalism and Cultural Studies: From Ireland to the American Midwest* (Gainesville: University of Florida Press, 1996) and Douglas Reichert Powell's *Critical Regionalism: Connecting Politics and Culture in the American Landscape* (Chapel Hill: University of North Carolina Press, 2007). For a response to Limón's essay, see Richard T. Rodriguez's "Glocal Matters: A Response to José E. Limón," *Literary History* 20.1–2 (2008): 183–186. See also Krista Comer's review essay "Exceptionalism, Other Wests, Critical Regionalism," *American Literary History* 23.1 (Spring 2011): 159–173.

26. The interested reader may wish to see Fish's more recent work on sentences, *How to Write a Sentence and How to Read One* (New York: HarperCollins, 2011), which was written for a general audience. In addition, though her socioformal analysis runs at a slightly oblique angle to the formalist analysis I undertake, I want to single out Paula M. L. Moya's proposal for using schemas, a model she adopts from social and cultural psychology, to carry out close readings of texts. Moya's methodology is wonderfully attentive to how meaning is produced in the act of reading. She notes, "[S]*chema* refers to the active organization of past experiences (physical and emotional) and past reactions (sensory-motor and cognitive-affective) through which a person apprehends and interacts with incoming stimuli. . . . They are central to cognition insofar as they allow a person to 'go beyond the information given,' to fill in the gaps, and to extrapolate from what is known or from what is given to what might be apparent or might not yet have appeared" ("Resisting the Interpretive Schema of the Novel Form" 127). These schemas affect both what readers bring to "the scene of reading" and what gets "embedded into the works of literature through various aesthetic features" (128). For a detailed explanation of schemas and how they affect our reading, see Moya's formidable new book *The Social Imperative: Race, Close Reading, and Contemporary Literary Criticism* (Stanford, Calif.: Stanford University Press, 2016).

1. BROWN LIKE ME? THE AUTHOR-FUNCTION, PROPER NAMES, AND THE RISE OF FICTIONAL NOBODIES

1. He has recently published a memoir, *Take This Man* (New York: Simon and Schuster, 2014), about growing up with these five stepfathers. I discuss this at greater length later in this chapter.

2. Of the novel's continued success, I should note that it remains in print. In 1997, the well-respected industry magazine *Booklist* chose it as one of its twenty best adult books for young adults written between 1980 and

1990 (Editors' Choices 832+). And as of this writing, the novel—for a thirty-year-old book—maintains a not unrespectable selling rank on Amazon.com.

3. It bears noting that the then struggling writer Arturo Islas (a wonderfully talented author who has only achieved a minor status, even in the Chicanx canon) did not champion Santiago's novel. As John Alba Cutler points out, Islas submitted his review for the *San Francisco Chronicle Review* (May 1983) with a letter to the editor, noting that he "had a hard time with the novel because it's been published for the wrong reasons, i.e. gangs are in . . . but there are so many better, more interesting Chicano writers out there treating subjects that aren't filled with stereotypes." The letter continues,

> Look at this pathetic fact: in the last two years, the 'major' presses have published two books by writers of Mexican heritage born and brought up and educated in this country. One of them [Richard Rodriguez] hates his heritage and capitalizes on the backlash against affirmative action and bilingual programs; the other [Danny Santiago] writes about victimized, absolutely helpless Mexicans in a barrio. And *that* is the image the rest of the country gets of Mexican-Americans and Chicanos. I know it doesn't bother you as much as it bothers me and the *rest* of us who do *not* fall into either category and who have been working our asses off all our lives to rise above such stereotype [*sic*]. I am completely demoralized by this sad fact. (Cutler 95–96; emphasis in original)

4. Matters of fraud in the writing of memoirs and autobiography are of another piece altogether, for they present themselves as works of nonfiction. Thus, the convention to invoke a willing suspension of disbelief does not obtain. Consider the recent uproar when it was revealed that James Frey fabricated or embellished many of the key sections of *A Million Little Pieces*. Nonetheless, these are complicated matters as well, and anything beyond easy moralizing over the act of invention requires a supple mind and a study beyond the scope of this project. Consider, for instance, the complex case of Rigoberta Menchu's autobiography, *I, Rigoberta Menchu*. It was revealed that some of the atrocities she recounted in the story as having happened to her had not in fact happened to her. Did this make the autobiography a lie, a fraud? Were not the atrocities she detailed in fact representative instances of acts of violence committed by the Guatemalan military during the Guatemalan Civil War (1960–1996)?

5. So comfortably and playfully did he become the persona that after the "scandal" broke, he wrote an article for the *Los Angeles Times* on August 15, 1984—"Danny Santiago Makes a Call on Daniel James"—in which Danny Santiago interviews Daniel James about the novel and James's use of the name Danny Santiago.

6. This function is so entrenched for well-established authors (particularly genre authors) that they sometimes have to write under pseudonyms to be able to try something different in their writing.

7. By way of some hypothetical examples, Foucault, again, offers some interesting thoughts on the author-function and the identity of the author:

> To learn, for example that Pierre Dupont does not have blue eyes, does not live in Paris, and is not a doctor does not invalidate the fact that the name, Pierre Dupont, continues to refer to the same person; there has been no modification of the designation that links the name to the person. With the name of an author, however, the problems are far more complex. The disclosure that Shakespeare was not born in the house that tourists now visit would not modify the functioning of the author's name, but, if it were proved that he had not written the sonnets that we attribute to him, this would constitute a significant change and affect the manner in which the author's name functions. Moreover, if we established that Shakespeare wrote Bacon's *Organon* and that the same author was responsible for both the works of Shakespeare and those of Bacon, we would have introduced a third type of alteration which completely modifies the functioning of the author's name. Consequently, the name of an author is not precisely a proper name among others. (122)

8. While I don't, by any means, want to confuse Daniel James, who penned a work of fiction under the heteronym Danny Santiago, with those who write works of nonficiton—especially memoirs and autobiographies—under pseudonyms, I would like to underscore that James's political *bona fides* are radically distinct from those of someone like Asa Carter, who published *The Education of Little Tree* (1976), a memoir of his Cherokee boyhood, under the pseudonym Forrest Carter. In 1991, Dan T. Carter, a historian at Emory University, revealed that Forrest Carter was really Asa Carter, who "[b]etween 1946 and 1973 . . . carved out a violent career in Southern politics as a Ku Klux Klan terrorist, right-wing radio announcer, home-grown American fascist and anti-Semite, rabble-rousing demagogue and secret author of the famous 1963 speech by Gov. George Wallace of Alabama: 'Segregation now . . . Segregation tomorrow . . . Segregation forever'" (qtd. in Browder, *Slippery Characters* 1–2). For a fascinating study of Carter and other autobiographical impersonators, see Laura Browder's *Slippery Characters Ethnic Impersonators and American Identities* (Chapel Hill: University of North Carolina Press, 2000). *The Education of Little Tree* is still in print, including even a Kindle edition. As of this writing (December 27, 2016), it ranks 19,674 in Amazon Best Sellers.

9. As reported in the *New York Times* on July 22, 1984, James, even after his identity was revealed, was working on another novel under the penname

Danny Santiago. It also dealt with "a Mexican American theme" and was, too, set in Los Angeles. (McDowell, "Noted 'Hispanic' Novelist," A1). James died four years later, and that novel has never been published.

10. For an account of some of these low points, see Marcial González's *Chicano Novels and the Politics of Form: Race, Class, and Reification* (Ann Arbor: University of Michigan Press, 2009), 130–133, which also includes interesting excerpts from Richard Rodriguez's and Rolando Hinojosa-Smith's defense of the novel.

11. See also Jonathan Culler's *Structuralist Poetics Structuralism, Linguistics, and the Study of Literature* (Ithaca, N.Y.: Cornell University Press, 1975), esp. Chapter 9: "Poetics of the Novel."

12. Such blind tests have a long history around all sorts of products. I remember them best from the Pepsi/Coca-Cola challenges of my youth, but they also have a tie to more pressing cultural matters. Indeed, Henry Louis Gates, Jr., opens his essay "'Authenticity' or the Lesson of Little Tree," in *The Henry Louis Gates, Jr., Reader* (ed. Abby Wolf [New York: Basic Civitas, 2012]) with the following jazz anecdote:

> It's a perennial question: Can you really tell? The great black jazz trumpeter Roy Eldridge once made a wager with the critic Leonard Feather that he could distinguish white musicians from black ones—blindfolded. Mr. Feather duly dropped the needle on to a variety of record albums whose titles and soloists were concealed from the trumpeter. More than half the time, Eldridge guessed wrong. (515)

13. I should note as well that much of the writing from the Chicana/o movement years speaks singularly of *the* Chicano experience, as if it were a monolithic, not multiply variegated experience. Consider, for example, Antonio Márquez's essay "Literatura Chicanesca," in *A Decade of Chicano Literature (1970–1979)* (Santa Bárbara, Calif.: Editorial La Causa, 1982). In praising John Nichols's novels *The Milagro Beanfield War* (1974) and *The Magic Journey* (1978), he writes, "[H]is point of view is not from without but from within *the* Chicano experience. . . . Nichols' point of vantage informs his fiction with authenticity and a compelling rendering of *the* Chicano." (77; emphasis added).

14. The two extended scholarly treatments of the novel also deal with matters of authenticity—not only in terms of the authorship of the novel, but also in terms of how narratives of authenticity work in the novel itself. In *Slippery Characters*, Browder analyzes the at times antagonistic relation between acts of cultural translation and assimilation, pointing to a number of scenes in which characters work against the ethnic expectations with which other characters try to freight them. She argues, "Chato's success will

ultimately rest on his flexibility, his ability to translate himself from one culture to another, just as James's own success rested on the degree to which he convincingly translated himself into a new culture, and his voice into Santiago's. The successful characters in *Famous All Over Town* triumph through setting up expectations about their own ethnicity in the mind of their audience, and then defying those expectations" (247). While I agree with the evidence she employs to support her assertions about these acts of foiled cultural translation in the novel, I disagree with her reading the novel as an autobiography or even as an autobiographical novel. There is simply no evidence to support the conflation of Chato Medina with Danny Santiago or, by extension, Daniel James. Chato Medina is nothing other than the fictional nobody he is, and to miss that mark is for Browder to entangle herself in a narrative of authenticity that she is otherwise brilliant at unraveling in her study of "ethnic impersonators." To my mind, Marcial González's is the most sophisticated and forward-looking assessment of the novel. He offers a detailed account of the publishing history of the novel and then goes on to argue that "despite its marginality within Chicano literary studies, *Famous All Over Town* contributes to a comprehension of the possibilities and limits of Chicano novels insofar as it simultaneously represents Chicano experience and contests cultural authenticity, by which I mean the reification of ethnic identification categories" (114).

15. The historian Patricia Nelson Limerick writes, "If we describe James's relationship to Mexican American ethnicity purely in terms of trendy antimodernism, romantic racialism, or even a kinder, gentler cultural imperialism, we give a deep story a shallow meaning" (272).

16. Regarding the "sightlines" through which we come to see and interpret race, see Matthew Pratt Guterl's fine study *Seeing Race in Modern America* (Chapel Hill: University of North Carolina Press, 2013).

17. Morrissey maintains an extensive fan base among Latina/os. Indeed, his cult status among Latina/os is the subject of the documentary film *Is It Really So Strange?* (2004) by William E. Jones. Morrissey also surfaces a number of times in Skyhorse's novel.

18. On the tendency to see Latina/os in future time and the complications that renders for the writing of a Latinx literary history, see Kirsten Silva Gruez's essay, "The Once and Future Latino: Notes Toward a Literary History *todavía para llegar*," in *Contemporary U.S. Latino/a Literary Criticism*, ed. Lyn Di Iorio Sandín and Richard Perez (New York: Palgrave Macmillan, 2007), 115–142. She writes, "Although there is as yet no single work [that] has dared to call itself a Latino literary history, the work of constructing temporal paradigms for Latino textual expression is in effect being done by anthologies, textbooks, and encyclopedic reference works" (127). Although

not a complete history of Latinx literature, Raúl Coronado's recent magisterial tome, *A World Not to Come: A History of Latino Writing and Print Culture* (Cambridge, Mass.: Harvard University Press, 2013), offers a complex history of Latinx writing and print culture in the nineteenth century, particularly among Texas Mexicans.

19. It remains unclear in the memoir if Paul Skyhorse Johnson is actually Native American or if that is a created identity by either Maria or Maria and Paul. For more on this topic, see *Take This Man*, 30–31.

20. Theorizing notions of *family* and *father* lie outside the scope of this project, but I should note that Skyhorse repeatedly questions what these terms mean. There is, of course, a wealth of scholarship on the topic of family. For more on how I see it operating in Mexican American literature, see Chapter 2 of *Brown Gumshoes*. For an even broader discussion of family in Chicana/o culture, see Richard T. Rodriguez's *Next of Kin: The Family in Chicana/o Cultural Politics*.

21. On the concealing of his Mexican identity, see also *Take This Man*, 148–149.

22. "As I suggested rather sarcastically in my review of *Decade [of Chicano Literature (1970–1979)]* and the Márquez essay ["Literatura Chicanesqua" in *Decade*], maybe what we need is yet another category of 'casi-casis,' or 'almost-almosts' in English, for those authors who cannot pass the blood test, but whose writing is culturally and ethnically Chicano. . . . Our inability to submit authors to a *prueba de sangre* before nominating them for canonization can lead to embarrassing *faux pas*. La Casa de las Américas thought it was honoring another Chicano when it granted an award to Jaime Sagel (Sah HELL), aka Jim Sagel (SAY Guell), an Anglo-American who has performed the Amado-Muro rites of passage and then some—he actually has an advanced degree in Spanish and writes in an interlingual mixture of Spanish and English" (*Retrospace* 141).

23. Halfon will, no doubt, be the subject of much scholarly writing soon, but, as of yet, there are no critical academic articles or books on his work. Assessments of his now nearly ten novels take place in reviews and in interviews.

24. Halfon sounds here much like the writer Rubén Martínez—a native of Los Angeles and of Salvadoran and Mexican heritage—who writes in his book *The Other Side: Notes from the New L.A., Mexico City, and Beyond* (New York: Vintage Books, 1993), "Mine is the generation that arrived too late for Che Guevara but too early for the fall of the Berlin Wall. Weaned on a blend of cultures, languages, and ideologies (Anglo/Latino, Spanish/ English, individualist/collectivist), I have lived both in the North and the South over my twenty-nine years, trying to be South in the South, North in

the North, South in the North and North in the South. Now, I stand at the center—watching history whirl around me as my own history fissures: my love shatters, North and South, and a rage arises from within as the ideal of existential unity crumbles" (3).

25. Raymund A. Paredes, a distinguished Chicano critic, once wrote, "John Rechy's essay 'El Paso del Norte' certainly should be considered Chicano literature, but his novel *City of Night*, which is virtually devoid of ethnic content, probably should not" (74). ("The Evolution of Chicano Literature," in *Three American Literatures: Essays in Chicano, Native American, and Asian-American Literature for Teachers of American Literature*, ed. Houston A. Baker, Jr. [New York: MLA, 1982]).

26. When asked whether the book should be read as a novel or a short story collection, Halfon replied, "Whatever works best for you. I really enjoy that there are readers who will fight to the death defending this book as a short story collection. And there are the same number of readers who will fight to the death defending it as a novel. Or as a memoir. Or as autobiographical fiction. Or as nonfiction. That's great. Wherever you want to classify it. In whichever bookshelf you want to stash it" (Murphy, "Origin Stories," par. 29). While I appreciate Halfon's desire to blur boundaries, to push limits, I would add the caveat that while one may position it as one sees fit, how one regards it formally will shape its interpretive horizons.

27. This is not the space to rehearse or review all of the relevant criticism on this score, but a good starting point would include Brian McHale's *Postmodernist Fiction* (London and New York: Routledge, 1993); Linda Hutcheon's *A Poetics of Postmodernism: History, Theory, Fiction* (New York: Routledge, 1988); and Fredric Jameson's *Postmodernism, or, The Cultural Logic of Late Capitalism* (Durham, N.C.: Duke University Press, 1992), among many others.

28. See also Halfon's interviews with Barry, "Eduardo Halfon and *The Polish Boxer*," *3:AM Magazine*, May 29, 2013, http://www.3ammagazine.com/3am/eduardo-halfon-and-the-polish-boxer/ and Barnes, "No Borders: An Interview with Eduardo Halfon," *Sampsonia Way*, December 10, 2012, http://www.sampsoniaway.org/literary-voices/2012/12/10/no-borders-an-interview-with-eduardo-halfon/ for similar responses to this question of the two Halfons.

29. Brozgal notes, "The term *Beur* is used in France . . . to designate the first-generation, French-born children of North African nationals" ("Hostages of Authenticity," *French Forum* 34.2 [Spring 2009]: 127, n 3). For further elaboration of this term, see the remainder of Brozgal's footnote.

30. With this final question, Foucault is returning to one of the key earlier moments in the essay in which he invokes Beckett in response to the ethical

questions raised by the relationship that holds between author and text: "Beckett supplies a direction: 'What matter who's speaking, someone said, what matter who's speaking.' In an indifference such as this we must recognize one of the fundamental ethical principles of contemporary writing. It is not simply 'ethical' because it characterizes our way of speaking and writing, but because it stands as an immanent rule, endlessly adopted and yet never fully applied. As a principle, it dominates writing as an ongoing practice and slights our customary attention to the finished product" (115–116).

2. CONFOUNDING THE MIMETIC: THE METAFICTIONAL CHALLENGE TO REPRESENTATION

1. The principal difference between the two volumes is that, in the McSweeney's volume, Plascencia was allowed to use die-cuts to efface a certain character's name, and at Harcourt they opted instead to black out the name.

2. The McSweeney's description reads as follows: "Amidst disillusioned saints hiding in wrestling rings, mothers burnt by glowing halos, and a Baby Nostradmus who sees only blackness, a gang of flower pickers heads off to war, led by a lonely man who cannot help but wet his bed in sadness. Part memoir, part lies, this is a book about the wounds inflicted by first love and sharp objects" (n.p.).

3. Navarrette is the author of the memoir *A Darker Shade of Crimson: Odyssey of a Harvard Chicano* (1994).

4. I use quotation marks here because, asked in another interview how he felt about "experimental novel" as a label, Plascencia indicated that he was okay with it unless it was being used "as a warning to readers" (Stubbs, "An Interview with Salvador Plascencia," *Bookslut*, June 2006, http://www .bookslut.com/features/2006_06_009056.php).

5. Plascencia is indisputably correct that it is a minority of "Latinx writers" who have been published by the major New York houses. Most Latinx writing comes out with independent presses. However, the number of Latinx writers with major commercial presses exceeds the three authors who come to mind for Plascencia. Indeed, given that the interview is from 2010, it is surprising that he does not name Junot Díaz, who won the Pulitzer in 2008 and who had received a great deal of acclaim for his short story collection *Drown*, published in 1996. Other Latinx authors with mainstream presses include, but are not limited to, Julia Alvarez, Rudolfo A. Anaya, Ana Castillo, Denise Chavez, Cristina García, Ernesto Quiñonez, Ana Menéndez, Kirstin Valdez Quade, Manuel Gonzales, Abraham Rodriguez, Richard Rodriguez, Benjamin Alire Sáenz, Carolina Garcia-Aguilera, Cristina Henríquez, Alfredo Vea, and Angie Cruz.

6. Jeffrey T. Nealon writes eloquently on this topic in his books *Alterity Politics* and *Post-Postmodernism or, The Cultural Logic of Just-in-Time Capitalism* (Stanford, Calif.: Stanford University Press, 2012).

7. He left before completing his degree.

8. To be fair, such an argument would require much more space than Saldívar has in an essay that is examining both Plascencia's novel *and* Díaz's *The Brief Wondrous Life of Oscar Wao.*

9. For a representative sample of the treatment of the rose workers, see page 34 of *The People of Paper.*

10. One cannot, of course, read these scenes without calling to mind Manuel Puig's first novel *Betrayed by Rita Hayworth* (1968).

11. Similarly, the character Quiñones, in trying to verify the marriage license of Saturn and Cameroon, discovers it is a fabrication. The location of the wedding ceremony written on the marriage license "existed only in the imagination" (130), just as does *The People of Paper.*

12. I refer, of course to the *Verfremdungseffekt* (or alienation effect) of Brecht's epic theatre. This would be a familiar strategy in the Chicano theatre of Luis Valdez's Teatro Campesino.

13. For more on point of view and the doubling of Paul Auster, see William Lavender's essay "The Novel of Critical Engagement: Paul Auster's *City of Glass* (New York: Penguin Books, 1987)."

14. There is, of course, the highly interesting phenomenon of an author taking another author's character or storyline and retelling it from a different perspective—John Gardner's *Grendel*, J. M. Coetzee's *Foe*, Jean Rhys's *Wide Sargasso Sea*. The list is too long to elaborate exhaustively. I will, however, be working on a book-length study of these networked texts.

15. Prior to this chapter, there are only occasional references to Saturn in the columns marked "Saturn," and they could be read as references to the planet, not the narrator, whose name we know to be Saturn.

16. See Jean-Paul Sartre's *"What Is Literature?" and Other Essays* (Cambridge, Mass.: Harvard University Press, 1988). This argument was then further elaborated in the 1980s with the rise of Reader Response theory.

3. FROM WHERE I STAND: THE INTIMACY AND DISTANCE OF *WE* AND *YOU* IN THE SHORT STORY

1. One of the reasons for its deep roots in the United States is, in part, because the magazine industry here was willing to print short stories. Nineteenth-century British magazines did not. They published only serialized novels (Brander Matthews, "The Philosophy of the Short Story," 1885, in *Die Amerikanische Short Story*, ed. Hans Bungert [Darmstadet: Wissenshaftliche Buchgesellschaft, 1972], 24).

2. One can, of course, think of exceptions to this bias. Alice Munro, for instance, comes immediately to mind. She has built her entire, acclaimed career—which includes a Nobel Prize in Literature—around the short story.

3. Though not the focus of this chapter, critics have argued that the short story form bears a special relation to emerging national literatures and to "submerged population groups." On the former score, see Mary Louise Pratt's "The Short Story: The Long and Short of It," *Poetics* 10 (1981): 175–194. On the latter, see Frank O'Connor's *The Lonely Voice* (Cleveland and New York: The World Publishing Company, 1962). It also merits noting that with the explosion of MFA programs in the United States, the form is perhaps more robust than ever, as it is one of the staples of the MFA workshop and the many literary journals attached to those programs.

4. The eminent literary critic, book reviewer for *The New Yorker*, and novelist James Wood remarks on the atypical use of first-person plural and second-person singular points of view. He writes, "The house of fiction has many windows, but only two or three doors. I can tell a story in the third person or in the first person, and perhaps in the second person singular, or in the first person plural, though successful examples of these latter two are rare indeed" (*How Fiction Works* [New York: Farrar, Straus and Giroux, 2008], 3).

5. This chapter is not the space to do a full review of the literature on affect studies, nor, given that the book is not organized around the concept of affect, do I want to belabor a comprehensive evaluation of the field. I do, however, wish to point out that, given the relative youth of this theoretical model (most date it back to Lawrence Grossberg's discussion of affect in *We Gotta Get Out of this Place: Popular Conservatism and Postmodern Culture* [1992], though he had been writing about affect and rock music since the 1980s), the use of even basic terms—affect, emotion, and feeling—are not uniform throughout the literature. Deborah Gould, in *Moving Politics: Emotion and Act Up's Fight Against AIDS* (Chicago: University of Chicago Press, 2009), is especially good at trying to nail down the distinction among the terms, but not everyone in the field observes the meaningful distinctions she generates. Many point to *affect* as the prelinguistic and precognitive feeling one has in one's body in reaction to a given event and that the conscious realization of that feeling is what we call *emotion*.
As Gregory J. Seigworth and Melissa Gregg note in the introduction to *The Affect Theory Reader*, "There is no single, generalizable theory of affect: not yet and (thankfully) there never will be. If anything, it is more tempting to imagine that there can only ever be infinitely multiple iterations of affect and theories of affect: theories as diverse and singularly delineated as their own highly particular encounters with bodies, affects, worlds" (3–4; loc 84–88). It is clear from their introduction that their own theorizing of affect

is greatly influenced by Deleuze and Guattari and Brian Massumi. As they rightly point out, Eve Sedgwick and Adam Frank's essay "Shame in the Cybernetic Fold" and Brian Massumi's essay, "The Autonomy of Affect," have greatly influenced the field since their publication in 1995. The two essays took their theoretical cues from Silvan Tomkins and Gilles Deleuze (5–6; loc 105–116).

I encourage the interested reader to peruse Seigworth and Gregg's interesting introduction. Given its publication by Duke University Press, its list of illustrious contributors, and its status as one of the first readers in the field, it will be an influential and oft-cited volume. Thus, I offer the following as a glimpse into their understanding of what constitutes affect: "Affect is an impingement or extrusion of a momentary or sometimes more sustained state of relation *as well as* the passage (and the duration of passage) of forces of intensities that pass body to body (human, nonhuman, part-body, and otherwise), in those resonances that circulate about, between, and sometimes stick to bodies and worlds, *and* in the very passages or variations between these intensities and resonances themselves" (1; loc 51–54; emphasis in original).

While I can appreciate the visceral, liminal, and relational qualities of affect, I cannot grasp from Seigworth and Geigg's introduction what precisely constitutes affect and what distinguishes it from feelings and emotions. Indeed, as relates to the current state of the field, I do not find the distinctions between affect and emotion especially clarifying. While I know as a living human being I have such corporal feelings in response to an event, I see no way to speak of a fictive character in such terms. Thus, when I speak of "affective dimensions," I mean the emotional experience of the characters. Furthermore, I often use *affect* and *emotion* interchangeably. I feel in good company here, for even Sianne Ngai, one of the leading practitioners of affect studies, in *Ugly Feelings* (especially the layout of her theoretical framework in the book's introduction) uses *feeling*, *affect*, and *emotion* interchangeably.

6. Janice Radway's *Reading the Romance: Women, Patriarchy, and Popular Literature* (Chapel Hill: University of North Carolina Press, 1984) remains a notable exception. In his *Life in Search of Readers: Reading (in) Chicano/a Literature* (Albuquerque: University of New Mexico Press, 2003), Manuel Martín-Rodriguez, has educated us on the readership of Chicanx literature. His is not, however, an ethnographic study. My former dissertation student, Dr. Felicia Salinas, has done an ethnographic study of Latinx readers in her unpublished dissertation "Latina Imprints and Impressions: A Study of Contemporary Popular Fiction for Latina Readers."

7. Please see note 26 in the Introduction, where the concept of "schemas" is defined.

8. Although I do not employ Moya's lexicon of schemas in my reading practice, I want to note that she produces an impressive interpretation of the title story of Muñoz's collection *Zigzagger*. She analyzes it as a retelling of the classic dancing-with-the-devil folktale and maintains, "[I]ts moral points not to the limits of Mexican American female desire and agency in a race-, class-, and gender-stratified world, but rather to a whole world of transformational possibilities—of alternative forms of Chicano masculinity; of the acceptance of homosexuality in Mexican American communities; of honest, open, and loving communication between family members of all genders and sexualities; and of gay Chicana/o self-love. The story further speaks to the importance of challenging our society's assumptions about what is good and what is evil" (105).

9. While I recognize that as a possible response, I am not, by any means, justifying such a hostile, homophobic reaction.

10. This is, of course, not an exhaustive reading of first-person plural and second-person-singular narration. It is, however, a suggestive and representative analysis.

11. For a reading that is wonderfully attentive to narrative technique in Muñoz's stories "Good as Yesterday," "The Unimportrant Lila Parr," and "Zigzagger," see Ernesto Martinez's essay "Shifting the Site of Queer Enunciation: Manuel Muñoz and the Politics of Form," in *Gay Latino Studies: A Critical Reader*, ed. Michael Hames-García and Ernesto Javier Martínez (Durham, N.C.: Duke University Press, 2011), 226–249.

12. Indeed, in the entire collection hardly a character, including minor ones, is introduced without making note of their nationality—the "Peruvian-Japonesa" maid (79), the McAllisters—"former Hell's Kitchen Irish folks" (81), Maureen Reilly who has "thick ankles and black hair from her Portuguese mom, freckled like a dalmation thanks to her Irish dad" (48), the Mexican and Nicaraguan "girls" Sabina beats out to be with her Hungarian boyfriend in the story "Vida" (119–120), the employee Sabina replaces in the story "Refuge" is referred to as "[t]he Polish girl" (32), and on and on. Engel, of course, describes her characters in other fashions, but there is a notable attention to nationality.

13. For a candid nonfiction exploration of eating disorders, see Marya Hornbacher's *Wasted: A Memoir of Anorexia and Bulimia*. It remains one of the most painful, revealing, and insightful accounts I have read on the topic.

14. While I am on the topic of envy, I should point out the connection of the story's title to envy. I think, however, it would be a bit much to take the color symbolism too far. We can and do associate the color green with both envy and new life (growth). They are themes that we see in the story. Furthermore, we know that everything about a story is an author's choosing.

The story is titled "Green" because it was the color of the sweater Maureen was wearing the day the two women met at the diner, and for that reason, Sabina will "always remember her in green" (55). Engel could just as easily have put Maureen in a different color sweater. The story could be "Orange," "Black," "Red," and so forth. Thus, one could make much of the authorial choice to title the story after the color of the sweater in which Engel has placed her character. Aside, however, from briefly making note of the color and its symbolic connections, I will leave a more detailed analysis of color and symbolism to a critic more interested in those matters.

15. We know nothing from the story about the gender of the partner, the *you*. Thus, when necessary in my analysis, to refer to the partner, I will use the gender neutral pronoun *they*.

16. We hear echoes here of the symbolic greenness that I said I did not care to make overly much of when analyzing Engel's story. See note 14.

4. THE LYRIC, OR, A RADICAL SINGULARITY IN LATINX VERSE

1. See also Jackson's working definition of the *lyric* in the *Princeton Encyclopedia of Poetry and Poetics*.

2. Virginia Jackson brilliantly shows how we came to read Emily Dickinson's poem 2 in the Thomas H. Johnson's *The Poems of Emily Dickinson*. That poem, which begins "There is another sky," was "'arbitrarily established' as a lyric in 1955." Prior to that, the "poem" existed as the final lines (absent the visual layout that aids us in understanding it as a poem) in Dickinson's letter to her brother Austin (*Dickinson's Misery: A Theory of Lyric Reading* [Princeton, N.J.: Princeton University Press, 2005], 3–6).

3. Phillips served as the contest judge the year Corral's collection won the Yale Series of Younger Poets Prize.

4. See, for instance, Corral's website, Lorcaloca.com. The assertion also comes up in numerous interviews with Corral.

5. In an interview with *Poetry* magazine, Corral speaks of Hayden's vexed relation to his sexuality and how he connects to Hayden as one of his queer forefathers: "Hayden never publicly acknowledged his struggles with his sexuality. Arnold Rampersad's introduction to the *Collected Poems* touches upon this reticence. The scholar Pontheolla T. Williams, in *Robert Hayden: A Critical Analysis of His Poetry*, mentions the 'wracking trauma that Hayden suffered as a bisexual.' I understand Hayden lived in a different time. Sometimes it was not possible to live as a gay/bisexual man. But Hayden also seemed to believe his sexuality was a sin. He believed the cancer that claimed his life was a punishment for his orientation. As an out-and-proud gay man, this saddens me. This sadness overwhelms me each time I read his work. To counter this sadness, to claim Hayden as one of my queer forefathers, I wrote

a poem in which Hayden has an intimate encounter with another man. Not a stranger, but a man he already knows. The pin in the shape of an ampersand speaks to this familiarity. Hayden, in this poem, doesn't fear or detest his desires. This comforts me as a gay man and as a poet who adores his work." http://www.poetryfoundation.org/poemcomment/243160.

6. Speaking of the importance of form to an assessment of African American poetry and aesthetics, Evie Shockley notes, "The deep attention to form that the investigation into black aesthetics invites is as critical as the emphasis it places on historical context and individual identity. Criticism of African American poetry too often treats the art as if it can be reduced to antiracist slogans" (*Renegade Poetics: Black Aesthetics and Formal Innovation in African American Poetry* [Iowa City: University of Iowa Press, 2011], 197).

7. Corral's full response is as follows: "Dear Young Chicano/a Poet, The literary life is hard work. Read, read, and then write. Revise. Poems can be biographical and imaginary, culture-specific and universal. Your Abuela is not special. Read the world. Open your mental veins. Synthesize. Absorb Hamlet. Read the African American canon. Note how African American poets incorporate their history, their vernacular, their music into their work. Steal, steal, steal. Distill. Absorb the literary work of your culture. Figurative language need not be pretty. Adopt. Duende is like the Force from Star Wars. Obsess over several poets. Absorb Robert Hayden. Reject some aspects of your culture. Language is Queen. Lie. It all has been done before, but not by you. Adapt."

Similarly, the poet Rigoberto González notes, "Those versed in Latino letters will recognize the obligatory 'abuelita poem,' which is by now nothing short of a poetic cliché: a poem that reaches back to the sentimentalized past in order to present a view of the 'old ways,' most likely back in the homeland" ("Introduction to J. Michael Martinez" 125).

8. Loffreda and Rankine also note in their introduction that "It should be difficult to write what one knows—and if it's too easy, it is worth asking if that is because one is reproducing conventions and assumptions rewarded by the marketplace of literature" (*Racial Imaginary: Writers on Race in the Life of the Mind* [Albany, N.Y.: Fence Books, 2015], 18).

9. This is the final stanza of MacLeish's "Ars Poetica."

10. The particular example that Fish uses to make his point is a sentence from Dylan Thomas: "This at least of flame-like, our life has, that it is but the concurrence, renewed from moment to moment, of forces parting sooner or later on their ways" (134–135). After a careful parsing of this sentence, Fish concludes that the sentence's "refusal to mean in [a] discursive way creates the experience that is its meaning; and an analysis of that

experience rather than of its logical content is able to make sense of one kind—experiential sense—out of nonsense" (135).

11. From Rosa Alcalá's "Mimicry," in *Undocumentaries* (Exeter: Shearsman Books, 2010), 48.

12. The poems from the chapbook are included in *The Lust of Unsentimental Waters*.

13. "Undocumentary," the single long poem that constitutes the section called "Undocumentary," cleverly and poignantly incorporates the title of the remaining four sections into itself.

14. In her recent memoir/autotheory *The Argonauts*, Maggie Nelson offers this useful reminder on presence: "Sometimes one has to know something many times over. Sometimes one forgets, and then remembers. And then forgets, and then remembers. And then forgets again. As with knowledge, so, too, with presence" (18–19).

15. On this wrestling with the contempt for contemporary poetry, see Ben Lerner's recent essay, "Diary."

16. It bears mention that in order to get the line from Whitman to work with this gendered critique, Alcalá has to remove the male worker—"the weaver at his loom"—from Wordsworth's original line, hence the ellipsis.

17. In *Orientals: Asian Americans in Popular Culture* (Philadelphia: Temple University Press, 1999), Robert G. Lee equates the cutting of the "Chinaman's pigtail" with the practice of scalping, and in so doing, dispels the myth of scalping. He writes, "The cutting of the Chinaman's pigtail allowed white men in the mid and late nineteenth century to reenact, at least at a symbolic level, an earlier savage eighteenth-century American ritual—scalping. Indeed, the cutting of queues in conjunction with the collection of taxes is reminiscent of the taking of Indian scalps for bounty, a popular practice among English colonists on the old frontier. . . . Just as the taking of Indian scalps by their colonial forebears was lost to historical amnesia and laid at the doorstep of the savage red man, the practice of cutting off the Chinaman's queue was an opportunity to bring the specter of the 'savage' Indian back into the narrative of race relations" (40).

18. Alcalá gleaned this dialogue from Neff's book *Victorian Working Women*.

19. Phone conversation with Amanda Calderon (June 26, 2015).

20. Though we are using it differently, I borrow this wonderful phrase from Bonnie Costello's essay "Jorie Graham: Art and Erosion."

CONCLUSION: THINKING BEYOND LIMITS

1. The poet and literary critic Harryette Mullen's words come to mind here. She writes, "As an African Americanist, I am aware that my scholarly

discipline depends, in part, on defining what is distinct, particular, and continuous about our literary and cultural heritage; yet it concerns me to see how frequently even editors and critics with the best intentions participate in draining the category 'black' or 'African American' of its complex internal diversity by removing from the category anything so eccentric or innovative that it subverts a 'traditional' or 'canonical' notion of black or African American heritage" (11).

2. Tom McCarthy, the author of the novels *Remainder* (2006), *C* (2010), and most recently *Satin Island* (2016), suggests, in his interview with Michael Silverblatt, that we conceive literature as an elaborate network. In her recent book *Forms: Whole, Rhythm, Hierarchy, Network* (Princeton, N.J.: Princeton University Press, 2015), Caroline Levine proposes a formidably engaging methodology to understand how both aesthetic and social forms act in the world together. Each of the items in her subtitle is an individual form, and she is interested in how these forms overlap, nest in one another, and often collide. "[N]o form, however seemingly powerful, causes, dominates, or organizes all others" (16). Thus, she defines the goals of her book as twofold: First, she wants to "show that forms are everywhere structuring and patterning experience, and that this carries serious implications for understanding political communities" and second, she wants to "think about the ways that, together, the multiple forms of the world come into conflict and disorganize experience in ways that call for unconventional political strategies" (16–17). This cursory description cannot capture all of the excitement and nuance of Levine's project. I encourage the interested reader to take up the book in its entirety. After carefully working through *whole*, *rhythm*, *hierarchy*, and *network*, it concludes with a chapter that shows her methodology at work in interpreting *The Wire*. Though it has had much less of an impact on my thought process about networks, I would be remiss not to mention Bruno Latour's book *Reassembling the Social: An Introduction to Actor-Network Theory* (Oxford: Oxford University Press, 2005). Similarly, in his much earlier *Literature as System* (Princeton, N.J.: Princeton University Press, 1971), Claudio Guillén analyzes literature as a system, but his interests are more literary historical than mine.

3. Information for this section has been gathered from their website (http://www.backporchcollective.com/) and from personal conversations with many of the authors, particularly with Dariel Suarez.

4. I have already mentioned some of the topics covered in Manuel Gonzales's stories. The Eric Garcia novels I have in mind are his Vincent Rubio detective ones, the conceit of which is that dinosaurs are not extinct, but rather roam the world in human drag. They include *Anonymous Rex* (2000), *Casual Rex* (2001), and *Hot and Sweaty Rex* (2004).

Abrams, Garry. "The Three Lives of Dan James." *Los Angeles Times*, June 19, 1988. Electronic.

Acosta, Oscar Zeta. *Revolt of the Cockroach People*. New York: Vintage Books, 1989.

Alcalá, Rosa. *The Lust of Unsentimental Waters*. Exeter: Shearsman Books, 2012.

———. *Undocumentaries*. Exeter: Shearsman Books, 2010.

Aldama, Frederick Luis. *Brown on Brown: Chicano/a Representations of Gender, Sexuality, and Ethnicity*. Austin: University of Texas Press, 2005.

———. *The Routledge Concise History of Latino/a Literature*. New York: Routledge, 2013.

———. *Your Brain on Latino Comics: From Gus Arriola to Los Bros Hernandez*. Austin: University of Texas Press, 2009.

Allatson, Paul. "From 'Latinidad' to 'Latinid@des': Imagining the Twenty-First Century." In *The Cambridge Companion to Latina/o American Literature*. Ed. John Morán González. New York: Cambridge University Press, 2016.

Anderson, Benedict. *Imagined Communities: Reflections on the Origin and Spread of Nationalism*. London: Verso, 1991.

Alvarez, Julia. *Something to Declare*. New York: Plume, 1999.

Aparicio, Frances R. "Loisaida Literature." In *A New Literary History of America*. Ed. Greil Marcus and Werner Sollors. Cambridge, Mass.: The Belknap Press of Harvard University Press, 2009.

Aragón, Francisco. "Latino/a Poetry Now: 3 Poets Discuss Their Art." Last accessed June 1, 2015. https://www.poetrysociety.org/psa/poetry/crossroads/interviews/roundtable_talk/.

———, ed. *The Wind Shifts: New Latino Poetry*. Tucson: University of Arizona Press, 2007.

Aranda, José F. *When We Arrive: A New Literary History of Mexican America*. Tucson: University of Arizona Press, 2003.

Arias, Ron. *The Road to Tamazunchale*. Tempe, Ariz.: Bilingual Press, 1997.

Arroyo, Rane. "The Book of Names." In *Home Movies of Narcissus*. Tucson: University of Arizona Press, 2002.

Auster, Paul. *City of Glass*. New York: Penguin Books, 1987.

Baker, Matthew. "An Interview with Salvador Plascencia." *Nashville Review*, April 1, 2010. Last accessed April 21, 2014. https://as.vanderbilt.edu/nashvillereview/archives/1084.

Baker Sotelo, Susan. *Chicano Detective Fiction: A Critical Study of Five Novelists*. Jefferson, N.C.: McFarland and Co., 2005.

Barnes, Joshua. "No Borders: An Interview with Eduardo Halfon." *Sampsonia Way*, December 10, 2012. Last accessed January 21, 2014. http://www.sampsoniaway.org/literary-voices/2012/12/10/no-borders-an-interview-with-eduardo-halfon/.

Barry, Des. "Eduardo Halfon and *The Polish Boxer*." *3:AM Magazine*, May 29, 2013. Last accessed January 22, 2014. http://www.3ammagazine.com/3am/eduardo-halfon-and-the-polish-boxer/.

Behar, Ruth. "Juban América." *Poetics Today* 16.1 (Spring 1995): 151–170.

Beltrán, Cristina. "Crossings and Correspondence: Rethinking Intersectionality and the Category 'Latino.'" *Politics and Gender* 9.4 (December 2013): 479–483.

———. *The Trouble with Unity: Latino Politics and the Creation of Identity*. Oxford: Oxford University Press, 2010.

Benavidez, Max. "Salvador Plascencia." *BOMB Magazine* 98 (Winter 2007). Last accessed April 21, 2014. http://bombmagazine.org/article/2877/salvador-plascencia.

Best, Stephen, and Sharon Marcus. "Surface Reading: An Introduction." *Representations* 108.1 (Fall 2009): 1–20.

Bhabha, Homi K., ed. *Nation and Narration*. New York: Routledge, 1990.

Biggers, Jeff. "More Than Measuring Up: An Interview with Alfredo Vea." *The Bloomsbury Review* 20.1 (January/February 2000).

Borland, Isabel Alvarez. *Cuban-American Literature of Exile: From Person to Persona*. Charlottesville: University of Virginia Press, 1998.

Borland, Isabel Alvarez, and Lynette M. F. Bosch, eds. *Cuban-American Literature and Art: Negotiating Identities*. Albany: State University of New York Press, 2009.

Bost, Suzanne, and Frances R. Aparicio, eds. *The Routledge Companion to Latino/a Literature*. New York: Routledge, 2012.

Brady, Mary Pat. *Extinct Land, Temporal Geographies: Chicana Literature and the Urgency of Space*. Durham, N.C.: Duke University Press, 2002.

Browder, Laura. *Slippery Characters: Ethnic Impersonators and American Identities*. Chapel Hill: University of North Carolina Press, 2000.

Brozgal, Lia. "Hostages of Authenticity: Paul Smaïl, Azouz Begag, and the Invention of the Beur Author." *French Forum* 34.2 (Spring 2009): 113–130.

Bruce-Novoa, Juan. *Chicano Poetry: A Response to Chaos.* Austin: University of Texas Press, 1982.

———. *Retrospace: Collected Essays on Chicano Literature.* Houston: Arte Público, 1990.

Burt, Stephen. *Close Calls with Nonsense: Reading New Poetry.* Minneapolis: Graywolf, 2009.

Bury, Liz. "J. K. Rowling Tells Story of Alter Ego Robert Galbraith." *Guardian*, July 24, 2013. Last accessed January 1, 2014. https://www.theguardian .com/books/2013/jul/24/jk-rowling-robert-galbraith-harry-potter.

Calderon, Amanda. "Composite Tiger." *Kenyon Review* 37.2 (March/ April 2015). Last accessed December 28, 2016. http://www.kenyonreview .org/journal/marapr-2015/selections/amanda-calderon/.

———. "Just Before the Ape." *Poets House.* Poetshouse.org. Last accessed December 28, 2016. https://www.poetshouse.org/programs-and-events/ workshops-classes-residencies/emerging-poets-residency/amanda -calderon.

Caminero-Santangelo, Marta. *On Latinidad: U.S. Latina Literature and the Construction of Ethnicity.* Gainesville: University Press of Florida, 2007.

Campo, Rafael. *What the Body Told.* Durham, N.C.: Duke University Press, 1996.

Cantú, Norma Elia. "Latin@ Poetics." In *The Cambridge Companion to Latina/o American Literature.* Ed. John Morán González. New York: Cambridge University Press, 2016.

Carter, Forrest (Asa Carter). *The Education of Little Tree.* 1976. Albuquerque: University of New Mexico Press, 2001.

Castillo, Ana. *I Ask the Impossible.* New York: Anchor Books, 2001.

Chabram-Dernersesian, Angie. "'Chicana! Rican? No, Chicana Riqueña!'": Refashioning the Transnational Connection." In *Between Women and Nation: Nationalisms, Transnational Feminisms, and the State.* Ed. Caren Kaplan et al. Durham, N.C.: Duke University Press, 1999.

Christian, Karen. *Show and Tell: Identity as Performance in U.S. Latina/o Fiction.* Albuquerque: University of New Mexico Press, 1997.

Cockburn, Alexander. "Naming as a Ritual." *The Nation* 4–11 August 1984.

Cole, Teju. "The White-Savior Industrial Complex." *Atlantic*, March 21, 2012. Last accessed May 23, 2016. https://www.theatlantic.com/ international/archive/2012/03/the-white-savior-industrial-complex/ 254843/.

Comer, Krista. "Exceptionalism, Other Wests, Critical Regionalism." *American Literary History* 23.1 (Spring 2011): 159–173.

Coronado, Raúl. *A World Not to Come: A History of Latino Writing and Print Culture.* Cambridge, Mass.: Harvard University Press, 2013.

Corral, Eduardo C. *The Border Triptych.* Last accessed July 15, 2014. http://
www.webdelsol.com/LITARTS/CORRAL/corralinterview.htm
———. *Slow Lightning.* New Haven, Conn.: Yale University Press, 2012.
Costello, Bonnie. "Jorie Graham: Art and Erosion." *Contemporary Literature*
33.2 (Summer 1992): 373–395.
Culler, Jonathan. *The Literary in Theory.* Stanford, Calif.: Stanford University Press, 2007.
———. *Structuralist Poetics: Structuralism, Linguistics, and the Study of
Literature.* Ithaca, N.Y.: Cornell University Press, 1975.
Cutler, John Alba. *Ends of Assimilation: The Formation of Chicano Literature.*
Oxford and New York: Oxford University Press, 2015.
Dalleo, Raphael, and Elena Machado Sáez. *The Latino/a Canon and the
Emergence of Post-Sixties Literature.* New York: Palgrave Macmillan,
2007.
Dávila, Arlene. *Latinos, Inc.: The Marketing and Making of a People.* Berkeley
and Los Angeles: University of California Press, 2001.
DeGuzmán, María. *Buenas Noches, American Culture: Latina/o Aesthetics of
Night.* Bloomington: Indiana University Press, 2012.
Delgadillo, Theresa. *Spiritual Mestizaje: Religion, Gender, Race, and Nation
in Contemporary Chicana Narrative.* Durham, N.C.: Duke University
Press, 2011.
Díaz, Jaquira. "The Next Literary Superstar: An Interview with Patricia
Engel." *Saw Palm: Florida Literature and Art* 5 (Spring 2011). http://www
.sawpalm.org/interview-with-patricia-engel.html.
Diaz, Junot. *The Brief Wondrous Life of Oscar Wao.* New York: Riverhead
Books, 2008.
———. "Introduction." *The Best American Short Stories 2016.* Ed. Junot Díaz
with Heidi Pitlor. Boston: Houghton Mifflin Harcourt, 2016.
Dimock, Wai Chee. *Through Other Continents: American Literature Across
Deep Time.* Princeton, N.J.: Princeton University Press, 2006.
Dowdy, Michael. *Broken Souths: Latina/o Poetic Responses to Neoliberalism and
Globalization.* Tucson: University of Arizona Press, 2013.
Dufresne, John. *The Lie that Tells a Truth.* New York: W. W. Norton & Co.,
2003.
Dunne, John Gregory. "The Secret of Danny Santiago." *New York Review of
Books,* August 16, 1984. Electronic.
DuPlessis, Rachel Blau. *Blue Studios: Poetry and Its Cultural Work.* Tuscaloosa: University of Alabama Press, 2006.
Engel, Patricia. *It's Not Love, It's Just Paris.* New York: Grove Press, 2013.
———. *The Veins of the Ocean.* New York: Grove Press, 2016.
———. *Vida.* New York: Grove Press, 2010.

Espada, Martín. *Imagine the Angels of Bread*. New York: W. W. Norton & Co., 1997.

Everett, Percival. *Erasure*. Minneapolis: Graywolf, 2001.

Falco, Susan. "Interview: Patricia Engel." *Gulf Stream Magazine Online*. No. 4 (2010). Electronic.

Fish, Stanley. *How to Write a Sentence and How to Read One*. New York: HarperCollins, 2011.

———. *Is There a Text in This Class? The Authority of Interpretive Communities*. Cambridge, Mass.: Harvard University Press, 1980.

———. "Literature in the Reader: Affective Stylistics." *New Literary History* (1970): 123–162.

Flores, Juan. *From Bomba to Hip-Hop: Puerto Rican Culture and Latino Identity*. New York: Columbia University Press, 2000.

Flores, Lauro. "El Pueblo: The Gallegos Family's American Journey, 1503–1980, and: Famous All Over Town, and: Chicano Poetry: A Response to Chaos." *Minnesota Review* 22 (Spring 1984): 145–148.

Forster, E. M. *Aspects of the Novel*. New York: Mariner Books, 1985.

Foucault, Michel. "What Is an Author?" In *Language, Counter-Memory, Practice: Selected Essays and Interviews*. Trans. Donald F. Bouchard and Sherry Simon. Ithaca, N.Y.: Cornell University Press, 1980.

Frey, James. *A Million Little Pieces*. New York: Anchor Books, 2005.

Gallagher, Catherine. "The Rise of Fictionality." In *The Novel*. Vol. 1. Ed. Franco Moretti. Princeton, N.J.: Princeton University Press, 2006.

Garcia, Eric. *Anonymous Rex*. New York: Berkley Books, 2000.

———. *Casual Rex*. New York: Berkley Books, 2001.

———. *Hot and Sweaty Rex*. New York: Villard, 2004.

Gardiner, Michael. *The Consitution of English Literature: The State, the Nation and the Canon*. London and New York: Bloomsbury, 2012.

Gardner, John. *The Art of Fiction*. New York: Vintage Books, 1985.

Gates, Jr., Henry Louis. "'Authenticity' or the Lesson of Little Tree." In *The Henry Louis Gates, Jr., Reader*. Ed. Abby Wolf. New York: Basic Civitas, 2012.

Genette, Gerard. *Narrative Discourse*. Ithaca, N.Y.: Cornell University Press, 1979.

Giles, Paul. Rev. of *Through Other Continents: American Literature Across Deep Time*. *Modern Language Quarterly* (December 2008): 569–572.

Giménez Smith, Carmen, and John Chávez, eds. *Angels of the Americlypse: An Anthology of New Latin@ Writing*. Denver, Colo.: Counterpath, 2014.

Gonzales, Manuel. *The Miniature Wife and Other Stories*. New York: Riverhead Books, 2013.

González, Marcial. *Chicano Novels and the Politics of Form: Race, Class, and Reification.* Ann Arbor: University of Michigan Press, 2009.

González, Rigoberto. "Introduction to J. Michael Martinez." In *Angels of the Americlypse: An Anthology of New Latin@ Writing.* Ed. Carmen Giménez Smith and John Chávez. Denver, Colo.: Counterpath, 2014.

Gonzalez, Veronica. "Interview with Michael Silverblatt." KCRW's *Bookworm.* November 1, 2007.

————. *twin time: or, how death befell me.* Los Angeles: Semiotext(e), 2007.

Gould, Deborah. *Moving Politics: Emotion and Act Up's Fight Against AIDS.* Chicago: University of Chicago Press, 2009.

Greenbaum, Sidney, and Randolph Quirk. *A Student's Grammar of the English Language.* Essex: Longman, 1990.

Gregg, Melissa, and Gregory J. Seigworth. *The Affect Theory Reader.* Durham, N.C.: Duke University Press, 2010. Electronic.

Grossberg, Lawrence. *We Gotta Get Out of This Place: Popular Conservatism and Postmodern Culture.* New York: Routledge, 1992.

Grossman, Allen. *The Sighted Singer: Two Works on Poetry for Writers and Readers.* Baltimore: Johns Hopkins University Press, 1991.

Guillén, Claudio. *Literature as System: Essays Toward the Theory of Literary History.* Princeton, N.J.: Princeton University Press, 1971.

Guterl, Matthew Pratt. *Seeing Race in Modern America.* Chapel Hill: University of North Carolina Press, 2013.

Halfon, Eduardo. *El ángel literario.* Barcelona: Anagrama, 2004.

————. *El boxeador polaco.* Valencia: Pre-Textos, 2008.

————. *La pirueta.* Valencia: Pre-Textos, 2010.

————. *Mañana nunca lo hablamos.* Valencia: Pre-Textos, 2011.

————. *The Polish Boxer.* New York: Bellevue Literary Press, 2012.

Hall, Stuart. "Subjects in History: Making Diasporic Identities." In *The House that Race Built.* Ed. Wahneema Lubiano. New York: Vintage Books, 1998: 289–299.

Hames-García, Michael, and Ernesto Javier Martínez, eds. *Gay Latino Studies: A Critical Reader.* Durham, N.C.: Duke University Press, 2011.

Herr, Cheryl Temple. *Critical Regionalism and Cultural Studies: From Ireland to the American Midwest.* Gainesville: University of Florida Press, 1996.

Herrera-Sobek, María. *The Mexican Corrido: A Feminist Analysis.* Bloomington: Indiana University Press, 1990.

Hirsch, Edward. *How to Read a Poem and Fall in Love with Poetry.* New York: Harcourt, 1999.

Horkheimer, Max, and Theodor W. Adorno. *Dialectic of Enlightenment: Philosophical Fragments.* Stanford, Calif.: Stanford University Press, 2007.

Hornbacher, Marya. *Wasted: A Memoir of Anorexia and Bulimia.* New York: Harper Perennial, 1998.

Howe, Marie. *What the Living Do: Poems.* New York: W. W. Norton & Co., 1999.

Hutcheon, Linda. *A Poetics of Postmodernism: History, Theory, Fiction.* New York: Routledge, 1988.

Jackson, Virginia. *Dickinson's Misery: A Theory of Lyric Reading.* Princeton, N.J.: Princeton University Press, 2005.

———. "Lyric." In *Princeton Encyclopedia of Poetry and Poetics.* 4th Edition. Ed. Roland Greene et al. Princeton, N.J.: Princeton University Press, 2012.

Jameson, Fredric. *The Political Unconscious: Narrative as a Socially Symbolic Act.* Ithaca, N.Y.: Cornell University Press, 1981.

———. *Postmodernism, or, the Cultural Logic of Late Capitalism.* Durham, N.C.: Duke University Press, 1992.

Jones, William E. *Is It Really So Strange?* 2004.

Journey, Anna. "Watermark and Fable: Eduardo Corral's *Slow Lightning.*" *Kenyon Review* (Winter 2013). Last accessed July 22, 2014. http://www .kenyonreview.org/kr-online-issue/2013-winter/selections/slow-lightning -by-eduardo-c-corral-738439/#.

Kanellos, Nicolás. *Hispanic American Literature.* NY: HarperCollins, 1995.

Kaplan, Amy. *The Anarchy of Empire in the Making of U.S. Culture.* Cambridge, Mass.: Harvard University Press, 2005.

Klein, Michael. "Five for Eduardo C. Corral." *Ploughshares Literary Magazine,* May 16, 2012. Last accessed August 8, 2014. http://blog.pshares.org/ index.php/five-for-eduardo-c-corral/.

Latour, Bruno. *Reassembling the Social: An Introduction to Actor-Network Theory.* Oxford: Oxford University Press, 2005.

Lavender, William. "The Novel of Critical Engagement: Paul Auster's *City of Glass.*" *Contemporary Literature* 34.2 (Summer 1993): 219–239.

Lee, Robert G. *Orientals: Asian Americans in Popular Culture.* Philadelphia: Temple University Press, 1999.

Lerner, Ben. "Diary." *London Review of Books* 37.12 (June 2015). Last accessed June 17, 2015. http://www.lrb.co.uk/v37/n12/ben-lerner/diary.

Levander, Caroline F. *Where Is American Literature?* Malden, Mass. and Oxford: Wiley-Blackwell, 2013.

Levine, Caroline. *Forms: Whole, Rhythm, Hierarchy, Network.* Princeton, N.J.: Princeton University Press, 2015.

Levinson, Marjorie. "What Is New Formalism." *PMLA* 122.2: 558–569.

Lima, Lázaro. *The Latino Body: Crisis Identities in American Literary and Cultural Memory.* New York: New York University Press, 2007.

Limón, José E. *American Encounters: Greater Mexico, the United States, and the Erotics of Culture.* Boston: Beacon Press, 1999.

———. "Border Literary Histories, Globalization, and Critical Regionalism." *ALH* 20.1–2 (2008) 160–182.

———. *Mexican Ballads, Chicano Poems: History and Influence in Mexican-American Social Poetry.* Berkeley and Los Angeles: University of California Press, 1992.

Lomelí, Francisco, and Donaldo Urioste. *Chicano Perspectives in Literature: A Critical and Annotated Bibliography.* Albuquerque: Pajarito Publications, 1976.

López, Marissa K. *Chicano Nations: The Hemispheric Origins of Mexican American Literature.* New York: New York University Press, 2011.

MacLeish, Archibald. *Collected Poems, 1917–1982.* Boston: Houghton Mifflin Harcourt, 1985.

Manning, Shaun. "Becoming Mexican." *Publishers Weekly,* April 5, 2010. Last accessed January 16, 2014. https://www.publishersweekly.com/pw/by-topic/authors/interviews/article/42694-pw-talks-with-brando-skyhorse.html.

Márquez, Antonio. "Literatura Chicanesca." In *A Decade of Chicano Literature (1970–1979).* Santa Bárbara, Calif.: Editorial La Causa, 1982.

Martín-Rodríguez, Manuel. *Life in Search of Readers: Reading (in) Chicano/a Literature.* Albuquerque: University of New Mexico Press, 2003.

Martínez, Ernesto Javier. "Shifting the Site of Queer Enunciation: Manuel Muñoz and the Politics of Form." In *Gay Latino Studies: A Critical Reader.* Ed. Michael Hames-García and Ernesto Javier Martínez. Durham, N.C.: Duke University Press, 2011: 226–249.

Martínez, Nina Marie. *¡Caramba!* New York: Vintage Books, 2006.

Martínez, Rubén. *The Other Side: Notes from the New L.A., Mexico City, and Beyond.* New York: Vintage Books, 1993.

Matthews, Brander. "The Philosophy of the Short Story." 1885. *Die Amerikanische Short Story.* Ed. Hans Bungert. Darmstadet: Wissenshaftliche Buchgesellschaft, 1972.

Maxwell, Glyn. *On Poetry.* Cambridge, Mass.: Harvard University Press, 2013.

McCarthy, Tom. "Interview with Michael Silverblatt." KCRW's *Bookworm.* 21 October 2010.

McCracken, Ellen. *New Latina Narrative: The Feminine Space of Postmodern Ethnicity.* Tucson: University of Arizona Press, 1999.

McDowell, Edwin. "A Noted 'Hispanic' Novelist Proves to Be Someone Else." *New York Times,* July 22, 1984. A1 (Late Edition [East Coast]).

McGurl, Mark. *The Program Era: Postwar Fiction and the Rise of Creative Writing.* Cambridge, Mass.: Harvard University Press, 2011.

McHale, Brian. *Postmodernist Fiction*. 1987. London and New York: Routledge, 1993.

McPherson, William. "Who Is Danny Santiago?" *Washington Post*, July 24, 1984. Last accessed December 27, 2013. https://www.washingtonpost.com/archive/politics/1984/07/24/who-is-danny-santiago/1fobfdf9-765e-40ee-9ff3-e0885fb74def/.

Menchu, Rigoberta. *I, Rigoberta Menchu: An Indian Woman in Guatemala*. London: Verso, 1984.

Menéndez, Ana. *Adios, Happy Homeland!* New York: Grove Press, 2011.

———. *In Cuba I Was a German Shepherd*. New York: Grove Press, 2001.

———. *The Last War*. New York: HarperCollins, 2009.

———. *Loving Che: A Novel*. New York: Grove Press, 2004.

Milian, Claudia. *Latining America: Black-Brown Passages and the Coloring of Latino/a Studies*. Athens: University of Georgia Press, 2013.

Morrison, Pat. "Pat Morrison Asks: Brando Skyhorse." *Los Angeles Times*, June 4, 2011. Electronic.

Moya, Paula M. L. "Resisting the Interpretive Schema of the Novel Form: Rereading Sandra Cisneros's *The House on Mango Street*." *Bridges, Borders, and Breaks: History, Narrative, and Nation in Twenty-First-Century Chicana/o Literary Criticism*. Ed. William Orchard and Yolanda Padilla. Pittsburgh: University of Pittsburgh Press, 2016.

———. *The Social Imperative: Race, Close Reading, and Contemporary Literary Criticism*. Stanford, Calif.: Stanford University Press, 2016.

Mullen, Harryette. *The Cracks Between What We Are and What We Are Supposed to Be: Essays and Interviews*. Tuscaloosa: University of Alabama Press, 2012.

Muñoz, José Esteban. *Cruising Utopia: The Then and There of Queer Futurity*. New York: New York University Press, 2009.

———. "Feeling Brown: Ethnicity and Affect in Ricardo Bracho's *The Sweetest Hangover (and Other STDs)*." *Theatre Journal* 52 (2000): 67–79.

Muñoz, Manuel. *The Faith Healer of Olive Avenue*. Chapel Hill, N.C.: Algonquin Books, 2007.

———. *What You See in the Dark*. Chapel Hill, N.C.: Algonquin Books, 2011.

———. *Zigzagger*. Evanston, Ill.: Northwestern University Press, 2003.

Murphy, Dwyer. "Origin Stories." *Guernica: A Magazine of Art & Politics*, April 15, 2013. Last accessed January 24, 2015. https://www.guernicamag.com/origin-stories/.

Navarette, Ruben. *A Darker Shade of Crimson: Odyssey of a Harvard Chicano*. New York: Bantam Books, 1994.

Nealon, Jeffrey. *Alterity Politics: Ethics and Performative Subjectivity*. Durham, N.C.: Duke University Press, 1998.

————. *Post-Postmodernism, or, the Cultural Logic of Just-In-Time Capitalism.* Stanford, Calif.: Stanford University Press, 2012.

Nelson, Maggie. *The Argonauts.* Minneapolis: Graywolf, 2015.

Nelson Limerick, Patricia. *Something in the Soil: Legacies and Reckonings in the New West.* New York and London: W.W. Norton & Co., 2000.

Ngai, Sianne. *Ugly Feelings.* Cambridge, Mass.: Harvard University Press, 2007.

Noel, Urayoán. *In Visible Movement: Nuyorican Poetry from the Sixties to Slam.* Iowa City: University of Iowa Press, 2014.

O'Connor, Frank. *The Lonely Voice.* Cleveland and New York: The World Publishing Company, 1962.

Ortíz, Ricardo. *Cultural Erotics in Cuban America.* Minneapolis: University of Minnesota Press, 2007.

Paredes, Raymund A. "The Evolution of Chicano Literature." In *Three American Literatures: Essays in Chicano, Native American, and Asian-American Literature for Teachers of American Literature.* Ed. Houston A. Baker, Jr. New York: MLA, 1982.

Pattee, Fred Lewis. *The Development of the American Short Story: An Historical Survey.* 1923. New York: Biblo and Tannen, 1975.

Pease, Donald. *National Identities and Post-Americanist Narratives.* Durham, N.C.: Duke University Press, 1994.

————. *Revisionary Interventions into the Americanist Canon.* Durham, N.C.: Duke University Press, 1994.

Pease, Donald, and Amy Kaplan. *Cultures of United States Imperialism.* Durham, N.C.: Duke University Press, 1994.

Pérez-Torres, Rafael. *Movements in Chicano Poetry: Against Myths, Against Margins.* Cambridge: Cambridge University Press, 1995.

Pineda, Cecile. *Face.* 1985. San Antonio: Wings Press, 2013.

Plascencia, Salvador. *The People of Paper.* San Francisco: McSweeney's, 2005.

————. *The People of Paper.* New York: Mariner Books, 2006.

Poblete, Juan, ed. *Critical Latin American and Latino Studies.* Minneapolis: University of Minnesota Press, 2003.

Porter, Carolyn. "What We Know that We Don't Know: Remapping American Literary Studies." *ALH* 6.3 (Fall 1994): 467–526.

Postman, Neil. *Amusing Ourselves to Death: Public Discourse in the Age of Show Business.* New York: Penguin Books, 1986.

Powell, Douglas Reichert. *Critical Regionalism: Connecting Politics and Culture in the American Landscape.* Chapel Hill: University of North Carolina Press, 2007.

Prashad, Vijay. *Everybody Was Kung Fu Fighting: Afro-Asian Connections and the Myth of Cultural Purity.* Boston: Beacon Press, 2002.

Pratt, Mary Louis. "The Short Story: The Long and Short of It." *Poetics* 10 (1981): 175–194.

Proulx, Annie. *Accordion Crimes.* New York: Scribner, 1997.

Puig, Manuel. *Betrayed by Rita Hayworth.* 1968. New York: Dalkey, 2009.

Quiroga, José A. *Tropics of Desire: Interventions from Queer Latino America.* New York: New York University Press, 2000.

Radway, Janice. *Reading the Romance: Women, Patriarchy, and Popular Literature.* Chapel Hill: University of North Carolina Press, 1984.

Rampersad, Arnold. "Afterword." In *Robert Hayden: Collected Poems.* Ed. Frederick Glaysher. New York: Liveright, 2013.

Rankine, Claudia, Beth Loffreda, and Max King Cap, eds. *The Racial Imaginary: Writers on Race in the Life of the Mind.* Albany, N.Y.: Fence Books, 2015.

Rivera, Tomás. *. . . Y no se lo tragó la tierra/ . . . And the Earth Did Not Devour Him.* Houston: Arte Público, 1995.

Rivera, Yezmin. "Eduardo C. Corral." *BOMB*, April 23, 2013. Last accessed August 8, 2014. http://bombmagazine.org/article/7062/.

Rodriguez, Juana Maria. *Queer Latinidad: Identity Practices, Discursive Spaces.* New York: New York University Press, 2003.

Rodriguez, Luis J. "Carrying My Tools." In *The Concrete River.* Willimantic, Conn.: Curbstone Press, 1991.

Rodriguez, Ralph E. *Brown Gumshoes: Detective Fiction and the Search for Chicana/o Identity.* Austin: University of Texas Press, 2005.

Rodríguez, Richard T. "Glocal Matters: A Response to José E. Limón." *Literary History* 20.1–2 (2008): 183–186.

———. *Next of Kin: The Family in Chicana/o Cultural Politics.* Durham, N.C.: Duke University Press, 2009.

Rody, Caroline. *The Interethnic Imagination: Roots and Passages in Contemporary Asian American Fiction.* Oxford: Oxford University Press, 2009.

Rooney, Ellen. "Form and Contentment." *Modern Language Quarterly* 61.1 (March 2000): 17–40.

Saldívar, José David. *Border Matters: Remapping American Cultural Studies.* Berkeley and Los Angeles: University of California Press, 1997.

———. *The Dialectics of Our America: Genealogy, Cultural Critique, and Literary History.* Durham, N.C.: Duke University Press, 1991.

———. *Transamericanity: Subaltern Modernities, Global Coloniality, and the Cultures of Greater Mexico.* Durham, N.C.: Duke University Press, 2012.

Saldívar, Ramón. *The Borderlands of Culture: Américo Paredes and the Transnational Imaginary.* Durham, N.C.: Duke University Press, 2006.

———. "Historical Fantasy, Speculative Realism, and Postrace Aesthetics in Contemporary American Fiction." *American Literary History* 23.3 (Fall 2011): 574–599.

———. "The Second Elevation of the Novel: Race, Form, and the Postrace Aesthetic in Contemporary Narrative." *Narrative* 21.1 (January 2013): 1–18.

Salinas, Felicia. "Latina Imprints and Impressions: A Study of Contemporary Popular Fiction for Latina Readers." Diss. Brown University. 2013.

Sánchez González, Lisa. *Boricua Literature: A Literary History of the Puerto Rican Diaspora.* New York: New York University Press, 2001.

Sánchez, Marta Ester. *Contemporary Chicana Poetry: A Critical Approach to an Emerging Literature.* Berkeley and Los Angeles: University of California Press, 1985.

Santiago, Danny (Daniel James). "Danny Santiago Makes a Call on Daniel James." *Los Angeles Times*, August 15, 1984 Part II p. 5. Electronic.

———. *Famous All Over Town.* 1983. New York: Plume, 1984.

Sartre, Jean-Paul. *"What Is Literature?"and Other Essays.* Cambridge, Mass.: Harvard University Press, 1988.

Scholes, Robert. *The Fabulators.* New York: Oxford University Press, 1967.

Shockley, Evie. *Renegade Poetics: Black Aesthetics and Formal Innovation in African American Poetry.* Iowa City: University of Iowa Press, 2011.

Silva Gruesz, Kirsten. *Ambassadors of Culture: The Transamerican Origins of Latino Writing.* Princeton, N.J.: Princeton University Press, 2001.

———. "The Once and Future Latino: Notes Toward a Literary History *todavía para llegar.*" In *Contemporary U.S. Latino/a Literary Criticism.* Ed. Lyn Di Iorio Sandín and Richard Perez. New York: Palgrave Macmillan, 2007.

———. "What Was Latino Literature?" *PMLA* 127.2 (March 2012): 335–341.

Silverblatt, Michael. "Hispanic Identity in Writing." *Bookworm Podcast,* July 21, 2005.

Skyhorse, Brando. *The Madonnas of Echo Park.* New York: Free Press, 2010.

———. *Take This Man: A Memoir.* New York: Simon and Schuster, 2014.

Soto, Sandra K. *Reading Chican@ Like a Queer: The De-Mastery of Desire.* Austin: University of Texas Press, 2011.

Stavans, Ilan et al., eds. *The Norton Anthology of Latino Literature.* New York: W. W. Norton & Co., 2011.

Stubbs, Angela. "An Interview with Salvador Plascencia." *Bookslut,* June 2006. Last accessed April 21, 2014. http://www.bookslut.com/features/2006_06_009056.php.

Viramontes, Helena María. *The Moths and Others Stories.* 1985. Houston: Arte Público, 1992.

———. *Their Dogs Came with Them.* New York: Atria, 2008.

Warren, Kenneth. *What Was African-American Literature?* Cambridge, Mass.: Harvard University Press, 2012.

Williams, William Carlos. *Asphodel, That Greeny Flower, and Other Love Poems.* New York: New Directions, 1994.

Wolfson, Susan. "Reading for Form." *Modern Language Quarterly* 61:1 (March 2000): 1–16.

Wood, James. *How Fiction Works.* New York: Farrar, Straus and Giroux, 2008.

Zenith, Richard. Introduction to *The Book of Disquiet* by Fernando Pessoa, vii–xxvi. Trans. Richard Zenith. New York: Penguin Books, 2003.

———. "Table of Heteronyms." In *The Book of Disquiet* by Fernando Pessoa. Trans. Richard Zenith. New York: Penguin Books, 2003: 505–509.